PRAISE FOR
THE NEW FREEDOM OF GOD

"A leader in spiritual guidance and energy healing, Ron Damico has written a master class complete with healing sessions in this amazing, transformative manual that delves into God *as* Source and how we as infinite, spiritual beings having a finite experience can become more of our true, Divine Source selves. I have witnessed firsthand how Ron's work profoundly changes lives, be it spiritually, emotionally, or physically. *The New Freedom of God* is an essential read for anyone seeking truth, personal evolution, and a greater understanding of God, the universe, and our place in it."

—CARA J. RUSSELL,
screenwriter, Netflix, Amazon Prime,
Hallmark Channel, Hallmark Drama, and Lifetime

"Ron's book is a spiritual game changer—a bold invitation to see reality with fresh eyes. He lovingly strips away distortions around commonly misunderstood core spiritual concepts—from duality to karma—with clarity, precision, and compassion. Reading this feels like unlocking a divine keycode into deeper truth—God reimagined in the most accessible and liberating way."

—DANI FREDERICK,
Divine Feminine Mystic and Spiritual Wayshower

"In *The New Freedom of God*, Ron Damico holds sacred space for the conversation that allows us to step back and look at our souls and their connection to the Universal energy and God presence. In reading this book, I was able to reflect on my own Source Consciousness and understand the message to really respect my own infinite potential and step forward in a higher dimension toward my true soul purpose."

—AMANDA ROMANIA,
metaphysical teacher and Master Akashic Record Oracle

"Every time I open Ron's book, I receive a powerful energy activation that goes far beyond words. Before I can even finish a page, I'm lifted into a state of expansion and pure consciousness. The experience is like being initiated into a living transmission of truth that unfolds into a profound communion with my own essence. Ron's work is truly remarkable, and I encourage everyone to experience its transformative depth for themselves."

—MYLÈNE PICHÉ,
founder, École d'Éveil Multidimensionnel (School of
Multidimensional Awakening); somatic practitioner

"This book opens a portal to the heartfelt sense of the divine moving in and through us. It gives an experience, not just an intellectual examination of Source."

—BOB WHITE,
initiated shaman, healer, and
transformational teacher, Shamanic Light

"What an important book for our time and conscious evolution! Ron addresses the importance of direct experience through presence in the moment and being with God/Source while systematically discerning the old and current pitfalls on the path of 'spiritual awakening' that may distract us from fully embodying our fullest potential. This book is not about knowing spiritual doctrines, dogmas, and teachings but rather pointing us to a path beyond, into a new freedom that emerges from remembering the truth of who we are. This evolution is our divine birthright! Ron includes simple yet potent affirmational meditations that assist in integrating the essence of the chapters within so that we may embody a loving, empowered, and peaceful vibration. This broadcasts a frequency that not only changes the way we experience life but puts us in a place of cocreation as we collectively dream a new world into being. Thank you, Ron, for being a clear conduit of these important transmissions."

—THREE TREES,
Master Sound Healer and Shamanic Energy
Medicine Practitioner; cofounder, Lineages Earth
Wisdom School; creator, SoulMonic™ Sound Healing

"*The New Freedom of God* is a blessed gift offering us a way back to the 'garden' and to the beauty that is all of life. This understanding and evolution of our idea of Source and our own connection to this consciousness feels of paramount importance in a time where the concept of God has become so inverted and abandoned."

—GRETA HOUGH,
educator and Shamanic Energy Medicine Practitioner;
cofounder, Lineages Earth Wisdom School

THE NEW FREEDOM OF GOD

Evolving the Most Powerful Word in the Human Language

RON DAMICO

Published by River Grove Books
Austin, TX
www.rivergrovebooks.com

Distributed by River Grove Books

Design and composition by Greenleaf Book Group
Cover design by Angela Damico
Author photograph by Nicole Lukas Photography

Publisher's Cataloging-in-Publication data is available.

Print ISBN: 979-8-90052-039-1

eBook ISBN: 979-8-90052-040-7

First Edition

This book is dedicated to my wife, Angela Jade.
With her love, dedication, and passion, she illuminated what this book could bring to people, as books were her greatest source of inspiration and healing at many points in her life. This book is a creation of our love and gratitude for life and each other.

And to our son Nate,
who came into my life when he was eight years old. Through our journey together, he has brought out in me the father I never had, and through his unconditional love and acceptance, has helped me to heal and become who I am today.

And to our soul family and global community.
I cherish every one of you.

"When no one is looking,
and I want to kiss God,
I just lift my own hand to my mouth."

—HAFIZ

CONTENTS

PREFACE

GOD IS A CREATION OF HUMANS.

People who have entered higher states of consciousness through meditation, spontaneous awakenings, or near-death experiences (NDEs) all express a similar idea—there are no words in any human language that can even begin to describe what God or any name we assign to "him" truly is. All we can do is apply man-made concepts, words, and labels to something that lies beyond what most people can grasp or experience for themselves.

Switching to using the word *God* for *Source* is not a new concept. What I am doing is giving you the bridge to step into a new way of knowing God for yourself, one that feels authentic to you. Once you have practiced this new way of seeing and thinking, Source Consciousness then becomes a feeling, naturally becoming embodiment.

In this book, I provide tools to help you let go of past and outdated frameworks of God, which are often characterized by viewing "him" as a person. Seeing God through this lens makes it easy to feel confused, hurt, and disappointed in our understanding of life and how the laws and truths of the universe operate. By recognizing ourselves *as* Source Consciousness (what is currently referred to as God) and gradually dissolving these past and present frameworks, we can experience God from a more fluid and authentic perspective. This upgraded vision can support us in our current state as a global community and offer a profound understanding that what is done to one of us affects all of us. We transition from an intellectual knowledge of God to a deeper inner knowing and experience of God. We encourage you to keep an open mind while reading, as this will help you absorb the transmissions of this book. (Remember, minds are like parachutes; they work best when they're open.) Awakening starts with abstract concepts.

Let's embark on a profound journey to evolve and upgrade our understanding of a word that has simply not grown with the times as higher understandings have emerged. A word that has not always been viewed through a modern lens of infinite light, love, and respect for all people. God is nothing but conscious creation and does nothing but create. Existence itself is nothing more than self-aware intelligence, as everything is of God, and there is nothing else from which to create. It is ALL that is.

Join me on this journey.

THE THREE-LETTER WORD THAT STARTED IT ALL

THE IMPETUS FOR THE TITLE OF this book came from watching my wife, Angela, observe her cousin Danielle's journey as she navigated ovarian cancer in her late thirties. Danielle posted her entire experience on social media, and what Angela compassionately witnessed was the fraught account of someone who was attempting to reconcile her belief in God with the reality that her body was quickly degrading. Danielle was dying, and she didn't understand how this could be, considering that her love for God was so paramount.

Danielle, like so many others brought up in the shadows of organized religion, with a general widespread misconception of God, was stuck in a painful contradiction: Although she didn't have a particularly religious upbringing, she had grown up awash in the mindset that God condemned humans for their sins; thus, if she was suffering, this had to be due to some kind of punishment she had brought upon herself. At the same time, Danielle was also clinging to the belief that God the "father" was the ultimate panacea for all the pain and suffering we experience on this earthly plane—and that the ticket to his benevolence had to be earned. And yet, Danielle felt she had all the qualities of a "good" person. So, why was any of this happening to her?

Angela and I watched as Danielle's struggle to comprehend her experience snowballed. Over time, she would share with her rapt audience that God was "speaking" to her directly and giving her guidance and healing messages. Surely, this meant that the cancer would go away, and she would be cleansed for good.

Unfortunately, that is not what happened. Danielle's battle with cancer ended five days after her fortieth birthday.

What struck me the most about her story was not the notion that she'd somehow "failed" by not beating cancer—a common misunderstanding that is often perpetuated in religious and spiritual communities but that I've come to know as inaccurate and even harmful—but that she'd been sucked into a spiral of mental suffering that was tragic, because it was unnecessary. That suffering didn't have to do with her cancer, but with a fundamental misunderstanding of what God is, and what our experience of God is meant to be.

Arguably, the most powerful word in human language is *God*. It can be used from one extreme to another, from upholding the holiest of holies—that which we know in our hearts to exemplify the sacred—to justifying a war. Religion might begin to move us in the direction of truth, but in its current forms, it will always limit us. This is because it is predicated on fear-based mechanisms meant to keep people in line with social norms (which are slow to evolve in support of the expanding consciousness of humanity, if they evolve at all), so it seldom offers a viable portal into truly knowing God. In addition, too many depictions of God tend to place "him" above us in the hierarchy of existence, separating the human from the divine in a twist on the Cartesian model of splitting body and spirit.

In truth, every single one of us belongs to the eternal Source that we have called "God"—the Source of all creation that is the seedbed of our very nature. This understanding of God is at the heart of the book you have in your hands.

Each of us is equipped with the ability to recognize that our human impression of an omniscient, omnipotent entity is severely limited, based in many ways on our own insecurities and misunderstandings. In other words, we have created God in our image—but we don't even know who we are, so how can this image be accurate?

We can begin to transcend this outdated version of God and develop a relationship with a Source of loving truth that allows all sentient beings to experience the soul's infinite potential (what I call *God 5.0*, which connects us to a fifth-dimensional reality that encompasses the one in which we live). This Source manifests a dizzying assortment of opportunities so that we can have the magical, paradoxical experience of ourselves as infinite beings in an experiential, matter-based form. Our ability to be present with our current reality, with our very breath, lets us connect to the deeper truths of existence instead of continuously creating painful realities for ourselves and others.

In other words, the very thing we often find ourselves running from (our finite human form) is the very thing that can lead us to the true meaning of "God."*

WHAT IS GOD 5.0?

Our social, cultural, and religious conditioning has created a limited representation of God that has been exploited over the millennia, with disastrous consequences. In addition, many spiritual seekers are

---

* Although I use the term *God* throughout this book, I am not attached to it. Many people are triggered by the word *God* due to their own experiences with organized religion and its attendant biases. However, the term you use doesn't really matter. We are using the word *Source* as a transition to letting go of the old paradigm of what God has meant. It is just a way to tap into the purest point of origin so that we can connect with that powerful energy that is inextricable from who we really are. You are welcome to use whatever word you feel most connected to.

disenchanted with these visions of God, which are so often utterly disconnected from our daily realities.

But if we were to replace the word and concept *God* with *Source*, we could come to the realization of what God really is: a field of energy, an essence, that is the source of all life, creation, and potential. It is devoid of judgment because it's not a person or deity, but an energetic field of unfathomable sentient consciousness that creates and emanates—as *us*.

When you replace the word *God* with the word *Source*, you're creating an opportunity to reframe and recreate how you see/feel what God is/means to you. As you shift from a human identity that you attach to God, to the energy/essence of Source, you begin to transition away from the old references into a space of opportunity. You start to see Source, as the conscious energy of creation, in a new and more embraceable light. Making this shift also makes it more difficult to see this divine energy as having "human" qualities. And when you stop seeing it as human, as a figure you can talk to and rationalize with, you transition how you talk, pray, and build a relationship with it. So, by changing your language from *God* to *Source*, you are automatically transitioning and transforming your relationship to this frequency.

As flawed and incomplete as the human constructs of God might be, we create them because we don't fully understand who we are, and so we continue to reach for some divine Source that we innately know we are connected to. *The New Freedom of God* represents a powerful process for communing with the higher aspect of life so we can develop the awareness that we are part of the divine network that constitutes Source energy. This awakening process, which I will systematically guide you through, is what allows us to bring our lives into balance and into our natural state.

Throughout this book, I use the term *God* to refer to the old, outdated paradigm, also known as *God 1.0, 2.0,* or *3.0,* depending on the period of human development we are referencing. *God*

4.0 is the transitional bridge that takes us to *God 5.0*, which is the true Source, or what we know as divine creative energy of the fifth dimension and beyond.

The various stages of our understanding of God coincide with our human development. We start with primitive humankind's God 1.0, which was connected to instinct rather than institutions. God 1.0 was all about survival. Because people were focused on feeding their families, evading large predators, and doing their best to perpetuate the species, this stage of human development was automatic and instinctive rather than conscious. There wasn't even a tangible view of God, beyond the awareness that nature was a brutal overlord. However, within God 1.0, humans began to recognize the importance and benefits of community banding together to thrive, which took us into the development of the limbic brain of early mammals, connected to emotions and altruism. This is how God 1.0 made the transition into God 2.0.

God 2.0 corresponds with the advent of civilization. This period of time spans the emergence of early ritualistic, magic-based traditions, as well as the major religions of the world. God 2.0 was rooted in the importance of the tribe, not merely because of survival concerns but because of the refinement of human consciousness that comes about when we are emotionally connected to others. Here, we see not only the beginnings of agriculture, but also of the arts, and of other practices that served to connect larger groups of people with one another, and with a shared focal point of purpose and meaning. While this tribal mentality certainly included "connecting" through aggression, conquest, and power over others, there was simultaneously an awareness of other values that enabled us to congregate on the basis of our desire for connection and cohesion. Thus, traditions were developed, and so were rules and regulations, to maintain reasonable order within a community or society.

This led to the era of God 3.0, which was when organized religion solidified into institutions and the so-called Age of Reason. This is when we moved from a tribalistic to a more individualistic mode of living. The essence of democracy and the importance of creating systems beneficial to all individuals arose (even alongside the consolidation of greater power within governments and religious institutions). In this time, which you could call the "modern" era, pure survivalism and tribalism gave way to innovations in science, medicine, and technology that offered humanity a new understanding of what it meant to thrive. Here, out of the more magical and mythical ways of envisioning God, we also began to see the emergence of human ethics based in the values ascribed to a "higher power"—such as kindness, patience, and altruism.

We are currently in the era of what I call God 4.0, a transitional phase in which we have the power to make a quantum leap in consciousness. In this era, we recognize both the value of the tribe and of the individual. Here, we see how the recognition of our interconnectedness and interdependence can help us to establish a world in which everyone can live with a greater sense of purpose—without having to be concerned about our survival. It is the largest and most significant evolutionary step we have ever taken, but it is a liminal space—a bridge upon which some of us are moving ahead at warp speed, and where others of us may be stalled because we fear the unknown. This is the era in which we are beginning to (messily) awaken to the fact that we cannot suppress another in order to thrive as an individual. And as a community, we've begun to realize that any structures based on domination and conquest—including the ways we use emerging artificial intelligence–based technology, and how we approach the climate emergency—are detrimental to our collective evolution. All of us are created to reach our potential, which will move us into a hierarchy of responsibility whereby everyone is equal even if our roles may be wildly different. In such a paradigm, there is no zero-sum game; a benefit to one must be a benefit to all.

God 4.0 helps us to transcend the power struggles inherent in the previous models, but this transitional period is inherently destabilizing. It's a lot like a brush fire, sweeping through and removing the debris that hinders our ability to grow. The brush fire can appear disastrous at first glance, especially because this is a major growth process that challenges us to cut toxic ties to our past references. But it has a cleansing effect; it's meant to unhook us from our tendency to repeat history, so we can look to the present and future with new eyes. Thus, it is necessary to metaphorically burn down all the barriers of our preconceived ideas so the brush fire of God 4.0 can release the nourishment we require to cross the bridge.

And this is how we come to God 5.0, where we get to experience the essence of what is possible at the level of spirit. In this phase, the past no longer binds us. We have done the work to shed the residue of our complicated human legacy, fully integrating those experiences to step into the essence of who we are, rather than the identities we created to survive. While our physical trappings hold some value, they don't determine our lives and choices. What we have no longer defines and limits us, because we no longer identify with material goods or the struggle for power and prestige. We fully take in every single experience that life has to offer, but these experiences, as well, do not define us; rather, they are expressive of us. Our reactions to each subsequent moment we encounter are not based on past references or the fear of loss, but on what we wish to experience as we continue to evolve into all of who we are: spiritual beings having a human experience.

In this phase of God 5.0, as we grow our creativity, curiosity, and passion, we step into more of who we are. God 5.0 is our transition back into the eternal nature of who we are when survival is no longer a preoccupation. In the absence of attachments, we are able to claim a greater range of the eternal essence of our spirit 100 percent of the time. (And since the nature of this eternal essence is evolutionary, we don't come to an ultimate destination.) At this point, we operate from peace, love, and joy, all expressed through wisdom, without effort.

We do not carry a sense of our brokenness, which means that we no longer rely on an external authority like "God" to save or redeem us, or to dispense judgment. In merging with our core spiritual essence, we ironically do away with the God label. Instead, we merge with Source Consciousness, and we move within and as this consciousness, exploring and bringing into manifestation more beautiful possibilities for ourselves and all of existence.

Regardless of whether we consider ourselves to be religious or not, the paradigms of God 1.0 all the way through God 3.0 each impact our biology and psychology, as they have made a massive energetic imprint on our way of viewing ourselves, life, each other, and the purpose of our existence. My hope is that, through this book, I can be a sherpa who will safely steward those of us who are stuck on the bridge of God 4.0 into a paradigm that allows us to live from a more expansive, harmonized perspective.

This entire book is a transmission that will enable you to feel and innately know the true nature of God as a radically inclusive Source that mirrors back to you your own capacity for feeling and experiencing everything—even the things that are difficult. When we willingly embark on this hero's journey, accepting and moving through the broad spectrum of experiences available to us, life becomes an adventure and living within *The New Freedom of God* becomes our faithful, steadfast copilot.

NO NEED FOR DETOURS— GO STRAIGHT TO THE SOURCE

Contrary to what many of us have learned, our most trustworthy path to Source isn't about following one spiritual path, or filling up on "love and light," or attempting to exert control over our lives through manifestation techniques. It isn't about gaining, acquiring, or proving anything to ourselves or some imagined deity. In truth, when we accept that life is an experience meant to be fully lived and loved; when we choose to navigate straight into our greatest pains and fears, to directly face and embrace them—all of this becomes our greatest tool for freedom and self-knowing . . . which is to say, a direct path to knowing Source.

If there is one thing I've discovered in more than twenty years of working with clients who are hungry for purpose and connection to a spiritual reality that transcends the one in which we're all living, it's this: *If we go to the "God" center first, everything in our lives becomes more bearable—and life becomes a sacred experience that we greet with love rather than fear.*

Abraham Maslow's hierarchy of needs comes to mind here. Maslow's theory states that our actions are motivated by certain physiological needs. It is often represented by a pyramid of needs, with the most basic at the bottom and more complex needs at the top. In this system, "self-actualization" (connected to self-awareness, spirituality, and our higher self) is at the top, while "survival" is at the bottom. But what if the need to know our true essence *is* a basic need? What if going to the center of our spirits is the prerequisite to living a fulfilled life?

The purpose of *The New Freedom of God* is to offer and support at a conscious level what it means to be a spirit having a human experience; to live in a state of beingness where we realize that the reason we're here *is simply to experience the full spectrum of who we are.* It's to consciously live a life that contains the marvelous and complex scope of our nature.

For many people, the goal of a spiritual path is finding happiness. Contrary to what most people believe, happiness isn't about getting what you want, or finding yourself, or figuring out your purpose. It's not about being a good parent or a high-level executive. It's not about gaining wealth or public recognition through social media numbers and other arbitrary indications of popularity. It's not even about doing what's "right" so you can feel like a "good" person. These are simply ways we express and experience ourselves in this world, but they do not ultimately define us. They are just part of living a life as an experiential being. We only come to know the full nature of our spirit self through the ways we choose to create and express ourselves.

Our willingness to embrace our lives and the many opportunities they offer for learning and self-discovery brings us to know the true nature of Source—not as a father deity who doles out rewards and punishments, not as a moral arbiter who stands watch over our every waking moment, not as a power whom we can beg and entreat in order to get what we want . . . *but as a living energy that is part of us, just as we are a part of it.*

When we open up to this truth, we are no longer afraid to feel whatever is possible to feel, and nothing can exert control over us— including some of the false narratives that have circulated for much of human history about God. For so many people, the vision of a punitive "father" God is ingrained in the way we grew up. Many of us are already very hard on ourselves—for our perceived failures, or our inability to live up to other people's expectations. Often, children are taught to bow down to an all-powerful God. As some of us grow up and observe the abuses of power that are rampant all around us, we come to refuse that image of God—but sometimes, we throw out the proverbial baby with the bathwater, choosing to reject our early experiences of religion and spirituality and to install "false gods" that have just as much control over us as the ones of our youth.

As this book shares, questioning and healthy skepticism are important aspects of reconnecting with what God/Source really is. However, we must learn to trust ourselves and our way of seeing the world; the more we come to know our true selves, the more clearly the world, and this energy we call "God," will present itself to us. Everyone needs a reminder of how to find their authenticity, which is directly tied to the energy of Source, and *The New Freedom of God* is a guide that helps readers to do this.

GUIDANCE FOR LIVING AS A SPIRITUAL BEING IN A HUMAN BODY

Everything I share in this book will not only help you to understand, embrace, and navigate your personal spiritual journey, but will also help you become deeply intimate with the nature of reality and the universe. You will be guided through a process that I have developed and personally lived through for more than thirty years, and that I've implemented with the clients in my spiritual healing practice for more than twenty years.

During this time, I have become intimately aware of how individuals function and how we all have the capacity to express both the best and most painful aspects of what we hold. Through my ability to find my own limitations and move into and through them to become more clear and skilled at working with higher truths and energy/frequency patterns, I am able to help people move to ever-increasing heights within their personal potential. It is these healing immersions,* techniques, and tools I wish to share with you.

The New Freedom of God is a spiritual manual divided into three parts, which are explained in greater depth in the brief introductions to each of the parts. These will inform not just your own journey, but also the journey of mentoring your children and teaching them to heal and awaken outside of the traditional human, linear timeline. This book focuses on what I call timeless space. If you take this path, you'll have

---

* I use the term healing *immersion* to assist you in feeling immersed and held in a state of higher consciousness, and therefore recognize, feel, and *know* this space for yourself. These are meditative intentions that you are setting for yourself to step into the expansive state that Source Consciousness *is* with you, *as* you. These frequencies are generated from that timeless space of Source essence, and my intent is to help the reader immerse themselves in the memory of who they are and where they come from.

measurable progress, but it's not the kind of progress that moves from A to B; rather, it moves from one moment to the next right moment, to facilitate the highest and best outcome for your transformation.

I have been told by the thousands of clients I've worked with that I have a propensity for opening people up to the richest core of who they are so they can live and breathe their essence. That is at the crux of *The New Freedom of God*. For it is through the experiential process that each of us gets to remember and reintegrate this powerful Source that we've so dramatically misinterpreted. We bypass the intellectual process of "understanding" God, and we come into a more honest and palpable relationship with the force that supports all of existence. We become a part of the sacred dance, knowing *it is us*.

Throughout this book, I present teachings, healing immersions, and stories about people who learned the true meaning of Source because of their willingness to descend into the most difficult experiences of their lives. I have often worked with people living with a terminal illness. While each of them comes to their own understanding of Source, I've been heartened to see how the decision to be at peace with all that is happening opens people up to the truth of who they are, and subsequently, the truth of what Source is. Just as I've done with clients, I've written *The New Freedom of God* to help you navigate any fear you might have and recognize that there is so much more to you than your physical reality.

You will come to recognize the unique gift and blessing of your life. Just as one of my clients, whose vital life force became beautifully apparent only hours before he passed away, realized, "God is not a person—it's home." Although my client did not survive his illness, his is a clear success story. His body didn't live on, but he received what he needed—he was able to die in a state of ease and peace, and he was no longer afraid of anything, not even death, because he was irrevocably connected to the power that is at the very center of who we are.

So many of us struggle with feeling lost in our purpose and place in this world. I wrote this book to help readers access sincere gratitude for the life they have been given, such that they will begin to see beauty and hope in places they previously had not. Just like my client, you will have an opportunity to experience the ecstasy of feeling whole and complete, just as you are.

In these intensely transformative times, when the suffering of the world casts a shadow over humanity's light, it's imperative that we have a road map for navigating the complexities of the world. From my experience, something inside us already knows the core spiritual truths, but few of us were raised with an experiential awareness of these truths—what the ancient Greeks referred to as *gnosis*, or direct transmission. Few of us have the direct experience of knowing that we are spirits having a human experience—so, naturally, many of our outdated concepts of God need an upgrade . . . such that we aren't regurgitating God in our own image, but we are viewing the essence of Source as clearly as we can in that moment.

My hope is that *The New Freedom of God* will offer a spiritual basis for a new kind of socialization that helps us to claim the gifts of this human existence so that we stop perpetuating the struggles and conflict that envelop the world. After all, our environment matches our consciousness, and the material world shifts to meet our new experience as we evolve and awaken.

We are all on our own hero's journey to get to know the best version of ourselves—but this book offers a new kind of journey: By walking through the pain we are trying to avoid, and by facing our "demons" head-on, we can become everything we innately know ourselves to be. We can express and live out our highest potential. In this way, I hope for *The New Freedom of God* to be an invigorating and inspiring conversation with all of humanity—with every child ever born and who is yet to be born into this world that we are individually and collectively creating.

A HEALING IMMERSION FOR CLEARING SPACE AND WELCOMING YOURSELF INTO THIS JOURNEY

Before you get into the chapters of this book, I've included what I consider to be a supportive intention setting of your own Source self. This is a wonderful way of metaphorically "saging" your inner space and aligning with the truest aspect of who you are. These healing immersions serve to awaken and activate your highest heart-centered consciousness. You can read these to yourself or out loud whenever you begin a chapter in this book, or even if you've simply been away from the book for a while.

Alignment is not about coming into attunement and resonance with an external source or space. It is about recognizing that the space around you is expressive of the space within you. As you step into your true power, your true potential, there is a purity that accompanies this process. There is an alignment that occurs to make the truth manifest. This initial transmission is meant to prepare you for the journey of this book; simultaneously, it is an opportunity to recognize that everything you seek is already within you, and all we're going to do together is walk into the remembering—in other words, the reintegration of that which has always been *you*. It's just that, most of the time, we don't consciously tap into and attune to this inner knowing, primarily because we weren't shown how. But you can take these healing immersions, which are also a wonderful practice to work with at the start of each day, as an opportunity to remember and reawaken your true essence, your pure spirit and nature.

As we step into this purification,
Honor that somewhere within you, you are complete.
You are whole, and you are one with God itself.

Now, begin to recognize that
Source essence,
Source Consciousness,
is you—and you are it.

Let yourself settle in.
Take a nice, deep, gentle breath,
Knowing that your breathing itself is an embracing of the truth.

And as you inhale, you're receiving the breath of Source,
as it reminds you of all that you are.
Every time you inhale, Source is breathing into you
all that you are, and all that you require
to remember and embody your true essence.

Breathe that energy into your heart center.
When you reach the peak of your breath,
pause and allow yourself to feel gratitude.
You may smile, or you may just feel content, complete.
Honor that as the gift received.

When you're ready, gently breathe what you received
from Source, through your body
and beyond your body, in all directions,
as it radiates and emanates from your heart,
from the soul center that is you.

Allow that energy to go beyond you,
out into this world.
And if you desire, let it go into the universe.

And then, breathe in another purifying breath.
And as you breathe that breath in,
you cleanse discordant thoughts,
imbalanced viewpoints,
inaccurate impressions of yourself, life, and others.

You're breathing into your consciousness,
into your body, the truth of who you are.

As you breathe that energy in,
you're clarifying yourself even more.
You're cleansing and releasing
all imbalanced, inaccurate,
and incongruent viewpoints of you, life, and others.

And as you continue to breathe,
the more you breathe,
the purer and more aligned you become.
Breathe in and remember your true nature.

As you become versed in this, over time, one single breath is
enough for you to come into alignment with your true self and
to feel your pure spirit essence as the very life that you live.

PART I

THE REVELATION: PREPARATION

WHAT DOES IT MEAN AND LOOK LIKE to embark on a journey of self-discovery that helps us to experience and know ourselves as Source Consciousness? It will be different for each of us, but there are commonalities in what I call the fundamentals. The fundamentals are the basics of spirit essence and our physical form, which we all share. For example, the human body has its basic operating systems we all have in common. There are ranges these systems operate within, but our place within those ranges is specific to each of us. Therefore, we must respect our process as our own but take in and honor those who have come before us, looking into the details of the process itself and not the exact way others went into and through it.

In this first section, which is the revelatory process that will help you prepare for your journey back to Source, you'll connect with the fundamental premises of this book, including some concepts-in-action that will impact your experience of God and of life itself. As you cultivate a vast understanding of Divine Source Consciousness, you will also begin to question the ways humanity has typically framed and categorized our ideas of the divine, and start to question, examine, and contemplate the norms we've all internalized to some degree. This will help you to receive new insights that open up the channels of communication between your human form and your spirit essence. Preparing yourself this way will lead to greater balance and ease, so you can begin to make healthier choices that are aligned with a new paradigm of Source Consciousness. Remember, Consciousness itself will always and infinitely continue to grow and evolve.

CHAPTER 1

THE TRUE SELF— KNOWING YOURSELF AS DIVINE SOURCE CONSCIOUSNESS

IN THIS FIRST CHAPTER, WE EXPLORE what it means to come to an understanding of what the true self is, which is integral to orienting you to the meaning of Source Consciousness.

Of course, when it comes to religion and philosophy, we have varying views about the self—what it is, what it means, and how we are meant to operate within and from this concept. Many view the self as the crux of personal identity, as well as the central mystery of existence. Others view it as a limited construct, or an outright delusion. Many Eastern ideas of the self regard it as an illusion altogether, or an ephemeral system that helps us organize our experiences as long as we are alive. In contrast, much of Western psychology and philosophy tends to think of the self as slightly more permanent—and of the individual self as a representation of the highest values in our culture: independence, free will and thought, innovation, and liberty.

Keeping all of this in mind, I encourage you to question every-thing you've ever held to be true about the self, based on what you've picked up from family, the media, religion, education, and so on. Most of all, question the beliefs about the self that you've internalized as being "true." Perhaps you can take a few moments to jot down your responses to the prompt, "The self/my self is . . . ."

Now, I want you to put all of that out of your mind, at least tem-porarily, while you are reading this chapter. Because we're about to redefine what the self is.

Why is it so important to get a deeper, more authentic understand-ing of the self as we come into greater alignment with the energy of the divine? Because when we feel safe and secure enough in ourselves to respect the full spectrum of who we truly are—to *feel* it, to *honor* it, in an embodied rather than a purely intellectual sense—we learn to sur-render to what *IS*. Once that occurs, we experience a newfound clarity of awareness. We come to recognize that we can organize ourselves and be present, gracefully, in a way that opens us up to the grandest truth there is: We have access to potential itself, and potential is the field through which creation occurs, *for we ARE creation itself.* We are not calcified fossils, stuck in fixed identities—but rather, we are a dynamic, fluid, ever-evolving process: a manifestation of Source's creative potential.

Few of us are shown the full capacity of who we are from the start. We are taught that we are human (and for many people indoctrinated by organized religion, this comes with the baggage of being inher-ently "sinful" and flawed). However, the spiritual maturation process involves a journey of exploration—the kind of journey that took us collectively from God 1.0 through 3.0 to where we are today, on the precipice of a breakthrough.

If we were raised with the awareness that we are a spirit creating and having a physical experience—and that we are so much more than our physical bodies (or, at least, our limited perception of what these bodies are capable of)—we would learn to view this earthly plane as a playground where we get to enjoy countless opportunities to harness the beauty and magnitude of our spirit selves. Can you imagine what this kind of exploration would look like, and how it could change the ways we interact with ourselves, others, and the world at large?

Fortunately, nothing is ever by chance. Even the experience of being out of alignment with the full spectrum of who we are has a purpose. Every action with a conscious intent (or not) creates a cause and effect, which brings about synchronicities due to the interconnectedness of all life. Because to understand the true self, we must know both alignment and misalignment. This is what helps us to calibrate and to respond proactively to moments that may seem like challenges, but which are only concealed opportunities for growth. Life is our creative palette, and we are given the opportunity from our spirit self to enjoy this process of getting to know our infinite nature in this physical manifestation of form. It is an honoring gift to yourself to play with that!

We were literally born to ask the question, "Who am I—on the most authentic and essential level?" and to find the answers, through the experiential journey that is life.

MY CHOICE POINTS

Before I go any further, let me give you some context as to how I got to where I am today. I grew up in New England, with a mother who was relatively religious and in a fairly rigid family structure that revolved around hard work and conformity. I clearly have the memory of being about two years old and realizing that I wasn't going to receive the support I required from the people around me. I had an extremely strong sinking feeling and an accompanying sadness. It was the most excruciating pain I could imagine, even as an infant new to this world. I felt that I was going to be alone for the rest of my life.

Even at the age of two, it is possible to have a certain awareness that doesn't make logical sense, because of course, we are coming into this life having experienced multiple lifetimes, meaning there are certain awarenesses that we bring with us. Many of us have formative experiences that set the stage for how we walk through life, even if nobody else in our family shares that same experience. There might be a particular feeling state that is so deep we cannot ignore it.

I came to the realization that most of the people around me were living in a perpetual prison that, for some reason, they couldn't see. They might shift from one thing to the next, believing they were moving toward freedom, only to create a different cage. I saw this with remarkable consistency, along with my realization of the self-imposed prisons that so many people seem to live in. In fact, just as most people do, my family had simply left one prison for another and handed down that inheritance to the generations that followed.

At the same time, I had a deep yearning for what I perceived God to be. This was the opposite of what religion had taught me. I was raised Lutheran, but when I went to church, nothing I experienced clicked into place. In church, I felt instinctively that I was in the house of God, the building itself being a manifestation of our core intent to create a physical resonance of God's heart on Earth. It was the one place where I felt reverence, where I felt something that was deeply real and pure. However, when adults began talking and filling the church, that feeling began to fade. Over time, although I never fully accepted it, I absorbed what others told me about God being a force that was above and apart from the rest of us. I traded one viewpoint for another and ignored my innate awareness of God as a loving and powerful Source Consciousness that lives within all of us.

Throughout my childhood, only one person truly supported my vision of what God was and could be. That person was my maternal grandfather, an unconditionally loving man who reflected the truth that my child self deeply understood: that we are meant to *feel* God rather than *fear* God.

I understood as I watched my grandfather move in the world that he was the kind of person who would give someone the clothing off his back if they needed it, without any effort or thought whatsoever, simply because it was the right thing to do. That was his relationship with God. It was not based on sacrifice, or compensation, or trying to gain approval in order to look good or to be accepted in heaven; everything he did came from a sense of the innate correctness of the action or behavior. He was the only person I saw who lived that way, and he was the only person who gave me the sense I felt at a very early age of what God actually was.

Throughout my childhood and late teens, my grandfather—who passed away when I was sixteen—helped me keep a spark of hope alive within myself. Even though I was constantly shown that I needed to be in a cage, there was something about his example that would keep Source Consciousness determined and alive within me, even if it lay somewhat dormant at times.

Over time, I realized that we all live in cages. It begins with our personal cage, and then the cage of our family, and then the cage of our society, our country or culture, our race, and so on and so forth. However, as I'd come to see, when we get to the core of why we placed that initial cage around ourselves, all of our defenses begin to fall away. In my late twenties, I came to an understanding of that initial cage I had set up when I was two years old, simply attempting to protect myself in a world I didn't know how to stay safe in. I recognized that I had systematically put one cage after another over me as a way of appeasing the people around me and keeping the guardians strong at the gate, so I wouldn't be attacked. It never worked, of course, but I did it, nonetheless, because the survival instinct is a strong aspect of our physiology.

This is how I came into my earliest gifts, which I would transmute further down the road of my life. That is, I learned how to accurately read the energy around me, for the sake of survival, as a highly sensitive child who was often picked on by peers and family members. I had to anticipate and recognize what they were feeling so that I could protect myself. I wouldn't realize until years later what a blessing this capacity was.

Growing up, I was also drawn toward many things that would unfold at later points of my life in totally different ways. For example, anything that was connected to sorcery, wizardry, magic, and martial arts immediately drew my attention. Of course, this was mostly for the sake of entertainment, but even as a child, I saw the distortions and misunderstandings that existed in stories about the magical and fantastical. I had a sense that I was being shown little pieces of a much larger and more meaningful truth.

I also had moments of recognizing the presence of angelic beings around me, but I somehow managed to shut out my connection to them. I didn't want an active and open channel to something that I wouldn't be able to talk about with anyone around me. The possibility of being shunned, especially by my father, who actively demeaned me in front of others, was too painful. And so, I shut the door to those beautiful visitations, but I could not completely keep them out of my heart. Some part of me sought a sense of purity, love, and peace, and after my grandfather passed away, I attempted to do my best to carry the mantle on my own.

Throughout my teens, I experienced one physical injury or imbalance after the other, and I knew that something wasn't right, but I just didn't know what it was. I delved into all aspects of physical healing, and I started to question reality and everything I had been taught about health, science, and religion. I pushed against all of it and went into full-throttle rejection of all the familial and social systems I had allowed to limit and restrict me. This was my attempt to take my power back and to live from my core essence. As I did this, I discovered my true strength. At some point, I announced that I was no longer going to church. I progressively went from being meek and quiet to having a voice, because I had accessed a primal memory of what I knew to be true. This was the thread of self-discovery.

I got to know who I was by unraveling who I was not.

I recognized from an early age that I had an opportunity to uncover my true self through even the trials and tribulations of my life. I withdrew from the world around me for the purpose of maintaining a connection with the God I knew in my heart to be true. As I got older, I still had a lot of pent-up pain and rage, and I would occasionally act out. Over time, I realized this was all because I hadn't had the environment in my formative years to simply express myself and to be supported in getting to experience and know my authentic nature.

In my early adulthood, I realized that any of the choices I made had to be lived through my body, a system that medicine and science continue to misunderstand. I took classes on psychology and religion when I was in college, and I came to the realization that psyche and religion create so many of the mechanisms under which our bodies operate. For instance, how we are raised to think and feel, and what we are taught to believe, directly affects our bodies and will influence how the body operates and how we feel. Then, as I continued to take classes in biology, science, and biomechanics, I realized that the truth of the body is much more vast than what most of us are taught. In fact, the body is simply a vehicle for the spirit to express itself, but so often, the systems and structures of our human societies get in the way of uncovering our full potential.

I went through many moments of evolution and setbacks over the years, until I no longer felt I needed my family's approval. I hit several choice points in my life where I felt the cages that had been placed around me simply ignite and blow up. Once the dust settled, I was challenged to figure out how I was going to live.

Three specific choice points helped me to go through a complete recalibration of my identity. Something in me made a monumental shift in both my viewpoint and my overall sense of beingness. Between the ages of thirty-five and thirty-nine, I had three powerful moments of completely blacking out and losing consciousness. Some people have compared them to near-death experiences (NDEs).

The first choice point happened when I was living in Maine, and I collapsed in my kitchen. I "woke up" in what appeared to be a tranquil forest with stone seats set up in a circular fashion around a huge fire. This space felt more real and comfortable than my everyday life on Earth. As I was getting myself oriented, I started sensing other presences and beings there. Some felt like ascended masters, *because they had human forms.* Other beings were just columns of light; some were white, others black, and some were rainbow-colored. There were angelic presences and what felt like highly evolved beings from other planetary systems that were universal and cosmic in nature.

I asked, "Why am I here?" They communicated very clearly, *You've exceeded in this lifetime what you came here to do.* Humans come in with a path to experience certain things, to evolve beyond what we have known. As we evolve, we remember who we are by going through a journey of feeling what it is to be aligned and misaligned. Misalignment can create survival-based thinking, and destructive types of expressions of life over time, whereas a thriving way of being is that which is aligned with the essence of who we are in relationship to God; those are lives that have more ease. It doesn't mean that everybody who lives those higher truths is free from experiencing difficulties. It's how they go into it, how they walk through it, and how they come out of it, that determines where they are within their evolutionary experiential journey. This all came through telepathically as a knowing. The coloration and energy of it was rich in detail yet carried no density, like nothing I have experienced on our human plane. I felt the fullness of everything, and I knew that this vast technicolor experience was far more real than my experience on Earth in a human form.

These beings said, *You can go back, or you can stay with us; if you pass now they will find your body.* And I said, "Stay with you; do you mean like dying?" And they simply communicated, *Yes.* I immediately felt a "no" stir within me and said I wanted to go back. And they asked me why, and I said, "I like being in the physical realm and having a physical body. It has caused me a lot of pain at times and has been very difficult, but I have a deep knowing within that I am here to help other people find their way back to themselves, which means I would also be able to do that on a deeper level for myself."

And then I simply woke up, face down on the floor and quite disoriented. It probably took me about nine months to really process everything because I didn't understand what that experience was. I had never heard of anybody going through that. I hadn't even heard about NDEs at that point. I wasn't really afraid to tell people, I just didn't know *what* to tell people. I now carried a knowing that life has more to it than accomplishments; life is about a deep tapestry and spectrum of experiences. It is about stepping in and feeling that you are more than your physical form, as your physical form is a gift and a blessing to be cherished and appreciated. Fully taking in those experiences felt by your physical form, no matter how painful or ecstatic, is a key to life that will open many doors to finding joy and peace.

The second choice point happened about a year and a half later when I was visiting Connecticut. I was in the woods on a run, and I could feel the same sensation coming over me as it had the first time. Suddenly it became difficult to keep the pace, and I collapsed mid-stride. I found myself in the same space I was in for the first choice point, except there were many new guides and beings unfamiliar to me. I knew it was the same space, as it had left a deep and profound imprint within me. The energy in that space was as vast and beautiful as I remembered, almost crystalline in nature. Again, I found myself in the center, being encircled by them, and I asked with awe and wonder, "Why am I back?" I could feel what I can only describe as a smile coming from them, and they said, *Because you've gone even further than was envisioned for you.* I asked, "But what does that mean?" And they said, *As humans live, they have options and opportunities. They set directions for their lives, and when you came back the last time, you set another direction for yourself.* I said, "I don't remember that." They replied, *Well, your mind wouldn't let you remember it, because you would have thought too much about it, but you made the decision to become more awakened, this time to begin the embodiment process. In this lifetime, you had not believed you would be moving toward embodiment, you just felt it was going to be toward awakening. So now you have awoken at a level where you are moving toward embodiment. Can you feel what this is for you?* And I said, "Yes, I could feel the differences that were happening in my life on and off since the first choice point." And they said, *You can continue, if you would like, or you can simply leave and be with us.* I said, "I really want to stay."

All of these beings were intently listening and holding me in the most amazing feeling of love I had ever experienced. I noticed more beings were showing up, and the space just got richer in love. And they asked, *But why do you want to be there?* I said, "I can't imagine not living until I can touch as many people as possible and for them to realize who they really are. For humanity to see what it really is. Because this, to me, is the single greatest gift I can receive, to not only embody what this is but to be able to share it with people who may be seeking it for themselves."

Then, that feeling of a smile came through again, and I was back. My face was in the dirt, yet I woke up laughing. I could feel the difference in my system, which was even lighter and less attached to our physical reality as we know it. I also noticed a more significant contrast between the energy that I felt being around them in that space and the energy of being human. The energy of being human was dense and uncomfortable, but the energy that I felt being around them without my body was a rich feeling that is far more vast and real than what we experience here on this three-dimensional Earth plane. I understood the concept of "waking from the dream." Who would want to leave that when you're in it?

From there, I did my best to take in what was happening and every shift that I made. I focused on embodying this experience as much as I could, and the same thing occurred as last time. My biological, psychological, and emotional reference points began shifting. References were released continuously, to the point where I couldn't even remember how to put a belt on some days. The way I would feel about things became profoundly different, and I found I couldn't relate to or feel the same way I had before about anything. The level of judgment I used to carry started diminishing rapidly, and I found myself being more aware, sympathetic, and compassionate.

One of the biggest shifts I noticed was that my life became lighter, and internal conflicts started to fade at a rapid pace. Another thing that began to occur was my ability to sense and notice things from a standpoint of awareness. Mine isn't just one particular way of registering things from a sensory perspective; it's an all-encompassing, heart-centered knowing of what is. I just became aware, and then I could put that awareness into a form that either made sense to me or that made sense to the person I was with. It became easier for me to work with people whom I was beginning to support energetically, spiritually, and physically. So my healing gifts, as people would call them, became more prominent and clearer, and I became more aware of how to access what was necessary to help somebody, even without having had any training. It became clear to me what they needed and how to introduce it into their systems. The clarity was astonishing even to me.

Choice point number three occurred when I was back in Maine in a different rental house. It was morning and I was alone. Something felt off, and because so much of me had changed, I just asked, "Can you show me the truth of this feeling?" It got more intense, and then

I became aware I was going to collapse again. I ended up back in the same place, except this time I was standing, and there were no seats. Returning to that richly cosmic space of love and divine truth felt incredible. There were even more beings than the first two times. This time, they weren't just around me in a circular fashion but hovering above as well; it felt like a huge dome of light beings. I could sense and feel that some of these beings had been working behind the scenes with me. There were new beings, but I didn't know who they were, and they were holding the most loving and supportive space—the kind that I can't put into words to this day. It is a type of love that saw me through and through, honored me for all I was, and could only support me by bringing more of who I was into the world. It was like they magnified a prism of light in my heart. And then I smiled, and I received the feeling of them smiling again for me, and they showed me that I had reached a level of purity and had again gone further than you or we could have imagined. It would take most people many incarnations to work through the deeper levels of seeking, finding, and awakening toward embodiment.

They said, *You can stay with us, and we can all support each other in our own growth, or you can go back, and we will still support each other in this growth, but if you go back at this point now, your life is yours to master and create.* In other words, my life script is mine to write. And I said, "What do you mean by that?" And they impressed upon me that when you come in for an incarnation, you and your support beings help you lay out a plan. When you get to a certain level, and you now have gone further, you get to choose completely every lifetime you have from this point forward. You're the one who gets to lay out the plan. I said, "How do I write a script when from my viewpoint, I don't even know what I'm doing?" And I felt that loving smile again, and this time, it permeated me. They said, *You are here to heal life, so life can realize itself. That is an unusual gift. Other beings have done that over your human centuries, and you know of them.*

You have chosen to follow in their footsteps. You have chosen to take every lifetime you've had of awakening and bring it all into form now in this life. If you go back, you can write a script for your life that is beyond anything you could imagine.

In other words, you are creating your life as if you are rebirthing yourself every time you make a choice. This is more about integrating who you have always been into the present, to dissolve the holding of any of the past that is still incomplete but not truly consequential. It will feel big when it comes up because you are now sensing, at a very deep level, the subtleties of what creates incongruence. You will feel it very deeply, but it's not significant. So if you go back, your life is yours. We will always be here. You will then meet with us as you choose, and we will all have a conversation, but the choice is ultimately yours. You will no longer look to us to make your choice and give you guidance. You will look to us for counsel, for you to make the choice you are drawn to make, and that is a very different life to live.

I said I wanted to return because I still couldn't imagine not coming back. From that point on, everything in my life began to progressively and rapidly become crystal clear. It was easier for me to move through some of the deeper things that my human flesh and my human psyche were struggling with and the lifetimes that were processing out. It was very easy for me to walk into everything I was experiencing, as I was no longer afraid. I wasn't afraid to feel any more physical, psychological, or emotional pain. I wasn't afraid of it anymore because the self loves to experience, and it's not afraid to suffer! I had hesitancies, but I wasn't afraid to feel what was there. It was easier for me to step into shame, regret, loss, grief, and those deeper feelings of emptiness and isolation. Those feelings were now easier to tap into because I grew up with a lot of shame in my life. Shame has always been scary for me, but it isn't anymore. It was simply a feeling that I needed to face, and I knew I had it in me to walk into it, and through it, and transmute it into love. So that's what began to happen. Energetically, things began to open up for me exponentially, and I literally felt myself evolve monthly, then weekly, and now daily. I have always known that I was meant to be here until every last human awakens.

I recognize in retrospect that these choice points occurred because there was something in me that was innately driven to do the work I am currently doing to help other people expand beyond their limitations, for the purpose of finding their true self. The guides gave me an opportunity to shed multiple skins of my own false self so my authentic nature could come out, and I could become more and more of who I am. Even today, I continue to go through these stripping-downs very rapidly, and the end result is always greater clarity.

Most of us will encounter such choice points, which are opportunities to move from intellectual knowledge to a heartfelt knowing and experiential awareness, which is a huge theme in this book. Something in me changed after my own choice points, and although it took me some time to reorient, I knew I couldn't go back to being the person I had previously been. I was ready to commit to a way of being that I felt represented our true human potential.

Anybody who is drawn to the kind of work that I do has, on some level, already chosen to awaken in this incarnation. They have chosen to remember who they are because they're no longer willing to live in a state of separation. This is why we see so many people moving in the direction of awakening. We are at a global choice point. It is time for humanity to shift and the new human to emerge. Many of us are no longer hiding our gifts but are choosing to live our full essence in ways we haven't before. It isn't possible to ignore a beacon that is this bright. It is an eternally expressive vibration that creates a disruption in the current dance of power we see unfolding on a global stage, among those who seek to take rather than engage in a reciprocal relationship with all of existence.

Today, all of us are starting to become more empowered from within. We are recognizing that no one can ever take away our true essence. We all have the power to help each other step into it even more. I realized after my own choice points that this was my path. More than that, it has always been my true self.

THE POWER OF SELF-TRUST

It's time to make a shift to accept the power that has always been within us. For many people, the "self" can feel like a living hell that is rife with judgment, loathing, doubt, fear, and loneliness. Many of us are, indeed, conditioned by our society to see ourselves as "less than," which perpetuates a victim/perpetrator paradigm that either keeps us from owning our true power or that puts us in a position of attempting to usurp power from others by force. Read any history book and you'll see this principle play out through the rise and fall of countless civilizations. But true power is always connected to self-trust and a deep acceptance of all parts of who we are, even our confusion (that is, if we're having trouble trusting ourselves). Power is the capacity to treat ourselves with deep compassion, knowing that our attention can move the unhealed parts of us into the light of our wholeness.

When we go through our lives in a state of fragmentation, detached from our innate self-worth, it can be really hard to trust the true self. This is because what we've construed as the self is only a limited aspect of who we are. Many times, the "self" is just a relationship between opposites, the dance of our true self and wounded self. These opposites are actually two sides of the same coin, moving to reconcile the pain that brought about the perception that we are separate from our true self and the world around us. The true self sits with eternal loving patience, connected to the wounded self that is looking for resolution as it moves away from the very thing that could bring it to inner peace—forgetting to pause long enough to realize the salve for the wound is right there next to it: the true self. But because the wounded self keeps looking outside itself for answers and relief, it gets locked in a continual pattern of looking for a different answer in the same place where no answer has been found. As a result of this pattern of pain, fear, and abandonment, resentment builds, amplifying the wound so that we move further away from the true self and the depth and beauty of what life truly holds.

The wounded self is also full of binary parts that are in conflict with one another. For example, the inner critic/critical parent aspect may be the one who berates and diminishes the wounded child who feels they can't do anything right. Maybe this dynamic plays out over and over again, and it serves to erode our sense of trust in ourselves— because we have two warring parts within us: one that believes it is worthless and incompetent, and another that reinforces this belief through constant judgment. How can we possibly develop a relationship of trust with ourselves if this is the dynamic we are stuck in, which amplifies two unhealed parts of the self that are not the full scope of who we are and what we hold?

We see this dynamic play out quite a bit not just on the individual level but on the global stage. Given the growing confusion around what "self" means, and the formations of self that we see arising from current politics, social norms, and religion, it is little wonder that so many people feel lost, fragmented, and incomplete—as if their core, essential being has been completely glossed over and forgotten as we fight internal and external wars that seemingly have no end.

Very often, even well-meaning attempts to fight for marginalized identities can result in the same gridlock and confusion that have characterized so many movements that initially started out with a good cause. When we swim in the waters of specific aspects of our human experience, we forget that we are *so* much more. We start to separate from our sense of wholeness and to drown in the particulars of our experience. We disconnect from our essence, which is inextricable from Source. We are much likelier to make decisions that are not aligned with our true self from this place, which can lead to feelings of failure and the inability to trust ourselves. Make no mistake, though—people who seem to be overly confident and who never question themselves aren't operating from solid self-trust, but more often than not, from an arrogance that has offered them protection from the possibility of self-doubt and shame, which would be too painful to face. Self-trust is curious rather than rigid, and it knows how to course-correct. In contrast, people who display unwavering confidence, even when it's clear that they're wrong, are operating in just one narrow bandwidth of the spectrum of infinite potential.

So, how do we get to self-trust, if our psyche is fractured (which it often is, as a result of living in an attention-compromised society)? Self-trust requires purposeful focus. We live in a world that is so full of variety and options that it can be very difficult to remain present with ourselves, and to make clear decisions based on a deep connection to what we wish to create in the world. We are constantly drowning in stimuli—from our phones, televisions, computers, and the world around us—that keep us stuck in comparisons. In such a state, fragmentation and confusion are more likely. We experience difficulty making even the simplest and most straightforward decisions. We dilute our ability to be decisive and clear in our choices about how we want to experience and express ourselves. Through all the noise, it becomes difficult to discern anything, much less the shape of our soul's yearning.

Keep in mind that although we, as pure creative potential, are capable of creating ourselves in an infinite number of ways, being scattered in our attempts doesn't yield the results we wish for. For the creative process to work, we must concentrate our focus. This is why it's important to check in with our gut and clarify our intent and awareness, so we don't get hijacked by the next distraction. If we want to steer our ship toward true north, we need to have a functional rudder.

This requires being really honest with ourselves. We must be willing to ask questions like, *How much of my life is just a distraction from things I don't want to face or feel? How much of what I'm moving toward is getting me closer to my full potential as a spiritual being, and how much of it is moving me further away?*

These questions might feel difficult or even painful to answer, but by doing the hard work of compassionate self-inquiry, we become loving parents to ourselves: demonstrating where we may have gone astray and setting boundaries that help us to be the person we want to be.

Keep in mind that a boundary is a limit. In this finite human form, we have limitations. This means the fear of missing out (FOMO)—which is an outward expression of not feeling connected with others—will likely continue to be there, if we operate under the false idea that we *should* be everything and everywhere all at once. Self-trust brings us to the "zero point" of *this* particular moment, because *now* is all we ever really have—and it is what opens us up to the essence of Source.

As we continue to be present and to ask ourselves questions that help us get to "true north," we do the necessary work of birthing our true self. But here's the catch: We aren't supposed to know what that's going to look like until it actually happens.

Think about the human gestation process. As an embryo grows inside its mother's womb, we recognize that something important is happening—but we don't know what the future of the embryo will be *after* it is born and navigates through each rite of passage, from infancy to childhood to adulthood. Uncertainty is inherent to the process of creation. Our potential is strategically hidden from us because it's supposed to be an unfolding process that is meant to occur moment by moment! As the old saying goes, the journey is more important than the destination, because it gives us clues as to how we might be able to use our creative energy in response to every opportunity or challenge that presents itself (and remember, even the so-called challenges are opportunities in disguise). The journey *is* the experience, and the destination shows us the moment has come to completion.

So, how do we tune out the distractions that abound so we can tune into ourselves and build self-trust in the face of uncertainty? This is where mindfulness practice can be particularly potent. The intention behind mindfulness is to bring ourselves into full alignment with who we are: our whole self. We do this by paying attention to the places where something feels "off." We don't even have to know what it is or figure out how to change it all at once. We can simply continue to pay attention to our energy levels and course-correct, as needed.

When we stop trying to put ourselves into some predetermined box created by society, organizing who we are in ways that can be defined by others, we come to a place of balance and harmony within ourselves. We start to feel better, and we experience the full extent of our wholeness. And our wholeness is the state of self-trust that our spirit is always gently leading us back to.

OWNING OUR FEELINGS

Here's the place where you might be wondering: Why are we discussing feelings in a chapter about the true self?

Because we can't know the true self until we tap into our wholeness. And we simply cannot know our wholeness if we do not *feel* our lives.

In addition, it's hard to exercise self-trust if we have no idea what we're feeling. Feelings are important when it comes to gauging our state of being and recognizing what is happening below the surface of our carefully constructed identity. However, in our world today, many of us have an allergic reaction or a conscious/subconscious aversion to the full scope of our feelings. Depending on factors like gender, age, socioeconomic class, culture, and so forth, it's likely you've been trained to believe that certain feelings are unacceptable to express, much less to internally acknowledge. And when we are forced to shoehorn ourselves into an "acceptable" model of what we are supposed to be, thereby neglecting the full scope of what it's possible for us to embody, there's no way we can understand or resonate with the magnificent largeness of Source Consciousness. Instead, we continue to receive a very small portion of the narrative of what Source is. It's similar to peering at the vast night sky through a tiny little pinprick in a sheet of paper and believing that's the entirety of the universe.

In order to understand and experience our complete existence, as microcosms of Source Consciousness, we must welcome rather than villainize our feelings.

I often explain this to my clients by noting that as beings of Source Consciousness, we created our human form to give us the experience of feeling what it is to be an infinite being in a finite form. Nothing in the domain of our existence is a waste, and this includes our emotions. The more we fully own and embody our "divine" humanity, the more we expand the scope of what is possible for us to feel and know—because our openness to each experience has an evolutionary function. The more we remain open, the more we expand and gain access to even more refined sensations and emotions beyond the survival-based ones (anger, fear, sadness, avoidance) that have come to mark humanity at this stage of our development.

To understand what it means to be survival-based, imagine yourself on a savanna during the dawn of humanity, with a wild animal at your heels. In this kind of situation, there's a raw, visceral, knee-jerk biological reaction that takes over, and it requires putting aside your true emotions and feelings to make it to the other side of the conflict in one piece. This mentality has become pervasive in our societies; that is, to navigate danger, to make it through the day, we are asked to set aside the inconvenience of *feeling*. The perception that dominates is that life is about survival—because we have zero concept of true "thriving," a state in which everyone is able to get their needs met. The only thing we can see through our tunnel vision is the sharp fangs of the animal that wants to make us its next meal.

The problem with a survival-based paradigm is that it puts us in a position of constantly attempting to gain the upper hand—to take advantage of the so-called weaknesses we see in others, through force, coercion, or by manipulating other people's emotions. There are individuals and groups that have utilized fear as a weapon to keep others in line. But fear is just one feeling, even though it has come to characterize so much of our daily lives because we have disowned or forgotten the other states of being that are possible.

Disowning our feelings is a rejection of our whole and magnificent self. The true self rejects no part of who we are. But the fragmentation of the self into a conditioned set of acceptable responses evolved from a social structure in which the weakest of individuals—by which I mean those with the least compassion and concern for others, which is a very different definition of "weakness" from the one we're accustomed to—were placed at the top of a chain of command, and everyone else was placed at the bottom. Living in a society that decries emotions as "weak" gives us a skewed sense of who we are supposed to be. Most of us who grew up in such a society are oriented toward survival rather than self-knowing. We learned to imitate and emulate this backward dynamic of cutting ourselves off from entire parts of our being, simply to get by. We also learned how to develop our observational skills and intellect, at the expense of our emotional intelligence. This is the framework for most aspects of Western civilization, and it doesn't take a genius to see where that's gotten us.

Despite the fact that we've largely disowned our feelings as a society, it's not as if we are operating on the basis of reason and logic. The most primitive of our feelings are still running the show; it's just that we are largely unaware this is happening because we don't have a meaningful relationship with our feelings. But we can't hope to master what we feel until we develop the strength and inner fortitude to feel absolutely *all of it*, even the uncomfortable emotions. Great heroes like Jesus, Gandhi, Mandela, and Dr. King were not heartless stoics; they experienced great anguish and often expressed it through tears and emotional catharsis. For when we feel the full gamut of our humanity, we learn to process and clear our emotions on a daily basis, so we can show up fully rather than slowly transforming into the very thing that caused us pain—which is often what happens when we get stuck in survival and cut off from our feelings.

When we honor all that we feel and avoid none of our feelings, there is nothing in this world that can control us. However, when we come to disown our feelings, we often end up projecting them out onto imagined enemies (whether these are ideological or simply other human beings), meaning it becomes very easy for people to weaponize our hatred and fear against us.

If you can see the essence of Source as the most whole, the most fulfilled "Being" in all of existence, you will see that people who embody Source Consciousness know who they are, through and through. There is a radiance, a self-confidence, that emanates *as* them, because it comes from the humility of learning to be with every sharp edge and rounded corner of their experience.

All of this still begs the question: How do we grow our comfort with the *feeling* aspect of the self when a lot of us were taught to cut off our emotions from a young age?

As I ponder this question, I think back to the day when my brother was diagnosed with cancer and my father said in a voice choked by numbness, "I want to cry but I can't." My father had always equated emotions with weakness, so opening the floodgates would have overwhelmed him. It would have meant the annihilation of everything he'd held himself up to be: "strong," "tough," "masculine."

Many of us are operating in a similar way, regardless of how much access we believe we have to our feelings. Even my clients, many of whom are already quite emotionally intelligent and who have done a great deal of spiritual work prior to meeting me, experience difficulty when it comes to making space for the truth of their hurt, their suffering, and even their joy, their wild wonder. Because we were all raised in a survival-based society, our sense of disconnection from our emotions is largely unconscious. This is why we must slowly accustom ourselves to carving out greater space for the parts of us that remain marooned in the darkness of our being.

One of my suggestions for doing this is to read a book that moves you, listen to music that tugs at the heartstrings, or watch a film that makes it impossible to emerge with dry eyes. Art is a powerful guide that reveals the self to the self, and I took solace in it from a young age. Because I was shamed by my family for being too sensitive and "weak," I also spent many of my early years in solitude and contemplation, in my bedroom, a closet, or the basement. In addition, I aligned myself with individuals whom I could trust to hold a space for me so that I could learn to be with my feelings rather than shoving them into a remote territory of my unconscious. And even today, when I stumble into the deepest pits of despair and I'm faced with the aspects of my being that I'm not fond of, one of the greatest gifts in my life is having my wife, Angela, hold me in the midst of it. It is a true source of refuge when you are blessed with the presence of a person who is strong enough to hold space for you as you surrender to the process of feeling. Such a person wouldn't dream of getting you to "move past" whatever you're going through; instead, they are the proverbial shelter in the storm, offering an anchor in the midst of the turmoil, in support of you moving deeper into and through the experience.

Amazingly, I think I've always sensed this. Even as a scared little boy, something in me understood that feelings are the language of the soul; they are the vibratory mechanisms of reception, expression, and animation—and when we surrender to them, we liberate ourselves, in turn creating a larger "opening" for our spirit to guide the creation of our life.

As sentient beings, we can feel with greater detail and vividness than other animals, because more of our spirit animates our existence.

Feelings are an interpretive system that helps us to determine whether or not what we are bringing into our bodies and the world is aligned with how our spirit wishes to express itself. Our feelings can help us figure out whether or not we are being congruent with our values and our deepest desires. It is only because we have misconstrued and underutilized our feelings that we have come to be threatened by them rather than to welcome the wisdom they have to offer us.

We typically don't feel safe enough to step into the ocean of what we feel, because many of us were raised to believe that we will not be embraced in the face of all our incongruities and pain. But as I learned at an early age, the experience of having a trusted friend, guide, or teacher who will be there to reflect wholeness and innate lovability back to us is so valuable—because at some point, we will be able to offer this kind of compassionate mirroring to ourselves. We will come into such a sense of communion and intimacy with our inner being that we ourselves will become a safe space for full self-expression. Playing this role for ourselves helps to generate greater self-trust, which is imperative in navigating a world fraught with instability and uncertainty. It helps us to operate with greater fluidity and to ease up on our rigid expectations. It helps us to truly *thrive*.

One thing to note about the capacity to fully feel our emotions is that this is not the same thing as being hyperemotional, lacking filters, and vomiting our feelings onto everyone around us. Hyperemotionality may be present for any number of reasons. Most often, it can be a way to gain attention from others, but the act of "venting" doesn't actually let people in, to the extent that our nervous systems can relax and we can be truly vulnerable. Genuine vulnerability requires stillness and receptivity, but hyperemotional people are often stuck in a relentless, churning wheel of "fixed" emotions (fear, rage, shame, disgust, etc.) and don't allow emotion to move through them. In a way, being hyperemotional is a mechanism that continues to keep others at a safe distance, which also offers us an excuse to push others away and stay locked in our own survival-based fears. But it becomes much easier to connect with others once we have learned to become a safe space for ourselves.

I recall a time when Angela and I were having an argument. I felt extremely emotional and volatile in the way I was expressing myself—until a thought suddenly came to me: *I don't need her to hear me; I need to hear me.*

When we truly hear ourselves and acknowledge our own feelings, it really does become easier to stay with them instead of seeking a stimulating experience or anything that might let us escape discomfort. Avoiding our feelings in favor of ecstasy is a common method of spiritual bypassing that even the most conscious people are susceptible to. In many ways, one of the escape valves for living in a survival-oriented society is pursuing distractive stimulation—in the form of thrill-seeking moments like high-risk sports, drugs, shopping, overeating, sexual distractions, video games, and other experiences of novelty. The problem is, the dopamine hit we receive from such experiences is temporary, and over time, it creates an equal and opposite indebtedness—because it's a false experience of happiness. The thrill-seeking, boredom, restlessness, hunger, and pain are not resolved, only postponed so that they eventually need to be dealt with at an even bigger cost to your spirit each time you choose to avoid what needs to be seen and felt.

We seek moments of relief and release in an attempt to work through the density of living on this earthly plane, instead of recognizing that ecstasy is temporary by design. Ecstasy is not meant to be a state we stay in forever, but rather, it is a portal to the awakening, presence, and openness that characterize Source. Ecstatic states aren't meant to be chased after, which only leads to disappointment; they are meant to expand our capacity for feeling even more. Ecstasy is a liminal state that facilitates our transformation into the next level of being, creating an opening to access our Source-based infinite potentiality.

Ironically, the only way to get to that next level is to move through all the feelings we're attempting to avoid; to feel rather than dampen our emotions, whatever they may be. When we do this, we come to that state of body, mind, and spirit in which everything within us is in perfect communion and our vibration is naturally high. We experience a sense of release that allows our entire being to relax.

People who end up being addicted to ecstatic states that are artificially or externally induced long for that sense of release, but they never actually *feel* what it's like to be there because they're too busy chasing after their next high. And that next high is always something they seek from the external world instead of recognizing that it's possible to generate it from within.

My stepson, Nate (whom I honor as my own son in every sense), experienced something like this when he developed an addiction to video games after spending time with his biological father. Many parents will let their kids succumb to a video game addiction because it's akin to giving them a pacifier, which keeps the home environment superficially level and steady. So even though Nate was stimulated, his attention was focused in such a way that he was essentially "reined in"—kept within a narrow emotional bandwidth that made it easier to predict and control his behavior.

Over time, Nate started to believe that without that constant level of stimulation (which can never truly be constant, as the desire for excitement always requires upping the ante and seeking even greater thrills), he wasn't okay. He was operating under the belief that he needed to be that stimulated all the time. Angela and I helped Nate realize that we all have the capacity to go within and explore the vital riches that already live inside us, rather than becoming overly dependent on external forms of stimulation. We did this by getting him to read interesting books, drawing, journaling, exercising, and going out into nature and observing it in its many shapes and forms, and by whetting his curiosity about the world in general, which helped him to stay connected to his feelings in a more sustainable and expansive way. He became more intentional about going inward, so that he could feel what was in there and what longed to be expressed. We taught Nate that in order to become familiar with the landscape of his feelings and his true self, he had to become more accustomed to living from the inside out, rather than the outside in.

MOVING FROM THE INSIDE OUT

We are accustomed to moving from the outside in (that is, basing our concepts of who we are and what we are capable of on the external input that is coming to us) rather than from the inside out (using our own intrinsic barometer for connecting to ourselves to navigate the world around us). Moving from the outside in offers us temporary relief and stimulation, as Nate discovered with his video games, but it's not sustainable and can only end up making us feel more lost, confused, and dependent on the world around us. Moving from the inside out is an important way of reorienting to the true self. We learn to be with ourselves and to express what is genuinely within the terrain of our spirit, the part of us that is connected to Source and wants to be expressed, when we move from the inside out. From this place, we are not simply imitating our friends, family, society, or social media; rather, we are acting from a space that is infinitely spontaneous rather than rigid, curious rather than self-conscious, engaged with the expression of truth rather than the perpetuation of artifice that is so present in the world around us.

Moving from the inside out is, in other words, a feature of the true self.

In fact, moving from the inside out is something that had its initial design in ancient humanity, back when survival wasn't merely a knee-jerk response but a creative, exploratory process. We had to come up with new ways of engaging with the environment, so we could initiate the process of understanding what thriving could be; this required going inward and perceiving our environment through a more expansive perspective. We found ways to practice different techniques to keep ourselves safe. But as civilization progressed, we started to project our own innate creative capacities onto other people, whom we praised as having God-like characteristics. We began to see this power as existing outside of us, instead of recognizing that all the answers have always been within us. Thus, our association with safety, stability, and satiation became chronically external. And, unfortunately, because the leaders we'd given power to failed us yet were lionized as gods despite their disconnection from their authentic self and relationship with "God," our concepts of who we are became even more distorted. Of course, people have used religion as a contemplative tool for going inward, and in some cases it works well, but all religions come with their own baggage, dogma, and distortions.

Getting back to our origins requires knowing that we *are* creation; we're already a part of everything! We need not depend on an external individual or institution to tell us this is true; we simply have to do the work of making that long voyage inward to innately know who we are.

So, how does this work? How can we come to live and breathe our true nature? For now, I will say that the process of going inward—which is not one that is modeled to us in most parts of our society—begins with recognizing what we are automatically drawn to. Think of the people, books, music, films, activities, and ideas that you feel innately connected to. Then, instead of moving out of yourself and toward those things (which most of us have been taught to do), pause for a moment and consider that your attraction is pointing you to something within you that you perhaps haven't yet activated or healed. We are always drawn to the things that most long to be stirred awake within us. And instead of idolizing those things, we have a choice to uncover and activate them within our own self. This is the beginning of living in a way that is truly authentic to who we are.

As a child, I was unusually sensitive, which was chalked up to me being "less than," or "not masculine enough," according to the values of the culture into which I'd been born. As much as I attempted to fit in, I continually had the experience of being rejected, ignored, and demeaned. At the time, I didn't understand that the best thing I could have done was to find a resonant environment that accepted me for who I was rather than trying to build a false persona in order to please others in an attempt to fit in. It would take me years to relax into my own specific talents and heart stirrings, and to recognize and accept that I didn't need the world to respond to me in any particular way. By moving from the inside out, I would come into contact with souls on a similar journey. I would come to recognize when I was behaving in a way that was incongruent with my true self and to reorient myself to a more internal barometer that allowed me to own my feelings without resistance.

How do people come into congruence with who they know themselves to be? Often, it's as simple as shifting our externally referenced sense of self from doing-oriented to being-oriented; we can become keen observers of our own mind and activities, by staying attuned to our feelings and accessing the perspective of our soul. This helps us step into a more constructive and expansive framework for the self. By going inward, we come to recognize that we are not separate, tiny beings who are meant to capitulate to an all-powerful external God; rather, we are a microcosm of the macrocosm. We *are* Divine Source: pure, creative, loving energy.

YOU ARE ALWAYS WHOLE

I keep referring to the power of recognizing that you are innately unbroken and whole, because it bears repeating. We may have an intellectual idea of this truth, but we rarely get a chance to feel it. In many ways, it goes against what we've been taught to believe about ourselves—that we are flawed, damaged, unlovable, unacceptable. But when we begin to attune to the fact that we contain all the potential of Source Consciousness, our entire perspective gets turned upside down. What we once viewed as our "imperfections" become beautiful idiosyncrasies that are meant to help us open up more deeply to the knowing that the Divine Source of all creation is within us, *AS* us.

This is why I always focus any discussion of the true self on a foundation of wholeness. Wholeness is ground zero for who we are, even if we can't remember a time in our life when we experienced it. However, even that is a false perception. Every single one of us has had at least a moment—even if it was fleeting or a really, really long time ago, perhaps when we were preverbal—when we felt complete, utterly safe, and at peace within ourselves and the world within and without. I often walk my clients through a process that enables them to remember this moment and amplify it in their bodies. I demonstrate how, when we align with this lived experience of wholeness, it becomes a guidance system that allows us to make decisions more easily and have greater confidence that our true self (which transcends labels and identities) is leading.

I have a client named Lily who came to me after many years of working with different practitioners. Like many of the people who end up finding me, she was at a crisis point; her life was falling apart, and she just couldn't figure out how to pull it all together. She was divorced and about to lose her apartment because she wasn't making enough money to pay the rent. Her kids were going to move back in with their dad because Lily didn't have the means to support them. I could sense during our first session that Lily's devastation had resulted in a kind of energetic fragmentation that made it hard for her to feel grounded within herself—because, for the most part, she didn't want to be. It was too hard to face the circumstances of her life, which she felt she didn't have the capacity to do.

However, her circumstances were not what had led to this state of internal chaos and confusion. I could recognize that Lily didn't know how to be at ease, because she had no memory of what this was like in her body. In her mind, things had been chaotic for as long as she could remember. She carried in her body an energetic makeup of a sense of being pain-riddled, disappointed, and heartbroken. Even when she was not conscious of it, this visceral reality that had been with her for so long had made her assume the mental and physical posture of someone who felt life was beating her down and nothing was lifting her up.

As tears began to flow, I asked her, "Was there ever a time when you felt your entire life was joyful? When it was driven by gratitude and contentment, even if only for a moment?" I asked.

Instantly, her entire energy field lit up when she identified a moment of pure ease that she'd experienced as a small child. She was about three years old, lying on the ground outside watching the clouds and feeling a deep sense of wonder and joy about life. In the next moment her mother had yelled at her, but in our session her tears stopped flowing and she was filled with a sense of wonder and peace when she remembered the experience of being one with the clouds.

Through our sessions, I helped her to feel and reintegrate this awareness into her psyche, energy, and biology. From this vantage point of ease and wholeness, it became easier for her to be with herself and her life, exactly as it was. She began to see that the pain she was experiencing was her own resistance. The problem was that, like so many other people, Lily didn't deep-down believe she was worthy of a life of grace, ease, and joy. She'd been shown repeatedly that life was about suffering and everything was a struggle—that she had to work hard even for crumbs. This is the mentality we adopt when we start to look to the world to mirror who we are, rather than looking inside ourselves.

Lily's transformation was beautiful to witness. Her self-trust and joy grew in spades. Her doubt faded, and she became more curious. She was now situated in a state of consciousness that would allow her to thrive, to claim her innate wholeness, peace, and love.

Our body and entire energy system will always find a way back to wholeness if it is given a way to heal, because it innately knows how to do this. However, wholeness is a practice that requires consistency. If it's what we want, we must consciously and consistently choose wholeness over disintegration. We must breathe our way back into congruence, which is something I'll teach you how to do when we get to Chapter 3.

After doing the work of coming back into congruence, Lily had emptied out enough of her old misconceptions so that it was now time to fill the space she'd cleared out. She ended up getting a great job out of state, and everyone in her family was on board with this plan. It's been nearly two years, and she's doing well, financially and spiritually. She recently finished a nursing degree, and she feels alive and excited. She is experiencing the will to thrive; this is nothing more than alignment with our innate nature, which longs to feel our wholeness.

Sometimes, I meet clients who can't remember a time when they felt whole. Sadly, this is often the case for people who carry an unconscious belief that they should never have been born. When this happens, I help them to regress to their origin—the moment of their first incarnation during which they came in cleanly from the realm of spirit and into form. This is a primal memory without any noise and judgment attached to it.

One thing I always try to emphasize is that we wouldn't be able to incarnate at all without a connection to Source Consciousness or the sacred awareness of our origin. So, when people are able to feel this moment through and through, it changes everything; they come to cultivate a sense of faith and trust that they are meant to be here, that they have everything they need to thrive. This can create a massive upheaval of unhealthy patterns that simply can't operate within the field of this memory, because those patterns are the antithesis of wholeness. Frustration fades: People begin to consciously recognize what they are choosing, as everything within them is in search of what will allow them to thrive rather than that which causes them to avoid greater pain (such as the many distractions we've generated in our modern world, from social media to other forms of consumption).

When we access the zero-point field of Divine Source Consciousness, the origins of creative potentiality itself, we recognize that ease and surrender are essential aspects of the true self. All that is required of us is that we remember this and learn to live within it. Once we experience how it feels to embrace our true nature, our Source-loving wholeness, the entire game transforms.

To clarify, reclaiming the true self is not about changing or "upleveling" everything in our life; it's merely about finding where the harmony naturally resides within us, and expanding from that point, while offering compassion to the "pain body" that has been masquerading as the true self. In addition, we don't need to do away with our thought processes, intellect, and capacity for reasoning. Rather, all of these become an extension of what we innately know but have not yet fully realized or experienced. Once you can fully take in that Divine Source Consciousness *IS* you and not outside of yourself, you begin to become innately aware of a sense of peace and joy that radiates from within. That is the point of origin of all you are and do in this life. You begin to feel at home within.

BREATHE IN YOUR WHOLENESS
AND REMEMBER WHO YOU ARE:
A HEALING IMMERSION

Breathe into the memory that you are,
and always have been, whole.

Pause and feel that breath of truth
as you bring it from the essence of Source
into your heart as you inhale,
remembering that your breath
is your direct connection with the memory,
that Source is only breathing into you
what it is that you require
to remember who you have always been.

Source has never forgotten who you are,
nor will it ever. As you breathe, you are receiving
exactly what you require to remember yourself.

As you breathe in that wholeness,
begin to feel the energy of love
moving within you, through you, around you.

Feel that gift, the beauty of the remembered truth,
knowing there is nothing special you need to do.
To feel this, to know this, to live this—
all that is necessary is that you pause
to take who you are deep into your heart of hearts,
as you stand within the awareness
of Source, which is within you always.

And as you exhale,
you are breathing that truth into your body,
through your body, and beyond your body,
to be shared across creation.

As you express the unique beauty
of your way of loving, caring, and serving
the process of life beyond the mind's understanding
begins to be known,
breathe and remember that life is meant to be felt.
It is meant to be experienced and expressed
through the heart and spirit essence of your body
and how you live aligned within that expression.

Breathe into active form
the memory of your first incarnation:
when you knew yourself as whole,
when you knew yourself as one with Source,
when you knew yourself as a spirit,
creating a new way to experience your infinite nature
in a universe that perceives finite as normal.

Breathe into your heart
and remember that with every inhalation,
you are breathing in from the essence of God
everything you could ever possibly want or require
to remember, embody, and live
the undeniable knowing that you
have always been and always will be whole,
for that which is of Source can never be anything
other than complete.

You are a spirit creating a physical experience.
Remember who you are.
Honor that truth: that you are love and wholeness itself.
Breathe, remember, and live.

CHAPTER 2

THE MEANING OF DUALITY

FROM OUR UNDERSTANDING OF THE TRUE SELF, we come to a frequently misunderstood concept that gets misinterpreted all too often in our exploration of spirituality: duality.

Duality is extremely important when it comes to getting a sense of who we are, why we are here, and our place in the universe.

So, what exactly is it?

Spiritually, many of us are probably familiar with the idea of duality in the form of the Taoist yin-yang symbol, which reveals the power of dynamic balance between two opposites, since a portion of the opposite element exists in each half of the circle. The balance of both yin (feminine) and yang (masculine) creates an indivisible whole that helps us to understand that the dichotomies we create when we judge something as "good" or "bad" are not real. They are the result of our misperceptions.

In the models of God 1.0 through God 3.0, duality has always been about judgment, which is based on the mechanism of survival. In essence, we turned an infinite palette of feelings, emotions, and mental and physical states into a "this or that" in order to navigate our massive universe and to survive. But how can we begin to live, to *thrive*?

Thriving is about taking all that we are and bringing more of it into the world because we have the desire to experience more of our potential.

Ultimately, duality isn't about preferences, or one thing vs. another. It is an energetic matrix for the entire planet; in fact, we wouldn't be here without it. Duality is the dynamic tension that allows the universe to exist. We get stuck when we fail to recognize that duality was never meant to create separation but to offer us an entire range of options that live between perceived extremes. When we're in survival mode, we tend to separate the world into binaries: good vs. bad, light vs. dark, feminine vs. masculine, left vs. right, and so on. But when we choose to thrive, we are able to recognize all the "grays" (grace!) that exist within polarity. It's almost like seeing a gradient of colors on a color palette and recognizing that there is a rich array of options between the beginning and the end. Unfortunately, in the activity of our day-to-day lives, many people don't see this at all, nor do they recognize that it is possible to play with the infinite field in conscious and intentional ways.

The yin-yang symbol is a powerful way to remember that duality isn't meant to slot us into extremes or create a world in which we are constantly fighting on a battlefield between two seemingly opposing forces. Duality is a vast field of potential in which things that have opposing or attractive charges coalesce to create what we call matter. This field of infinite potential also happens to be neutral—it sits in wait for us to excite certain areas and energetics so as to manifest how we desire to express and experience ourselves.

We move away from limiting and binding concepts of either/or when we recognize that within the process of creation, there are no positives or negatives; there is only the choice around what we wish to create, and what the ideal conditions are for nurturing such a creation. Of course, I've had some people ask me, "Well, isn't the desire to create *anything* a preference?" My answer is no. Creativity is simply our nature as humans; it is a choice to make ourselves manifest as experiential beings who are playing within that field of infinite possibility. And of course, this is a process of experimentation. We usually know what we want to create in terms of the feeling we want to have, but it can take practice and diligence to determine whether our outcomes match our intentions.

This is where the color-gradient metaphor becomes useful. The process of course-correcting requires more options than "black" or "white." (This is also where thinking about the sheer variety of art that has been created over the course of human history is useful, in that our innate creativity works to reveal to us how much variety is possible within duality.)

The current model of duality is such that we generally don't see the field at all; we only see the extremes at either end. This is a severely limited way of engaging with our potential—and it's one that has been especially damaging with respect to our ideas about God.

The move to define Source Consciousness may very well be the birth of our current model of duality. The perception that we were not doing what "God" wanted us to do, which would draw "his" condemnation and judgment, is one of the most destructive aspects of duality as we know it.

To which I say: Source Consciousness isn't a personality, a deity, or a limited awareness that separates the world into "good" and "bad." It is a field of infinite potential in which all possibilities must be available—otherwise *nothing* can be made available.

This is a scary prospect only for the mind that is separate from itself—and separation from our true Source is a major reason so many of us are reaching for the light without recognizing that darkness is part of creation's package deal.

IT'S NOT ALL ABOUT THE LIGHT

Most of us who have been on a spiritual path are probably accustomed to the idea of "love and light," which is a common email sign-off and all-purpose mantra meant to ward off the possibility of . . . well, anything that might be deemed "low vibes." I'm not going to knock the power of honoring the light, but it would be false to say that Source Consciousness is all light. After all, the darkness and mystery of the vast Cosmos are also a beautiful part of Source.

Our orientation to "love and light" is usually based on the extent to which we have resolved our traumas. If we have been determined to see everything about our experience with the utmost objectivity, openness, and compassion, it becomes possible to see the entire panorama of beauty and ugliness without the weight of our judgment, which comes from avoidance of our own pain. I've discovered that the mechanism that tends to move us toward avoidance (which typically means avoiding one end of the spectrum of infinite potential and focusing all our attention on the other) is the inability to accept certain aspects of our reality—namely, the trauma and pain that continue to linger in our nervous system, body, and mind. Avoidance is always accompanied by the sense that something has not yet been resolved.

Why is it so hard to accept that terrible things can happen to us? Often, it's because we mistake acceptance for looking the other way and condoning that terrible thing. It's difficult to live with this, so the solution a lot of people resort to without even realizing it is to pretend that terrible things *don't* happen.

Our perspective shifts when we come to see all of life, the so-called "good" and the so-called "bad," as part of an experiential process. This does not mean that violence, coercion, and any number of horrible things a human might experience in their lifetime are acceptable. However, creation is meant to bring forth that which helps a person evolve. The messy and rapturous act of cocreating with a vast number of other beings means that we will always be presented with opportunities to navigate complex situations; to fail; to hurt others or to be hurt in return; to ask ourselves the million-dollar question: *Am I aligned with my highest potential or not?*

Tragic events transpire when we fail to ask this question. In fact, even those who make hollow declarations about love and light are contributing to a destructive pattern of avoidance that does not make the possibility of change viable. It is only by clearly seeing and looking at what is destructive and challenging, by coming to acknowledge the ways in which our societies and cultures have shaped us and contributed to this dynamic, that we actually get somewhere.

But to do this, we can't simply bask in idealistic fantasies about turning toward the light. We have to own up to the ways we've given our power away. We have to look at what lives in the shadow of our unconscious. We have to cultivate the humility to admit that we've made mistakes and perhaps we've even been complicit in destructive patterns that have hurt ourselves and others.

There is an important existential lesson when it comes to understanding that Source Consciousness is the summation of all possibilities—the infinite field in which light and darkness dance. The feeling of being separate from Source is the greatest pain anyone can possibly fathom; it is the origin of all our feelings of abandonment and inadequacy. When we experience this form of darkness, we automatically think, "This should not happen." We might find ourselves wallowing in that feeling or spiritually bypassing our way out of the despair. We forget that such moments (which St. John of the Cross referred to as the "dark night of the soul") are necessary experiences. They are meant to clearly show us what we are *not* and what we *do not want*. Again, this can be hard to realize when we're so busy fighting the feelings that come up instead of offering ourselves deep compassion and empathy in the midst of these difficult moments.

The thing is, darkness is the place where love can show up the most vividly, the most passionately, the most unconditionally.

Of course, this doesn't automatically take away or justify the pain and sorrow we've experienced, or the times in our lives when we may have been victimized or thrown for a loop. However, it *does* mean that what we choose to do with our experience is up to us. Every single one of us carries wounds, so we must do whatever we can to honor ourselves—by choosing to heal. We cannot heal without confronting the reality of darkness. More important, we cannot heal without in some way healing the world in its current manifestation and bringing out the very best of ourselves. This is a powerful way to move beyond the swinging pendulum of "good" and "bad" and to honor all aspects of our experience as catalysts for our transformation and evolution.

This is how we begin to navigate the pain so that we come to understand love, light, and truth in ways we previously haven't. We are no longer debilitated by our pain, because we are actually seeing it and acknowledging its reality. In doing so, we begin to recognize how we may have been taken out of alignment, how we may have fallen prey to the falsehood that we are separate from Source Consciousness. This is a vital opportunity to return to love, which is a large enough container to hold the entirety of our experience and come back into alignment.

This is how we come to see that the conscious intention to come into alignment is the organizational force that helps us navigate the field of infinite possibility. We literally begin to see and sense this vast potential, and to understand through experience that mastering our intent can help us to bring forward whatever we choose to.

And truly, your intention can be as simple as coming back into alignment. Instead of repeating a positive affirmation to yourself that your subconscious mind can't process or feel because it doesn't actually believe it deep down, you can reach inward to Source Consciousness and say, "Please show me a way to come back into alignment. I don't know what that is right now, but I am willing to remain open to the answers. I am willing to see what is true."

The true essence in nature of all these spiritual practices is to embody what the "master" has become. There are many examples throughout human history of enlightened beings, such as Jesus and the Buddha, who transmuted suffering into understanding and knowing—not by denying its existence but by aiming their awareness right into its very center.

Today, more and more of us are choosing awareness. The old paradigm, which fed on extremes, is in the process of decaying, even though its death knell is loud and relentless. Again, we don't need to involve ourselves in the skirmish by fighting it. All we have to do is cultivate the staying power to be with our greatest pain, with the utmost love, tenderness, and clarity, before we come out on the other side.

TURNING DIVISION INTO BALANCE

The idea of nonduality as monism, or pure consciousness that has no subject or object or sense of separation between phenomena, is often contrasted with duality. Duality is usually defined as the view that the universe is made up of two distinct realities, such as God and the Devil, mind and matter, male and female, and so forth. The unfortunate thing about duality is that it is often employed to suggest that one part of the binary is better or more acceptable than the other—which doesn't take into account that Source Consciousness is radically inclusive.

In truth, nonduality and duality aren't clashing ideologies. As I noted earlier in this chapter, duality is the way the world is organized into matter—between two seemingly "opposing" forces (at least when they're viewed through the lens of our distorted perception) is an infinite array of possibilities. Nonduality is simply the attitude of nonpreferential awareness we take when considering this field.

The essence of duality is nothing more than particles, light waves, frequencies, and thoughts that coalesce into possibilities from potential. Our evolution is all about learning to create something that brings us into the right balance—similar to what the Buddha said about choosing a "middle path" that helps us to truly understand who we are—and to choose the simplest and most fulfilling route, which is ultimately what will serve all beings.

It is possible to approach duality with a nondual consciousness, but the process of getting there is one of undoing a personal and global identity, not only in relationship to self and others but also to self and God. Instead of looking to an external father figure or other personification of Source, we must dive deep within and begin to ask ourselves some difficult questions about what we have deemed of value and importance: *If God doesn't exist, who am I? How do I really feel about myself? How do I feel about life?*

Our perspective becomes nondualistic when we cease to see ourselves and our lives as "less than" or "inferior" to some imagined ideal. Rather, we begin to experience the intricacies and beautiful particulars of everything we've navigated through. We appreciate every instance of our life. Nothing is perceived as a gain or a loss. We recognize that the field of matter is infinite, and we can choose to create a different experience—not because we're stuck in comparison envy but because we are interested in new possibilities.

It's also important to recognize that when we inhabit nondual awareness, morality ceases to exist in the ways it used to. After all, morality is merely a dualistic framework that dictates what's right or wrong, acceptable or unacceptable. In contrast, a nondualistic viewpoint is endlessly curious and good at asking questions like: *Is who I am and how I choose to be, as well as what I wish to manifest, something that elevates the quality of my life? And not only that, but does it also elevate the quality of life for every form that exists?*

With nonduality, a moral compass is unnecessary; you simply choose that which involves, engages, and supports all life. At this point, duality is all about looking at the energetics of matter and determining the particular charges, amplitudes, and movement patterns associated with any given object or situation. You might choose a little bit of this with a dash of that, and with each choice, an expression of a particular flow of truth comes forward. This process of creating is exhilarating and joyful, because it is exploratory.

In contrast, separating the world into a series of ever-conflicting opposites places us in direct conflict with ourselves. A true recognition of duality would reveal to us that all of life is possible through a balanced interaction of opposing forces: night and day, male and female, light and darkness, passion and logic, pain and pleasure, liberal and conservative, etc. Each part of the pair is meant to complement, not cancel out, the other. After all, we cannot fully understand one side of the duality without understanding the other.

While we tend to label certain qualities and ideas as acceptable or unacceptable, all of it is essential—all of it is life. Indeed, separating the world into good vs. evil hasn't done us any favors, as the tendency to stack everything into categories of "us" and "them" often leads to and has been responsible for some of the most horrific atrocities imaginable.

We are able to shift out of this inherently conflict-ridden framework when we recognize that, in order for us to bring anything at all into form, we must use two different yet complementary forces. There has to be an expressive quality that radiates out and an attracting quality that magnetizes in. It's like the negative and positive ends of a battery; nothing happens until both are present. This translates to everything we label "positive" or "negative," including our emotions. If we decide that rage and fear are "bad," we miss out on experiencing the full range of what is possible—and we miss out on catalyzing these feeling states in times when they may be appropriate. Nondual awareness teaches us that no feeling should ever be off the table; instead, true happiness is a balance between the extremes/dichotomy of ecstasy and pain. It's only how we use, view, judge, and identify with certain feeling states that can end up crippling us such that we end up forgetting that any feeling state is simply a tool to work with when the time calls for it.

With this recognition, the way our world operates ceases to

make sense in the way it used to. Even our ideas of world peace become less fraught with ideology and self-righteousness. After all, from a nondual awareness, peace is not what we typically define it to be—rather, it is an environment where space is held for everyone's viewpoint to be honored.

Let's say you and I are experiencing a conflict. In a nondual model of peace, I would wholeheartedly honor all that you feel and all that you've lived—but in order to come into this loving, neutral space, you must be willing to surrender your attachment to your pain. Likewise, I must be willing to surrender my attachment to my definition of peace or my idea of the ideal resolution to our conflict. With this understanding, the power struggle that may have been present is eradicated, and we can come together to recognize that we may have a similar concern but different ways to go about resolving it.

In this case, peace is not an ultimate destination but a dynamic state of presence that helps us to work through conflict. And even the most difficult conflicts can be worked through if we have individuals and groups who are willing to relinquish their viewpoints, which are based on preferences that may have little to do with an underlying support for all of life. Peace honors all of life. When we engage with it, we are no longer attached to one specific outcome. There is simply a recognition that the aim of this wild roller-coaster ride may very well be to learn from our experiences of being misaligned so that we can realign and evolve into a new state of balance.

Angela once asked me how she should send love to someone she no longer had a relationship with but still very much cared for. She knew this person was in a difficult situation and wondered if sending them love actually helped. I told her to simply pray that they are at peace, as peace encompasses everything she wished for them.

THE PRACTICE OF INTEGRATING DUALITY

As I've mentioned, holding a nondual awareness of duality requires a depth of surrender that enables us to let go of any stubborn attachment to our viewpoint and desired outcome. We don't need to start with the most complex or troublesome conflicts, such as ending war, poverty, or hunger. We can start with our reactions to more mundane stimuli.

When Angela and I were in Hawaii on a recent vacation, we took a boat ride. Angela tends to get seasick on boats, so prior to the excursion, she took a homeopathic remedy to alleviate any potential nausea. Unfortunately, the waves ended up being more severe than we'd expected, and Angela was throwing up throughout the trip.

Someone in the throes of motion sickness is typically going through a deep emotional churn, not just a physical one. What made Angela's experience even more challenging was the contrast between her bodily and emotional state, and the lush beauty (and even rainbows!) of the surrounding environment. Talk about duality!

But instead of getting angry or frustrated, Angela went through a process of progressively surrendering to what was happening. She'd primarily been attempting to stave off the possibility of her nausea getting worse, but eventually, she was able to let even that go. If she needed to throw up, she'd throw up. Thus began a two-hour process of crying and laughter, as Angela continued to cede control over the situation and let her body go where it needed to. As I attempted to support her through this journey, I could tell that the tears, laughter, and vomiting were part of a major release—especially since Angela had always found it difficult to cry in front of other people because of the messages she'd received as a child. But here and now, Angela was letting go of her fears and plunging into the present moment.

As she discovered, wellness was not about a specific outcome—like not getting nauseous and keeping everything contained. Wellness is the middle road we walk when we are able to balance ostensible extremes. As Angela allowed herself to fully feel both the pain and levity of the situation, she came to navigate her experience with more grace and curiosity. In her own way, she was contributing to a world that is capable of embracing wholeness and complexity.

Angela's motion sickness is such a simple example, yet it's profound because few people are able to achieve this sense of balance during a difficult moment. This is in large part because we tend to assign value to our preferences, which usually look like perfect health, perfect happiness, etc. We have fallen prey to the misconception that if we don't have these things, we are doing something wrong. We forget that it's impossible to experience great joy without great sorrow, so people get stuck in the rather prejudiced notion that they're supposed to be healthy and happy all the time—and they are absolutely beside themselves when a perfectly normal thing like getting sick on a boat ride happens.

The magical thing about being an infinite spirit in a finite form is that we always have the ability to bring a disharmonious scenario into a state of harmony. And all harmony really means is *balance*. If we feel sick, it's perfectly natural to want things to be different; however, we don't get to that different experience by resisting what is happening to us. Rather, we must address whatever it is that is being triggered within us. For example, Angela's fear of vomiting or crying in front of others was connected to her fear of expressing intense emotion, as she'd learned from her childhood that this was unsafe. But as she leaned into the literal and metaphorical turbulence, she discovered that she could naturally move into balance—*by moving with her experience instead of resisting it.*

It takes conscious practice in a range of scenarios, but when someone has mastered the essence of duality, they have an innate awareness of what the highest state of alignment is in any given moment. Alignment occurs when we find ourselves in a self-sustaining state that drains nothing and no one, but rather, gives to everything and everyone as a natural state of being. Amid this awareness, we recognize that we are more than a finite being; we are eternal awareness itself. When we come to trust in this, we automatically gain clarity on organizing our life in a way that orients us to our wholeness.

Many of us can spend decades ricocheting back and forth inside the walls of a very narrow bandwidth of experience in which we've gotten stuck. However, if we can let go of our attachment to our viewpoint, we'll be amazed with what we find. It has nothing to do with effortfulness and striving (although at first it might feel that way, since getting out of our own way takes dedication!); it is simply about being present with ourselves and being the peace that so many of us long for. In the face of such a stalwart power, conflict starts to crumble on its own. Rigid viewpoints melt away and we are faced, once again, with the majesty and inexplicable beauty of the infinite field. What we choose to create from there is up to us.

REAP THE GIFTS OF DUALITY:
A HEALING IMMERSION

Breathe in, and remember:
Duality is a gift. It is a grace from God
that helps us remember our infinite potential.

Duality is not conflict, but merely the physical universe's
palette of possibilities for experience.
It is our way of knowing the vastness of God's love and truth
in physical form.
It's not a curse. It's not a burden. It's a joy—
because it is the ability to recognize your gift of creating
through your infinite supply, of everything you need
to manifest a physical life that your spirit longs for.

This is the gift of gifts.
As you open to see and feel and innately know it as such,
you awaken so that you may live and breathe the knowing that
when you are in your heart of hearts,
when you are connected with Source itself,
all that you wish to experience is birthed from this sacred
relationship,
from this eternal truth.

Remembering this,
you can shift from survival and judgments and limitations
into using duality as a palette of infinite potentiality.
You can appreciate the beauty of light
as much as you can the beauty of darkness,
and embrace the letting go as much as the welcoming.

You are here to experience not only what you choose,
but to realize that what you choose within this field of duality,
from a place of thriving, is an opportunity to elevate all of life.

Duality is the gift of limitless creative possibility,
directed and guided by the heart and soul of your essence,
to manifest all that it wants to remember of Source in form.

Breathe, and embrace the gift that duality is.
Play in the field of potential,
without preference or prejudice, only curiosity,
and you will know peace, love, and joy
as your true nature.

CHAPTER 3

LIFE IS AN EXPERIENTIAL PROCESS

AND NOW WE COME TO THE final chapter in this section—and one of the primary themes of this book. Life is an experiential process. We are infinite beings who are innately drawn to experience ourselves as form, so that we can express ourselves as an emanation of Source. Our spirit is meant to be aligned with our biology so that we can have the experience of bringing Divine Source Consciousness into form. But due to the way humanity has developed, our awareness of how to step into alignment can seem just as elusive as the search for "God."

How do we become aligned? We open up to the full range of experiences that are possible for us to navigate on this planet. This is, in fact, our destiny.

To be clear, when I use the word *destiny*, I'm not talking about some kind of preordained fate. Rather, I'm talking about the inner barometer that recognizes the direction in which we must move because it intuits that *this* is how we can align with our true self.

Every human destiny is interdependent with the web of unresolved experiences one is born into, but overall, our destiny is to live the *truth* of who we are and to move toward whatever will help us bring that truth into the world. Karma (what we are here to resolve) is a way to experience where our strengths and weaknesses lie, what brings us into a state of harmony, and what might be creating disharmony or dis-ease. But each of us has the opportunity to put to rest the imbalances we carry from previous lifetimes; after all, we are here to become whole and unified, to awaken to more than just the physical world, and to embody Source Consciousness. In other words, we're meant to realize who we are at every level of our being—not by sitting alone in a cave trying to reach enlightenment, but by embracing the raw material of our lives so we can experience what we are and what we are not . . . and to eventually begin shaping that material with greater intentionality.

I came into the experience of being an infinite being in a finite form early in my life—and it started with a deep sense that I didn't fit anywhere. Fortunately, that sense of isolation and bewilderment was accompanied by a recognition that in some way, the world into which I was born, which was so fraught with contradiction and conflict, was not the only world that was possible for me. Thus, my journey became a journey of shifting into experiences that would help me live a truly healing and evolutionary life, rather than simply accepting what I'd been given as "the way things are." And let me tell you, some of those experiences were extremely painful. At the same time, they were necessary, because the pain of living in an illusion, of adopting a life with values that didn't align with my own, was much worse.

As I reflect on my life, it has been a journey of uncovering, healing, awakening, and becoming. It has been long, deep, and at times challenging beyond description, and I regret none of it. I truly find my life in its entirety to be a blessing and a gift. As I become more aligned with my authentic self, I allow myself to embrace everything I encounter. I resent no one, nor do I reject any part of my experience, no matter how painful or disagreeable; rather, I take it all in. Even when it doesn't fit my preferences, I see that everything in my life is moving me toward evolution. Even when it hurts, it helps me to become intimately aware of *who I am*, through the realization of *who I am not*.

It can be easier to recognize that everything that is happening is "for" us rather than "against" us when we come to the awareness of just how powerful we are. Every single one of us is creating our reality, and every aspect of this reality we are creating is meant to help us realize that everything we are and do is creation itself—especially because we *are* Source Consciousness. But because most of us have been cut off from the reality of Source, we fail to see that we play an active creative role in devising the greatest stage performance that has ever existed: life!

In fact, there is nothing we do that is *not* creative, whether that is devising a company structure, a piece of equipment, an educational system, a plan for parenting our children, or even an act of calculated deceit or manipulation—all of these are instances of using our creativity to create something. The act and art of living *is* the experiential creative process; that is, we take the essence of infinity and channel it into something we perceive as finite and limited. Life starts to become interesting when we move through a process of spiritual self-actualization. We recognize that we can intentionally live our lives however we want to, but this only happens when we are able to surrender the mechanisms that bind, distort, and limit our creative power.

To heal, you have to let go of your perceptions and reference points for what a "good" or "successful" life looks like. For when you cling to these ideas, you place a ceiling on your own growth. You follow in the footsteps of those who came before you rather than recognizing your own potential to carve out new paths that will bring the unique being you are into a greater sense of alignment and presence. You mistake potent cathartic processes for "failure" and end up choosing one end of the spectrum of duality at the expense of your own wholeness.

Of course, on this earthly plane, we must learn to skillfully navigate and negotiate our way in and around a variety of complex factors. The challenge is, most of us are navigating to avoid—similar to how a ship on the ocean attempts to avoid hitting rocks and icebergs. Unfortunately, while this can be a way of staying "safe," it severely limits the vividness and scope of what you could experience.

At a certain point, I began to recognize that true wellness and vitality come from the willingness to see the highest truth, the greatest capacity for joy, love, and peace, in my ability to open up to *all* aspects of my life—including the pain.

Accordingly, when we begin to see life as an experiential process with the power to bring us back into alignment, we can dive into every experience life presents us with. This is how we get to the purest essence of what we are carrying within us, which helps us identify which aspects of the self must be resolved so we can all come together in the way we are meant to and consciously cocreate an even more incredible experience that will anchor us in Source. I look forward to the day when truth is no longer an individual adventure but a conscious and collective one!

NO REFERENCE POINTS

As I've been emphasizing throughout this book, we need to be fully present—and willing to fully feel if we want to heal and live in the most vibrant, soulful, Source-fueled way possible. And there, precisely, is the conundrum. We *don't* fully feel, because we *don't* allow ourselves to surrender to life; and we *don't* surrender to life because we *don't* allow ourselves to fully drop into our feelings. And so, a vicious cycle ensues.

Why is it so difficult to simply navigate our lives with a sense of surrender that helps us welcome the perceived good and bad, ups and downs, peaks and valleys, of life? It isn't that we fear the accompanying losses (of security, loved ones, identity, etc.) that might come when we are receptive to the journey. It's that we become rigid and clamp down on our desire for control because we fear the accompanying feelings associated with loss and acceptance.

I went through my own dark night of the soul during a period when I felt like I was in stasis and nothing was moving. I was going through a deep personal review of why things were so difficult for me and why I was struggling to feel more relaxed and at ease in my life. I recognized that I did everything very mechanically, very methodically, as a way of controlling my environment and myself, so I could feel safe and like I had some say in my life. However, I realized that having my proverbial ducks all lined up in a row was causing me greater pain. In truth, I was always holding back and preparing for the worst to happen.

The moment of realization was almost laughably mundane. I was in the parking lot of a laundromat, having a conversation with somebody about this. I literally stopped what I was saying, and I just looked up in the air at my invisible ducks. At that moment, I pulled the pin on an energetic hand grenade and threw my hand up in the air, as if I were tossing it out to the powers that be. In my mind's eye, I could see everything blowing up—the ducks that had symbolized my sense of "safety" shattered into a million pieces. I was in shock. And then, I started crying and laughing simultaneously. Both emotional responses were coming out of me at random intervals. I simply didn't know how to organize myself with respect to what was happening.

In that moment, I declared to myself, "I'm done with this!" Once that happened, I found myself no longer operating with intellect as my navigational GPS. I started to realize that those orderly ducks had been obscuring the vitality and beauty of my true essence. I began to realize that by controlling my life in order to limit pain and fear, I was limiting love and joy. A limit is a limit. It can't be specific; we are either open or closed. There are degrees and nuances to keep in mind here, of course, but if we are afraid to feel something in one particular area, we limit all areas.

This was a massive turning point for me. Without the safety of previous anchors and definitions of who I was and who I could be, I felt like I was starting from scratch. The old operating system—which, frankly, didn't work all that well to begin with—was in need of a massive overhaul. The reference points of the past, which had given me a sense of false assurance, no longer worked for the person I was swiftly becoming. But for most of us, it is the past that gives us a sense of who we are: our roots, our personality, our likes and dislikes, our yardsticks for measuring the present and future.

Letting go of reference points is frightening because it can feel like we're on a raft in the middle of nowhere, and we've just released our oars. It can kick up a lot of chaos as the mind struggles to find a speck on the horizon that resembles land. This is why, even when people go through massive changes, backsliding into familiarity can be just as common as taking a quantum leap into the unknown and growing as a result. Reference points give us a sense of (temporary) certainty; they help us predict the future and make sense of our life path up until now.

But if we want to have the sacred experience of touching Source, which is the current that runs through everything, we must be willing to let go of reference points now and then—at least, until we get to the state where we feel comfortable doing away with them altogether and allowing life to be a spontaneous emergence rather than a narrow path toward a preconceived set of desirable outcomes.

This is the paradox of surrender: We must be willing to feel eternally lost in order to be eternally found.

Spiritual awakenings occur when people realize that they are limiting the breadth and depth of their experience of life, and thus, their ability to fully interface and intimately exchange with Source Consciousness. When you come to the understanding that I came to so many years ago, playing it safe is no longer an option; in fact, you'd rather give all of it up because you are painfully aware of the fact that you are not living as you should and you are not experiencing the "you" that is ready to be expressed.

My "awakening" moment wasn't a one-and-done deal, of course. My choice points, which I described in Chapter 1, simply precipitated moments wherein I continued to realize I needed to surrender even more deeply. As I moved through these difficult moments, I came to realize that there is something in me that has a desire to facilitate *all of life* awakening to its true self. I realized that I could do this for eternity. From there, everything changed rapidly for me. I began attracting experiences into my life that helped me to heal wounds I didn't even realize I was still carrying.

As I opened up even more and allowed more of my spirit to guide and infuse my life, I found I was receiving more of the essence of Source. And more of me was inviting it in. My desire to know Source more deeply and richly started to become the center of everything. I also recognized that if this required demolishing my life to its very foundations and starting over from ground zero, I was willing to do it. What I had previously feared—the feelings accompanying loss, which would have reduced me to a state of annihilation—was nothing compared to what I was letting in: an experience of Source, living through me, as me, in dynamic motion on this earthly plane. If that meant the "Ron" I knew yesterday would cease to exist, I wholeheartedly welcomed it.

Again, this was the paradox: The more of "me" I was willing to give up, the closer to my essence I became.

Then, life became . . . well, actually enlivening! It was no longer a set of concrete reference points I could turn to every time I felt flustered or bewildered. References are useful in that we look to them for help in making a decision, but they become cumbersome when we revert to them out of fear that we'll make a mistake.

Connecting with Source Consciousness helps us to release our fear of falling into error. It is a fluid, relational dance in which even our mistakes can be purposeful. For me, the fear of making a mistake was a moot point, because I recognized that every experience, no matter how difficult, could be turned into an expression of wisdom—a way to check whether I was living in or out of alignment.

I came to see that fluidity is required for anyone to be authentically connected to Source and to themselves. When you're in the dance, you don't need reference points; you organically respond to each moment as it arises. This becomes life as art: taking the essence of what you are and working with it, within a matter-based reality.

Gradually getting rid of reference points altogether would create a completely brand-new world, and we'd see massive shifts in the relationships between individuals and societies. But all of us are familiar with people who get stuck in their paradigms and ways of seeing and interacting with the world; often, these are the ones who resist change and who cling to "old ways" of doing things and perceiving reality.

Certainly, this survival-based form of human consciousness is alive and limping along in our world today, but we are also beginning to see more and more people who are choosing to awaken to their full potential. They, too, are rapidly contributing to the creation of a new form of consciousness on this planet that is beginning to spread its compassion, peace, love, and wonder far and wide. As we move into a paradigm of God 5.0, we will see this becoming the dominant consciousness; more and more people will be initiated into a higher path of joy, acceptance, gratitude, and fluidity. And even if we encounter people who continue to hold on to survival-based modes of operating in the world, there will be a loving space that the dominant consciousness holds for them. Even if people rooted in fear-based reference points never shift out of this paradigm, they will be exposed to the love that is Divine Source Consciousness—so that when they die, they can take the old paradigm with them and weaken the construct that has kept so many people stuck in fear and rigidity.

The new consciousness we are stepping into is an innate sense of presence that holds the universal matrix or pattern in a completely different light. It is not about survival or domination or having power over anyone else. Nor does it drain us as we bring it into existence. There is no deficit that occurs, as it is pure life giving birth to pure life. When we become the conduit for this new way of being, the propensity to cling to the way it "used to be" automatically dissipates. We come into a natural state of harmony that takes us on a new adventure, in which our evolution is the journey rather than the destination.

PAUSE, FEEL, SHIFT

Most of us are raised to see ourselves as human, first and foremost. However, if we were raised to realize that we are spirits creating a human experience, and *that* is the essence of who we are, we would be moved to bring this essence into form in an infinite number of ways. Through this perspective, the end goal of life wouldn't be happiness, or success, or any of the things we are encouraged to aspire to in our survival-based world. We would recognize that life is about expressing and experiencing everything we are drawn to express and experience.

Because the nature of existence is pluralistic, and because it is meant to walk us home to Source, we would easily see that there is no such thing as failure. For when we engage with life in a deeply embodied way, even if something doesn't go according to our preferences, we would likely say, "Ah, this is showing me an imbalance I need to correct by bringing my loving attention to it. I'm so grateful it showed up, because it's pointing me to something within me that I need to look at, honor, and heal through loving it into wholeness."

It can be difficult to step into that state of receptivity, but through my own work with clients, I've developed a powerful three-step method I call "Pause, Feel, Shift," which I've witnessed in action in the lives of so many people.

One of my clients, Leanne, grew up in a family dynamic in which she was almost invisible. It's not that she was a black sheep, but more that her family had rejected her whole self, and she experienced an alarming amount of neglect. When she attempted to come out of the shadows, as some part of her longed to align with her authentic self, her family would knock her down. This turned her into an individual who was personally and socially very withdrawn. At the same time, her Source-based self continued to shine through and assert her innate value. She developed a business wherein she helped people find the right kind of home for themselves. Not only was she offering a valuable service, but she'd found a way to transmute her deepest pain (feeling out of place within her "home") into a beautiful offering so others could experience the kind of sanctuary and sense of welcome that she'd longed for at a young age but had never received.

Leanne was, unsurprisingly, drawn to a spiritual path. However, she ran into something that most people on such a path will run into at some point—it was typical Spirituality 101, which urged her to "find the positive in everything" and to take full responsibility for every aspect of her experience. (This misinterpreted aspect of the Law of Attraction forgets we are all cocreating our experiences, and that something "bad" doesn't happen because we unconsciously drew it in but because it's one of Source's generous opportunities to come back home to ourselves.) Leanne found it difficult to sit with heavy emotions or be with anything that weighed her down. Although she put on a cheerful face, it was all surface-level, and her avoidance didn't make her any happier. She recognized that she was in search of something deeper than the facade of happiness. What she wanted was the authenticity of joy—of being effortlessly kind and comfortable inside her own skin. But she lacked true confidence due to the insecurity she'd dragged around over the years. No matter what she ended up doing, she always found herself wondering if she'd failed or succeeded in her endeavors. Had she done right by the people in her life? And ultimately, did this mean she was "good enough" now?

In general, Leanne's pattern shed light on the fact that so many people seek out success because they don't have the skill set to walk into failure, which is associated in part with shame and inadequacy. So, this is where I asked Leanne to really *pause* and *feel* her pattern of looking for either success or failure. She realized that everything she was engaging in was more of a thought-based perception of what feeling was. She didn't actually feel very much at all; she had intellectualized her way into what she thought she was supposed to feel, which is common for people on a spiritual path looking for a formula to fix their problems. A lot of this could be traced back to her family, who had taught her that she wasn't allowed to feel, but to keep her emotions to herself and project the image of her best self.

Experience is just a multifaceted process or way of being that takes into consideration all that makes up each of us: our visual, auditory, cognitive, and kinesthetic reception, as well as how we feel when we're in any given situation. In order to fully be in our experience, *we have to feel it*. So many of us are trained to be like robots moving through our process, but this harms us because it keeps our spirit from guiding our actions and fully animating our finite forms. Thus, we end up depending on the intellect, which also gets disconnected from our spirit.

Connecting with our feelings, the language of the soul, helps us to become more spirit-directed and to get to know our body as an expressive tool that is an extension of our spirit. Our intellect is merely one way of gauging the "how" of expressing our spirit self and then recalculating and course-correcting if we haven't quite gotten it. But we must first and foremost trust our feelings. We must fall into what we are and what we are feeling with unconditional acceptance and love of ourselves and life, before we can begin to perceive the truth of who we are and what is possible. As Leanne learned, this takes an enormous amount of surrender as we gradually let go of the reference points and all forms of knowledge and safety that we used to believe in.

It's like the mind is saying, "Okay, spirit, I'm willing to go into that chrysalis and dissolve everything I've known myself to be, so I can know myself even more deeply. I'm going to go into the unknown—but is it okay if I make mistakes?"

As we sit in the space of the pause, the space of the feeling, something happens. We start to know from a deeper place. We start to recognize the message that Source has always transmitted: "There are no mistakes, only opportunities." As we become aware of the eternal nature of our spirit, we *shift*.

Together, we kept peeling back the layers of the pain Leanne carried, which she gradually allowed herself to feel. She began to progressively feel good about herself, and to feel better about her life. All of this helped her to work diligently to become aware of who she was and how she was feeling. First the pause, then the feeling, then the shift.

Over the next several months, Leanne remarked, "I feel more alive than I've ever felt before! I feel so much better about myself!" She was no longer numbing herself through "love and light" spirituality, avoidance, or addiction.

You can also practice what Leanne did and be assured that the body always knows when something in our life isn't working for us. You will feel the sense of misalignment and discontent that is calling for your attention. There is no need to push it away or power through. All you have to do is pause. When Leanne paused, a complex mixture of feelings came up for her, including the sadness associated with everything she'd wanted to push away. She didn't push it away, though. She rested within it. The more she sat with her feelings, she began to sense something that wasn't intellectually tangible—it was the essence of life, which is no different from Source Consciousness. It was as if the tightly balled-up fist that was her entire being could finally relax, and through this relaxation, she could feel her spirit communicating with her. She could then begin to take cues from her spirit, step by step, gradually, and to make massive shifts. Leanne continues to thrive in her life, due to her willingness to step into the unknown—and to feel and grow.

LEARNING TO BE WITH ALL OF IT

Of course, the breakthrough Leanne experienced doesn't happen with everyone. I once had another client, Michael, who was a recovering addict participating in a twelve-step program. He once came to me and said, "What's going on with me? I'm starting to feel things that are really freaking me out."

I told Michael that while his twelve-step program was giving him a powerful, useful tool to stay sober and remain stable, he had not fully allowed himself to feel the deeper feelings that were calling for his attention. I encouraged him to pause and feel, but his response was, "Fuck no! Why would I want to feel that hell?" This was indicative of the struggle he'd been through. He was frightened that opening up to his dark and troublesome feelings would cause him to relapse, which would then cause him to hurt and possibly lose his family.

"What if you were able to move through this in a very progressive way, in bite-size pieces?" I inquired.

He shook his head. He wasn't having any of it. "No way! I don't want to put my family through this again."

I said, "Then I'm not sure I can help you."

I knew it wasn't my place to push past Michael's resistance or take him somewhere he wasn't ready to go. He was very clear that he didn't want to feel what was lurking beneath the resistance, because he feared he would just end up losing everything.

That may seem like a legitimate fear, but it never is. It is just a choice that must be honored.

Even when we feel lost, confused, or disoriented, the willingness to *stay* with our experience is what will allow us to navigate through the discomfort and bring more of our whole self forward. Michael was caught in the web of a strong ideology—that of his recovery and sobriety journey. It had given him a new sense of purpose, but all ideologies are based on the need to protect some aspect of ourselves; rarely are they created to expand us and free us from our inner turmoil. This is where an ideology can become a crutch—when it keeps us from looking honestly at ourselves and evolving.

Part of accepting that life is an experiential process is learning to come into more intimate contact with it and ourselves, such that we are no longer hiding behind a veil of protection. Rather, we are passionate about experiencing the naked essence of this earthly dance, which includes the terrain of our feelings—the dark and light, the high and low. In welcoming this, we learn to be with all of it.

We are truly here to experience everything we can, but we are so caught in survival mode that we cordon off entire parts of our being because we fear they would submerge us in pain and suffering if we let them out. But we cannot embrace life unless we are fully able to embrace ourselves. We cannot offer love and respect to others if we cannot love and respect all parts of ourselves. We cannot respond to our deepest yearnings if we shut off the valve to whatever it is they are communicating to us.

There is something about this kind of deep acceptance—which is not the same as indulging our "demons," yet another form of avoiding our pain—that has the power to open us up to all of life. I think of someone like the Dalai Lama, who lives and breathes this acceptance as the only true way of being. To be around that kind of vibration changes us on a cellular level, until we are ready to step into the initiation—and to be honest with ourselves about what we are avoiding.

What Michael couldn't understand is that if we are having a hard time with pain, it's important to walk through how that pain feels. We resort to avoidance because we are tired of suffering, but the problem with this tactic is that it keeps us from being able to accurately interpret our experience (a side effect of cutting ourselves off from our feelings). We step into more of our creative potential when we honor and embrace whatever is presenting itself to us. However, our resistance only ensures that we continue to see our pain in a distorted way. It also keeps us from being able to experience joy and ecstasy, which is simply a grounded embrace of the entire range of our sensory capacities.

One of the tools I offer to clients who have a difficult time stepping into and being with pain is something I call "Just Get Me Through This." This was my literal entreaty to God when I was younger and confronted with experiences that threatened to knock me off my center. Even at a tender age, I wasn't looking for a free pass. I was simply looking for the capacity to get through my challenges, moment by moment.

I believe this is what helped me to expand into even greater states of flow and allowance. I realized that happiness wasn't about being ignorant and protected from pain. It was about the inner freedom that comes from recognizing we can navigate even the most tumultuous storms.

We are by our nature meant to vibrate ecstasy, which comes from our recognition that it is safe to expand into whatever life is presenting to us. We become truly happy and vibrant when we release the limitations and external references that a mindset of avoidance creates. We can look at things as they are rather than as we wish for them to be, and this opens us up to a remarkable aliveness, even in the midst of our greatest pain.

There have been moments in my life when I felt broken down and even shattered, but those moments ultimately created a feeling of relief that gave way to a sense of being broken open. Ironically, it was in those moments that I actually felt the most alive.

In truth, life will break our hearts over and over again, but the goal isn't to keep this from happening. It is to feel the depth and breadth of *all of it*—to allow the pain to expand our capacity, so we open up to even more compassion, love, and empathy. During such times, we are given the opportunity to recognize what our human mind cannot always comprehend: that what appears to be a destructive process (for example, the end of a relationship, the death of a loved one, or the grief associated with what is happening to our planet) is corrective. It is life's way of clearing imbalance. From a human standpoint, we might choose to fixate on all that has been lost, but often, being broken open frees us up to a new perspective. We can even begin to find gratitude within this process. This doesn't mean we stop feeling grief or loss. But in some ways, our love deepens when we experience loss.

I have worked with many clients who describe an almost ineffable sense of love that washes over them after the death of someone who was very close to them. I believe this occurs because, when people are alive, we do not let them in (or ourselves out) completely—often, this is because we may be more focused on what we have to *do*, rather than how we are *being* with them. Death can be an opportunity to appreciate what may have been taken for granted, consciously or not, or what may not have been fully felt when the loved one was alive. It breaks our heart open even more, so we can feel what they meant to us. And then, as a result, we get to have the sacred experience of an innate knowing that they are always with us, even though they're no longer physically present. When our heart is broken open, we come to fully feel our losses, but we also get to receive the gifts in ways that may not have been previously accessible to us.

I might even take this further to say that the experience of "heartbreak" only occurs when we do not accept what has happened. But when we stay with our experience of grief and suffering rather than attempting to change it or to turn away from it because it's too much to bear, what is ultimately broken open is our sense of limitation, as well as the viewpoints that keep us captive in a state of fear and smallness. We recognize that what is breaking open is our own prejudice and the ways in which we have held on to a belief or identity that is too small to hold the person we are evolving into. It can feel terrifying to face, but when we allow our hearts to keep breaking wide open, we come into contact with the eternal nature of our connection with Source. We come into a calm acceptance of the feelings we have attempted to avoid or bypass—and when we go into them, we discover that the profound intimacy we have always yearned for lives right there, at the center of what we once believed was too painful to touch.

When we stop trying to protect ourselves from our pain, we come to honor what has been. We allow ourselves to feel what we feel for as long as we need to, and our hesitation and resistance fade altogether. The fortress we've built around our heart reveals its weak spots, and then we realize we can dismantle it altogether. We no longer need to protect our pain, because we have come to see through the eyes of our own resilient heart.

SEEING THROUGH THE EYES OF THE HEART

There is a practical way to learn to be with all of it—and it does not involve even an iota of using our intellect to muscle through or endure difficult situations. Rather, we give up the robotic intellect of the mind that is cut off from its feelings and step into the intellect of the heart, which always opens us up to the magnificent scope of reality.

The literal and energetic heart is a powerful organizing principle that brings the essence of who we are into focus in such a way that it helps to generate the frequency and patterning of our life on this Earth. The heart brings together the higher chakras (associated with intuition and our connection to spirit) and the lower chakras (associated with our biology and physiology), synchronizing these seemingly disparate spheres of experience. The heart is what lets us come forward as a unified presence, so we are no longer simply trying to survive or striving to touch God. When we live from the heart, we realize that we are the essence of existence itself! Life becomes a joyful game, replete with beautiful discoveries and playfulness.

The heart is, in fact, an instrument that helps us to navigate this earthly plane. Think about our planet—everything that is alive has a specific vibrancy. If we look at life on this planet, we will see the color green more than anything else. Not coincidentally, green is the color that is associated with the heart chakra. It is the vibration of life itself.

Currently, on our planet today, there is a painful schism between the human body and our spirit essence. Few people are truly grounded within the body, as their experiences of trauma have resulted in a split. The human psyche is in a state of crisis, as we are walking around in an atomized state that makes it very difficult to recognize and live within our true nature.

The more heart-centered we become, the more we come to heal this split. The heart is the merger point between the body and our spirit; it is where we come into a state of union with ourselves. Physically, psychologically, and spiritually, the heart weds the knowing of the higher self and mind (which are not the same as the intellect) with the states of presence that are possible when we come to fully inhabit our bodies. The heart takes the awareness of the physical and nonphysical planes of reality and channels the intent of our spirit into our present reality.

The heart is a powerful center of gravity (something the old myths and fairy tales knew well, even though this can be communicated in overly sappy ways when people discuss the importance of "following your heart"). It is a muscular force, in that it helps us to fully engage with the process of turning our choices into form and matter. It is the fulcrum of our attention.

So, if we focus on feeling everything from the heart, we are attuning ourselves to hearing and knowing our spirit essence first and foremost. This information then gets filtered through the gut, the mind, and the intellect, for there must be a negotiation on how to bring together the core intent of spirit, make it manifest in the physical world, and put it into action. But unlike so many other models of living, in which the wisdom of the heart is sidelined and thought of as frivolous, we place it at the center of our lives so that everything in our physiology, psychology, and spirit can begin to work together harmoniously.

This is also a wonderful way to reverse a common misunderstanding that many of us are often unconsciously operating under: the notion that feeling through the heart is the primary reason for our pain and suffering. The survival-based intellect (which my client Michael was grappling with) resists the idea of being vulnerable, so it causes us to resist opening up to and trusting our hearts. However, the heart, which is a conduit of spirit, is the gateway to knowing Divine Source Consciousness and ourselves more intimately and truthfully.

Remarkably, we used to be much more connected to the heart, prior to the development of civilization and the onset of the Age of Reason. We lived on instinct, and although some of this was connected to our primitive survival instincts, we were much more open to the serendipity that is associated with feeling things as they are, without resistance or internal blockages. As our cultures advanced and we developed a higher intellectual capacity and sophistication in our approach to life, we became more closed off to the spontaneity that is inherent in being an animate being in a world that is fully alive. For the majority, our knowledge became references that froze the world around us into a lifeless version of itself.

The heart has a vibrational knowing of our eternal nature that contributes to the creation of our bodies, but we've become so intellectually charged over the centuries that we've moved away from the sages, wisdom keepers, and shamans—who brought the world beyond "ordinary reality" into the present moment, because their hearts guided their minds, bodies, and voices into creating stories that people could feel as true, on every level. One of the greatest reasons we struggle as much as we do is that when we have an experience, we do not allow it to fully animate us, through our hearts. Rather, we mechanically attempt to resolve what's going on or direct it in the way we think it should be directed.

The heart is the quickest path to any true kind of "resolution," in that it knows what the spirit wants to experience and bring into this world and can communicate this information to us in such a way that we can make that desire manifest. When we open the heart, we open the gateway to Source Consciousness itself.

Fifteen years ago, I noticed through my own intuitive awareness that the heart center is growing significantly stronger in some people. As we evolve, we are moving into a more unified state of consciousness, which allows our physiology and biology to be a direct reflection of our spirit essence. As this happens, life can truly become an experience in which there is no separation between matter and spirit—and our survival-based world can ecstatically surrender to the joy of living in infinite potential, the way Source always intended.

THE DIVINE POWER OF OUR BREATH

One of the greatest tools we have for connecting with the heart, and for being in a state of open receptivity to life itself, is recognizing the role of the breath as a conduit that connects us to Source Consciousness and the open heart. It is little wonder that so many spiritual traditions refer to the "breath of God" being the force that breathed us into life. Breath is our ultimate tool for aligning with our core self. The remedy for all that ails us is the breath of truth, which connects us to our true nature. In the dance of life, we are meant to inhale the essence of all that we need, and to exhale the expression of what our spirit wishes for us to know ourselves as. Breath is the animating principle of the universe, a way for creation to radiate out into the world (the exhale) and to draw itself back into the zero point of consciousness (the inhale). This is the fundamental operating principle of the universe. The Big Bang was the exhalation that set everything into motion, but at some point, even the universe will retract back into itself as Source Consciousness inhales this whirlwind of activity and evolution back into the zero point.

As we learn to really engage with our breath, we come to understand our true nature and that we ourselves are an emanation of the active principle of creativity. We inhale all we require, and we exhale the bounty of the gifts we have been given. In the stillness and pause between the inhalation and exhalation, we come to know the timeless, boundless spirit of Source.

Whenever we need to put the noise and commotion of the world around us to rest, we can always use our breath as a reorganizing, recentering, and calming tool. It's so simple, yet we often forget it. We breathe all day long, but if we can remember in a moment of conflict or resistance to simply take a breath, we can reawaken and ignite our innate ability to come back to a state of self-unity, of ease, of connection with our core essence. Certainly, it might not take a single breath—it could take five, or ten, or a hundred. But as we surrender to our breath, we come to see that it has a powerful function that is Divinity itself.

Namely, breath is an exchange of energy. We draw in the nourishment we require, and we exhale what no longer serves us but can nourish other parts of creation. It's similar to breathing in the oxygen that the trees give off, as the trees breathe in the carbon dioxide we give off. The act of respiration is essentially an act of nourishment that extends to all beings. In this way, we see that sacred reciprocity and balance are laws and truths of the universe. There is nothing in this universe that is a waste, even what we view as the release of our "toxins." When we breathe through the lens of balance, everything we have to offer is a gift.

In this sense, breath is the essence of Source and its creation. All matter is simply the breath of Source in a specific and tangible form. Divine Source Consciousness breathes us into aliveness, and there is no life form that is more or less sacred than another. If we can acknowledge this, we can come to gather our true essence, which we have scattered across this and other lifetimes. We can bring ourselves back to a state of union with ourselves and all of life, with every conscious inhalation and exhalation. As we come into synchrony with our breath and learn to breathe more deeply, we find a way to bring spirit into our physical form and transmute the places within us that hold on to patterns that limit us. As we do so, it becomes harder to live within an illusionary frame.

We know when someone is out of alignment when we observe their breath—if it is shallow, ragged, or short. Often, many of us live without utilizing the full capacity of our breath, and this becomes natural and normalized. But when we surrender to the breath and allow ourselves to breathe, we come to be one with the breath of God. What does this mean in a practical sense? It means we are committed to harmony, to alignment, to coming back into our true nature every time we step out of balance. When we breathe in that which only knows itself as the purest essence at the center of all things, and if we honor and respect it, the whole of us will move in that direction.

If we do this multiple times a day, it is possible to disperse certain patterns that hold us back from experiencing the full spectrum of life. We begin with the easiest and least destabilizing patterns, and then, we gradually move into more complex patterns. This expands our bandwidth for life. The way we breathe can literally change our experience. With our breath, we begin to summon what we require to remember and awaken who we truly are. With our breath, we translate our state of being into pure presence, which is the most genuine form of prayer there is. We become available to the wild ride of experience and are then equipped to surf that wave to the best of our ability.

BE BREATHED BY THE BREATH OF GOD: A HEALING IMMERSION

*Your breath is your single greatest and most sacred tool
to remind you of who you are.
Your breath is your way of remembering your connection with
the Divine.
Your breath is your way of receiving everything and anything
you require
to not only remember your true self and your true nature,
but to bring it into form—
because it is YOURS to bring into form.*

*With your breath, pause, and be still.
On your exhale, feel that resting point.
Feel your intent of what you would love to receive from God,
to remember you are complete.*

*And when you are complete, breathe in,
knowing you are receiving from Source itself.*

*Once again, feel God breathe into you all that you are.
Draw that into your heart center until you feel your lungs and
your body
receive as much as you can in this moment.*

*Pause . . .
and rest in the gratitude that comes with that reception,
with that gift of the reminder that is you.*

*And when you are ready, breathe that energy to your body,
through your body, beyond your body,*

from your heart center, in all directions,
gifting to all life everything you just received and honored
as you.

And when you feel that exhalation,
and you find yourself more complete,
stay with the pause and experience gratitude once more.

You can use your breath to remember
the true essence of what it is to be unconditional love
and to receive everything you feel you require
to remember yourself as whole.

Use your breath to receive from God all that is necessary
to be whole and harmonious in every moment of your life,
in the joyful moments and the challenging moments—
for we're not meant to receive from Source
only within periods of difficulty.
We are meant to receive from Source
a constant reminder of our vastness
and the depth and breadth of love, compassion, and joy
that we can bring forth in this universe, through these bodies.

Breathe in,
and remember and receive an exchange of love and truth.
And then, breathe that into the world, for all your sisters
and brothers,
so that you know yourself as part of a whole,
and choose to love for and with all, because that is your essence.

Breathe in whatever it is you require
to remember your wholeness.
Breathe, receive, feel.

PART II

THE REVOLUTION: CLEARING

A REVOLUTION CAN BE DEFINED AS an overthrow of an existing order in favor of a new system that brings about greater balance. The reason so many revolutions throughout history haven't worked and have indeed only ended up replicating the same conditions they were fighting, is that so few of these revolutionaries understood that true transformation begins on the inside. In the next few chapters, I will guide you on the most effective practices for clearing out the systems and structures that were handed down to you and beginning the important work to consciously change.

Revolution moves us into a new cycle that begins with recognizing the aspects of what we have inherited that are harmful or simply no longer serve us. Most of us have already mastered the pain cycle—that is, we know how to be in pain but we don't know how to be in joy.

Clearing away the old can be terrifying because it leaves us in a space of uncertainty and emptiness, like we lost a dear friend. However, uncertainty is one step on the way to erecting a new foundation of joy, peace, and love. This is how we move out of desperation and survival mode (and with it, all the ways we've grasped at "power" from our perceived sense of inferiority and inadequacy) and into the wholeness that we are.

As a species that is on the cusp of ushering in God 5.0 (the next highest expression of God Consciousness), we recognize on some level that the societies we've built were created for the purpose of survival. As we yearn to evolve, we are drawn to create a different relationship with life. Everything we've ever known or unconsciously accepted must be placed on the altar for review. And even if we find ourselves on our hands and knees in pain because the world as we have known it is crumbling around us and we're terrified, there is hope. The altar, despite its religious connotations, is an essentially sacred space where we can place everything in our human experience before Divine Source Consciousness and ask for the truth. And as Jesus said, "Ask and ye shall receive."

CHAPTER 4

OVERCOMING TRAUMA, FAMILY LINEAGE, AND PAST-LIFE INFLUENCES

BEFORE WE PROCEED ANY FURTHER, I want to ask you a question: Do you feel safe now, at this very moment? Chances are, you haven't really stopped to think about it. Or maybe, on deeper reflection, you realize you've always walked around with a low-grade sense of uncertainty and insecurity, of feeling the world is a place dotted with land mines, and at any moment the rug of security will be pulled out from beneath you. If you're anything like most of the eight billion people on this planet, it's quite possible that you've already experienced forms of unsafety: violence, war, abuse, and many other difficult ordeals that all of us are subject to in different ways. Some people might say that the experience of trauma is a universal human experience. This may well be true, but as infinite beings having and creating a human experience, we have the power to transmute our wounds so that they don't become our destiny.

At this point, you might be wondering: *Why the heck are we talking about trauma? I'm here to talk about God—or Source—or whatever it is we're calling it. I'm here to figure out how I can get free from all the stuff that's been holding me back from my true essence!*

To which my answer would be: Well, you've answered your question, then!

A book about "God" would be incomplete without a deeper exploration of the impacts of trauma—which encompasses the gifts and curses of family lineage; the transformation of personal demons (including guilt, shame, doubt, and unworthiness) that are the result of traumatic experiences; and the ways in which past-life influences may be clouding our judgment and interfering with our current energetics so we don't have access to that wholeness. Trauma is essentially a quality of fragmentation that keeps us from wholeness, which keeps us from opening up a line of communication to Source—to our truest, most authentic self.

So, as you can see, our experience of trauma has everything to do with our relationship to Source Consciousness.

For many people, sadly, trauma begins at home—in the subtle and overt ways that domination and control get enacted through the family system. In many ways, our experience of God (at least, the God that is broadcasted to us by organized religion, family, and society) is based on our relationships with the parental figures we view through our young and innocent perspective as all-powerful, all-knowing, and perfect. Often, this perspective gets transferred onto God; hence the number of religions in the world that characterize God as an omniscient, omnipresent (usually male) being who is there to discipline and punish us for our shortcomings. This becomes "motivation" for us to please and be perfect. We tend to ascribe a consistent and palpable relationship with God to our own worthiness. That is, if we are disconnected, that means we've displeased God—or, similar to early experiences of family unrest, that we have been abandoned by God. Even those of us who were not raised within the confines of institutional religion are impacted by this pervasive rhetoric of God

1.0, even if only on a subconscious level. In and of itself, this is a story that paints a picture of a God who will punish or abandon us if we're "bad." Many of us carry this fear around long after we've decided that the God we grew up with doesn't fit into our belief system. But the trauma continues to linger.

Trauma is a hot topic these days. What exactly is a trauma? Again, it can be defined in a number of ways, but it's generally a subtle induction of disruptive energies that accumulate before you can recover. A lot of times, many traumas can build on the first one until all of that energy gets frozen in a person's system. That's why a trauma can make itself known years after that first experience that crystallized into form—and it might even feel just as fresh as it did that first time. It's important for all of us to heal from our trauma in order to know our wholeness, but the term *trauma* is becoming a challenging arena to traverse. Quite often it can be used to avoid and validate a personal viewpoint or experience, rather than moving into healing. That's because a lot of people aren't interested in feeling their trauma; they want it to be recognized and respected by others. They want to be recognized and validated for what they have gone through, almost like a badge of honor.

Of course, it's important that we never diminish our experiences. Everyone's experience is rich in opportunities for growth. However, we don't have to nor should we define ourselves on the basis of our trauma; after all, trauma is an experience, not a defining moment or reference point we are meant to live our lives from. All we have to understand is that it's the result of an incomplete experience that got stuck in our physiology, energy, psyche, and persona. It can arise from something seemingly "small" (like being scolded by a parent for doing something they deemed dangerous or an unwanted behavior) or from an event that had lasting and dramatic repercussions (such as being the victim of rape or abuse). Sometimes, we humans have an unfortunate tendency to label one thing more traumatic than another, but in all sincerity, we must see our experiences as being unique and incomparable to someone else's. If we can honor the pain we felt and the ways it may have destabilized and triggered us down the line, we can learn to be with the feelings we may wish to push away: the grief, the fear, the rage, and whatever else might come bubbling to the surface.

It wasn't until I learned how to surrender and feel the depth of my trauma that I came to heal it, which paved the way for a healed relationship to myself and Source Consciousness. At first, I didn't realize that I had these congested energies within me. All I knew was that I was holding on to something that interfered with my ability to be more authentic and more clear. I didn't realize I had created a defensive armor and system of coping that kept me from fully feeling my pain. The ironic thing is, the defense didn't keep me safe. I constantly viewed myself through a lens of being wrong and less than. But one day, I allowed myself to access the deep pain I'd had on lockdown. I was having a conversation with Angela about something that triggered me. I chose not to defend, react, or respond to what she was saying, but to simply be with the feelings of trauma that had come rushing to greet me. I realized then and there that the defensive mechanism was what had kept the trauma stuck. But now, it was just pouring out for me to see and feel it. I simply allowed myself to sit with it for three full days until it felt (key word being *felt*) resolved.

Angela later asked me what I thought the root of that particular trauma was. When had I first felt it? I told her I didn't think it actually mattered. Sometimes, we want to understand our trauma before we work through it. I knew I just needed to feel it until I couldn't feel it anymore—and then, perhaps I'd be ready to talk about the root, if that provided me with any benefit for further healing and growth. But I learned an important lesson: When you resolve a trauma that has been frozen in time, you don't have to understand it, because you won't be repeating it again. The incomplete experience is complete. In fact, sometimes the act of attempting to understand it short-circuits the experience of actually feeling it. It's like we're trying to find a back door to resolution, but resolution doesn't often come from understanding. It comes from the embodied experience of feeling. This is similar to our experience of Source Consciousness—it's not a theoretical construct, the way we've been taught God is, but a felt experience that requires our full surrender.

HEALING THROUGH THE FAMILY LINEAGE

As I've previously shared, I grew up in a challenging family environment—which, as a highly sensitive person, was at times a living nightmare. As life progressed, I learned to shut down my heart center and channel through my intellect. I learned how to operate from a materialist lens that was fixated on the physical reality of what I could touch, sense, and know through my five senses. Even though I was becoming more successful, I began to experience one physiological issue after another, and my body began to show signs of illness.

Through a long foray into the realm of allopathic medicine and holistic healing (a world from which I emerged a brand-new person), I realized I had the ability to help others heal and to open the door to them healing themselves. Through the clients I encountered, I also realized intergenerational trauma that is passed down from parent to child in an uninterrupted cycle of violence and self-denial is one of the primary instigators that causes us to shut down our hearts, which can contribute to all kinds of physical and emotional issues.

Trauma is a significant disruption in the psyche, as well as our biology and energy systems, to the extent that it can alter our DNA. I began to recognize that when people shared their life stories with me, their birth and lineage also became clearer. I began to recognize energetic patterns that had been around since their gestation, including how that vibrational patterning had started to merge with their genetic material. I also began to see how "unfinished business" in the lineage and from a client's past lives can have an impact on their well-being today. I had a chance to experience this firsthand when I married Angela and became a father to my stepson, Nate. I was initiated into parenthood—and in learning to become the parent I'd never had, I healed my own early childhood wounds and also stepped into a more joyful relationship with my wife and son.

Again, honoring early trauma associated with our family of origin is crucial to healing—because if we grew up in a dysfunctional family environment, this is invariably tied to the way we relate to God, consciously and unconsciously. If punishment was the way we were taught to see love, it's likely that our ideas about God are rooted in the mistaken belief that "he" is going to punish us for our sins. If we were taught to be ashamed of our bodies and sexuality, our ideas about the sacred and about spirituality will most likely be based in shame, even if we vehemently deny it. Even if our intellectual constructs are totally different, the trauma that got frozen in our energy, psychology, and physiology is going to tell a different story. Overall, it'll be hard to find a way through the pain when your model for spiritual guidance is just a reflection of the model that traumatized you. You can't look for hope in a God that is based in hopelessness. Despite the religious connotations, salvation is nothing more than being walked through your deepest pains, horrors, and fears so you can grow into who you really are and put that burden down, once and for all. This is why I often walk clients through a separation process where they can finally extricate their ideas about God from their experience of their parents, family of origin, and social paradigms.

It's true that, on an energetic and symbolic level, our parents are meant to be an embodiment of the essence of God—a source of love that can steward us toward being our most whole and authentic selves. Most of us are not gifted with parenting that is rooted in this understanding of Source Consciousness; most of our parents never searched to discover who they were on the deepest level. The world of God 1.0 through God 3.0 is centered around survival, and this is the paradigm of family that has been handed down to us over and over again—a paradigm that's more about domination and ownership than truly unconditional love and heart-centered freedom.

In some ways, the exploration of how trauma has impacted us is positive, because it's an indication that people are taking steps to confront the past—because we are collectively tired of being in survival mode. Ideally, the search to heal trauma helps us dig for the source code—to find God beyond logic and survival. It can also help us recognize that our trauma holds certain gifts. For example, I grew up haunted by the feeling that I didn't fit in—not into my family, my peer group, or society in general. I learned to embrace my idiosyncrasies and unique way of seeing the world to greater degrees, and to recognize that as painful as the sense of nonbelonging was, it also carried its own wisdom—because only when we fully accept who we are, outside of what society tells us we should be, can we be fulfilled. This is why I encounter so many people who did everything the "right" (in other words, the culturally mandated) way but who still felt miserable. Through my own experiences of healing my feelings of being rejected, abandoned, and ridiculed by my family, I can be clear and compassionate as I sit with my clients and help them to hold their own suffering to completion and integration. But this compassion also comes from the fact that I am on the other side and know what it means to live in my wholeness. This compassion is integral to my work because it helps me create a field that dispels resistance and invites healing.

It's ideal when that compassion comes to us directly from our parents or caregivers at an early age. When a child is brought into the world, their caregivers' presence should be able to reflect the light of the child's preciousness, as if to say, "This is what you really are. Even when you forget, we are here to raise you to become whole again—because we can see and sense all the wisdom and also all the pain you are carrying from your previous lifetimes as well as our lifetimes, which we haven't yet healed." Wouldn't it be beautiful if all families committed themselves to a healing path right from the very beginning? This kind of approach to Source-based parenting would help us navigate a course to get to know ourselves in concert with one another. We'd be encouraged to bring the best of ourselves forward—and also to heal our own trauma, so we can set ourselves and each other free.

That's the essence of a parental role, and it's what having Nate and Angela in my life showed me. Amazingly, stepping into the parental role also helped me to heal the imbalances and misperceptions associated with my upbringing that I still unknowingly carried. I also healed my own ideas about what it means to be a husband and father, based on what I'd been handed by my dad and my family. As all my old ideas unraveled and I gave the grief of my early years a chance to be fully seen and expressed, I came into a deep intimacy with myself—the kind I'd never known before. For the first time I could remember, I began feeling truly whole, at peace, and grateful to be alive. I had learned to embrace myself and life.

That intimacy is what's possible when you start to heal from trauma. Family is the place where most of us are harmed, but it's also the sacred ground through which we can learn to walk with grace and compassionate strength. And even if we were not held with such grace and strength by those who raised us, we can begin to give the true spiritual essence of family to ourselves. This awareness is also one of the hidden gifts of trauma. Many of us develop the wisdom of compassion, empathy, and deep listening because we know what it means to suffer—of course, it isn't until we catalyze this legacy through our own healing, acceptance, and transformation that we can begin to share these gifts with others as a way of living and being. It is difficult to interrupt trauma when we haven't come to recognize what it is and how it shows up.

In our relationship, Angela and I have our own distinctive stress patterns that let us know where and how our past is showing up. Because we are both committed to healing and have no desire to bring these patterns forward in our relationship with each other and with our child, we have become adept at protecting others from our pain. We can both trust that we've created a safe space within ourselves to be vulnerable and open, to hear what needs to be heard, to respect what we and others feel, and to process through it. If there is anything to say, we do our best to lovingly or at least neutrally express it; if not, we honor the silence and peace that is available so we can create something new. In this way, our presence is speaking all the time, whether it says a word or not!

In my experience with Angela and Nate, and in the work I've done with countless clients over the years, I know that family can be one of the most potent transformers of trauma, even though it is often the primary site of trauma. However, while family has the capacity to walk us home toward the truth of who we are, this does not necessarily mean it's advisable to remain in close contact with family members who display toxic and destructive patterns. I have healed my relationship with my parents and sincerely wish them well, but I recognize I've had to set up solid parameters that require me to maintain a healthy distance from them. Everyone's situation is unique to them, and there are multiple ways to honor yourself, forgive those who harmed you, and heal your trauma. Some of these ways will entail creating fresh new relationships with your family members, and others will challenge you to remain in a place of love, truth, and sovereignty that will not be drawn into unnecessary stress and drama.

NAVIGATING AND TRANSFORMING TOXIC FAMILY DYNAMICS

I have a number of clients whose issues reflect the trauma of living within a dangerous or toxic family system, which can compromise their relationship with Source Consciousness. Some of these dynamics seem fairly innocuous at first glance, but as I dig deeper into the energetics, I see how destructive they are, even though they may be seen as socially acceptable. We are not normally conditioned to see strict, controlling parents as "abusive," but the truth is, on an energetic level, seemingly normal parental behaviors can wreak havoc in a number of ways.

I worked with one particular family for a few years. The dad, Dave, came to me because his wife, Anna, had pushed their children away with her controlling behavior. Anna had grown up in a family where there was alcoholism and abuse. She'd internalized these behaviors, just as many victims do, and became a perpetrator. She'd instilled a sense of terror in each of her children from a young age. If she sensed anything that could be labeled addictive patterning, she became extremely controlling and abusive. One of their daughters, who had addictive patterns (since such patterns can be hereditary), had moved far from home as soon as she got married, because she couldn't bear being around her mother, whose out-of-control rage and judgment had created a number of ruptures in the family. Dave and Anna also had a younger son, Brandon, who was still living in their house and was just as belligerent as his mother. This family pattern of belligerence was an expression of a deeply rooted pattern that continued to persist because Anna was not willing to look at her trauma and how it was terrorizing her family, rather than creating a foundation of love and stability.

Understandably, Dave was heartbroken. As he told me, "I know I can make things work. I can't just leave her." Yet, nothing had improved. At the time we were all working together, and I was helping Dave to look at his own complicity in the situation. I was also helping Brandon to find self-honoring ways to express himself while being respectful of others. I helped Brandon to see that this wasn't about blaming his mother. I also helped Dave to be a loving parent who held space for Brandon to fully be himself. Brandon didn't engage much with his mother, sadly, because most conversations tended to fall apart before they could even get off the ground. "I've learned to walk away from her when I'm upset," Brandon said. "I also see how my addiction isn't something she did to me. I hated her enough to destroy myself, so she could suffer for what she did to me."

Brandon knew he was harming himself emotionally, physically, and spiritually when he drank to excess, which is why he had moved back under his parents' roof to begin with. He continued to stabilize his life and develop the skills to hold his inner counsel in the presence of a person who didn't respect his ideology or sense of self. As I have shared with Brandon and many other clients, it is absolutely crucial to learn to align with our true self—not just when we are around people who love us, but when we are in the presence of an antagonist who is doing whatever they can to make us doubt ourselves and our reality.

For an adult dealing with an abusive parent, it is crucial to be clear on when it's time to walk away, rather than continuing to be the small, beleaguered child who gets stepped on. It used to be that Brandon was easily goaded into arguments with Anna, but this was only because the wounded child within him desperately needed his mother to hear and see him—even if the only way that could happen was through a fight. I said to him, "You want her to hear you so badly—but are you hearing yourself? Are you being true to what you know is right? When you start to do that, it becomes less about getting her to be the person you want her to be—instead, it becomes about being an expression of the highest truth that everyone can benefit from."

The dance I see so many family members dealing with is one that revolves around a single question: Will the one who is instigating so much of the drama and trauma have the awareness to actually go inward to see what they are doing to the family system? Sometimes, I do see breakthroughs—but more often than not, there is one person who is driving the healing of the family system, and one or more people who are resisting this process. While we have no control over whether a family member will heal and move forward with us, we have the option to change our behavior and break free of negative hereditary patterns, regardless of what they do and how they react.

My client Olivia is the daughter of two Holocaust survivors. While her father had emerged through the suffering of the past with a reasonably healthy and empowered perspective that allowed him to show up for his daughter, Olivia's mother had emerged from it with bitterness and resentment. She felt like she'd been victimized, and as a result, acted in controlling and demeaning ways toward everyone in her life. Olivia's dad had built a successful and thriving business, but her mother wasn't happy for him. She felt the loving attention he gave to his children and his employees detracted from her security. Her most revered form of security was to buy her way into and out of everything, and even though she lived a lavish lifestyle, nothing was ever enough. Olivia's mother became severely ill later in her life, and Olivia made the difficult decision to care for her as her health deteriorated. At the same time, I could see that Olivia continued to hold out hope that her mother would extend the same understanding to her.

I said, "Expect nothing—only do this because it's the person you wish to be." I was speaking from firsthand experience. I'd come to see that my own parents could not respect who I was as a human being because they refused to understand me. I maintained my relationship with them until I was no longer willing to alter who I was in their presence, or to be treated poorly. This was when I separated from them completely. I recognized that, as an adult, if I was willingly putting myself in an abusive environment, I had to accept whatever occurred.

I told Olivia, "You'll have to dig deep to respect that she is going to vomit her pain onto you because you're the safest person in her life, the only one who actually loves her." Sadly, Olivia's mother had two sons who took advantage of her by manipulating her into giving them large sums of money, which she would gladly hand over if they praised her or said things she wanted to hear. Olivia told me that she just wanted to be respected in the same way that her mom respected her brothers. I explained, "In truth, your mom doesn't respect them. She gives them money because she wants something from them."

Over time, I've had to walk Olivia through her own bitterness, resentment, condemnation, and general pain and anguish toward her mother. I showed her that, at times, the way she verbally slapped down her mother was exactly what her mother had done to her and so many others. Olivia had to learn to forgive the woman who had caused her so much pain. As she began to do this, she became more accepting of her mother and of herself. She no longer needs anything in particular from her mother, although her own sense of self allows her to stay connected while maintaining a healthy emotional boundary.

Sometimes, the adult child who is looking for acceptance from an unloving parent by whom they've been traumatized receives what they want—but not by fixating on the desired outcome. While transformation is possible at every stage of our lives, many people who have become hardened by and habituated to trauma cannot find their way out of it.

My client Tom was able to cultivate the relationship he wanted with his abusive mother, but only after his father died. Tom's father was a passive man who became aggressive when drunk, while his mother was a rigid and controlling woman who was never happy with her husband or her son. Like his father, Tom also developed addictive behaviors—a common response to trauma. After all, trauma affects our capacity to cope with stress. If stress feels difficult or impossible to bear, people will attempt to escape the downward spiral of despair through addiction.

However, when Tom's mother developed cancer after his father's death, he had a change of heart toward her, although she'd always blamed him for her troubles. He wanted to show up for her in a different way. I told him, "This is good, but don't look for anything in return. Instead, give to her what you wish you'd been given. Expect nothing from her but be everything you can be for yourself and for her." This approach was extremely healing for Tom, who felt empowered to act in the way a loving parent might. Remarkably, he and his mother are now closer than ever. They have frequent conversations that are more dynamic and open, with much less judgment and condemnation. Tom has said, "I feel more love and acceptance for her, but I am also feeling it from her." This doesn't mean that the pain of the past has completely melted away. Tom has continued to delve into and clear his own pain so that when he connects with his mother, he is doing so from a place of wholeness. He is not grasping for her approval; in fact, he has found that he wants less and less from her. Rather, he is focused on all the good things he wants *for* her. But this forgiveness is only possible because he has continued to process and accept his own experiences of trauma, and to transmute the pain associated with those experiences into love and acceptance. If life is an experiential process, as Tom now understands it to be, all of our experiences, even the most painful ones, have the ability to bring us back home to Source Consciousness and wholeness.

WHEN PAST LIVES IMPACT THE PRESENT

Some of the trauma we carry with us in this lifetime doesn't necessarily come from experiences in our developmental years. Certain phobias, limiting beliefs, and an overall sense of disconnection from our true selves might be rooted deep in the subconscious, and may even reach as far back as a past life. Sometimes, you might be paralyzed by a phobia or a dysregulating core belief without having any idea how it came to be. While I don't necessarily get into the "cause" of a trauma (as I've mentioned earlier, the need to understand can diminish our capacity for feeling what we need to heal), I often share with clients who display signs of trauma from a previous lifetime that it isn't essential to know how their suffering came to be. Instead, I focus on easing their nervous system so they can have an experience of healing here and now. If further wisdom, growth, and healing can emerge from knowing the cause, it will come forth. Sometimes, knowledge relaxes the guard at the gate, which frees the traumatic energy to allow the experience in and through, with less resistance.

No matter how long we've been carrying trauma around, healing usually is not a one-shot deal. It's not as if we are given a single lifetime to figure everything out, and that's all there is to it. The topic of karma can also be an energetically complex one, and it can derail our process of healing when we get caught up in the strange calculus of how it all works out. However, the most important thing to remember is that we are tasked with dealing and feeling and healing right now, in this moment. We don't need to know where our issues come from; we simply need to acknowledge and feel what it is like to be misaligned with our true self.

The remarkable thing is that all healing takes place inside eternity—the place where timelines melt away and we are squarely in the ever-present moment that is now. This means it's possible to release and transcend previous experiences of trauma at any moment, even on our deathbed. Even if we have eons of trauma from past and present lives, we don't have to wait several more lifetimes to "figure it out." Remember, trauma isn't something that we can work our way out of using our intellectual constructs and ideas about being a "good person." When we get to the deep core feelings that are tied into our pain; when we can look upon those feelings without flinching, and indeed, with love and acceptance rather than disdain or disgust—we come to free up something that has become congested in the stream of our essential self.

In this way, the subsequent lifetimes we come into become more open and we are better able to remember and embody our true self, which is sourced in pure consciousness. When this primal memory is awakened, healing becomes easier and easier, although it's always a matter of free will as to whether we choose to heal or not. When we are in the presence of an embodied truth, it will touch us even if we reject it. So, there is something to be said about the wisdom we carry with us from previous lifetimes, which is how we run into the phenomenon of old souls in young bodies. Because of these experiences, some people in any given lifetime will simply be more awakened than others. Fortunately, more people than at any other time in human history are choosing to awaken; they are moving toward feeling, healing, and embodiment, and they are sharing this with all life on this planet through their vibrational presence.

Many people are also stuck in a trauma loop that continues to play out through their lifetimes, because they are scared of what they believe will be the annihilation of who they are. However, getting to the core of our deeply rooted pain is what actually enables us to access the joy and peace that are inherent to the true self, which knows it is always connected to Source because it *is* Source. Although the forecast for Earth can seem dire when viewed through a limited lens, those who are stuck in a trauma loop and continue to perpetuate their own and others' pain because it gives them a sense of power are a dying breed. Such energy cannot withstand the evolution of the human spirit, so rather than continuing to play out its drama on the world stage, it will gradually fall apart and reintegrate with Source Consciousness rather than stepping on the merry-go-round of repeating the same old story.

FROM PAIN TO SURRENDER

By now, you're probably aware of one of the most important antidotes to trauma: surrender. Surrender is also key to coming back to our core self, which is Divine Source Consciousness. We get caught up in the idea of surrender because the paradigms of God 1.0 through God 3.0 equate surrender with powerlessness (which is ironic, given that

Christ consciousness is pure surrender, but the Christian church and the culture of conquest and "power over" have largely misinterpreted the message that Jesus gifted the world with). However, surrender is actually a gateway to the most authentic power we could hope to have, because it brings us home to who we truly are.

Most of us have been seduced by the notion that the external world is more powerful than we are, so we set up elaborate defenses to protect ourselves. The true meaning of surrender is that we are no longer willing to hold ourselves in a pattern of fear, pain, and terror. Surrender offers us a more stable base for being; if we walk into our healing process in a state of surrender, we will ultimately heal.

I recall a period of three days when I went through the experience of feeling like I'd been run over by a truck: physically, mentally, and emotionally. By the time it was over, I'd come to see the light at the end of the tunnel—not because I was "saved" by anything in particular but because I was willing to go all the way into the darkness and simply stay with it. There were certainly times when I felt tempted to turn away, but I didn't give in to that temptation. I knew the experience had something important to reveal to me about how I'd held myself up to that point in my life. But more than this, it had information about the person I was deep down, without the burden of all that armor surrounding the feelings I hadn't yet felt all the way.

My question to you, if you are dealing with unhealed trauma, is: Can you let your body weep? That is, can you allow your body to mourn, to feel shame, to feel empty, to feel hopeless? Will you truly feel that feeling, as much as your survival instincts will fight you tooth and nail so they don't have to?

This process doesn't require that you know or relive the source of your suffering. (Collective trauma is very real, too, and all of us carry a piece of it simply by being alive on this planet—it's much harder to determine where that comes from, because it's not transmitted on an individual soul basis.) The only thing you have to do is feel it until it's complete. If you truly go down into the depths, you won't be doing this forever (something I often assure my clients about, as one of their most frequent concerns is, "If I feel all of it, what if it tears my life apart and never goes away? What if I get lost in this and I can't find my way out?").

When you allow the cycle that was cut off to finally complete, I promise you will gain clarity that will not arise from the meaning-making of your mind. It will be an embodied clarity, something you will know in your heart of hearts, through and through. This clarity will include what you absolutely know you will no longer allow in your life—whether this is abuse, addiction, or living out of alignment with your purpose. Your clarity will be gentle rather than aggressive—an energetic radiance that will know when it's time to shift, rather than a permanent wall that shuts out the love of the universe. Whatever once had a hold on you may be there in some form, but it will not be so tight and constricting that you continue to see it as the only possibility available to you. You'll be able to poke holes in your own narrative. You'll be able to honestly say to yourself, "I won't let myself step into that same situation again." This won't come from defensiveness or anger; it will come from a simple, gentle honoring of what you experienced and learned, and how you grew from that painful moment. Finally, it will be time to move on to something different.

When I experienced this, there was such a sense of relief. I was dealing with the trauma that was still frozen in my experiences of being a little boy with no place to turn for safety and positive mir-roring. But I had to stop protecting myself from what I was feeling; from the people and situations that had been involved in that pro-cess and were no longer in my life. I had to recognize that one of the greatest gifts of being a physical being is that we are not meant to stagnate in a continuous puddle of the same feelings—which might include loneliness, despair, fear, rage, or powerlessness. Our emo-tions are temporary, but only when we feel them rather than shove them into the dark closet of our past. When we feel all the way, what's left is our core essence: the part of us that we are meant to live as; our vibrant self; the peace, love, and joy that are intrinsically a part of our being. The lower-vibration feelings are just part of the experiential process that's meant to help us figure out who we are and who we are not. The path to awakening helps us make full use of trauma, in that it invites us to feel the breadth and depth of all we've experienced as human beings.

What we sometimes fail to realize is that a traumatic event can be transformative if we don't put a label on it. This is because it allows us to feel at a magnitude and amplitude that we might not have otherwise experienced. The ability to feel at a higher amplitude is what opens us to the vast capacity we have for the thing we call love—which has been inside us all along, even though we've continued to seek it in the outer world.

True peace, which we come to when we allow the stream of feelings to just keep moving, is not the absence of feelings—it is the presence of everything, a place of neutrality where all potential sits in wait to be realized in whatever fashion we choose to bring it forth. Love is that peace formatted as action. If you look at the vibration of peace, it is high and refined, and it has the ability to relax our very cells and thought processes, so we become more efficient. The unwillingness to move all the way into our feelings robs us of our efficiency; after all, it takes a lot of energy to avoid something so monumental. This doesn't mean that we won't go through moments of feeling ill at ease or being in a state of suffering. But if we ceased to play on the back-and-forth pendulum and simply experienced ourselves in one location or frequency of the spectrum, we could more easily embrace ourselves and others when we're hanging out in the mud of difficult emotions. We wouldn't have to personalize it or turn it into a personal failure.

From this perspective, we become better at withstanding our capacity for intensity. For someone who has experienced any kind of trauma, intensity (even intense love) can threaten a pattern of self-protection. But we build our capacity step by step every time we honor however we feel about what is happening to us. We don't simply push away the love that feels too big to withstand; we willingly admit, "I'm scared of this experience because it feels like more than I can handle." And we stay with ourselves through that.

I know a lot of traumatized people who tend to get caught up in their bitterness toward their idea of what God is. They insist that if God were a truly benevolent being, "he" would never have allowed this to happen. They resent what is being asked of them with respect to healing. When I encounter this, the question I invariably ask is, "What God are you looking at?"

More often than not, we are looking at the human creation of God: our projection of our ideas about ourselves onto an external deity. These human perceptions, of course, are severely limiting. God doesn't make anyone pay for their sins. What we refer to as "sin" isn't something that is deserving of punishment but of forgiveness; it's a sign that someone forgot who they are and stepped away from their pure, true nature. If we saw ourselves through the eyes of Source Consciousness, we'd be totally different in how we expressed ourselves and how we integrated our human foibles into this deeper understanding.

What I am seeing is that more religions and spiritual people are stepping away from the human perspective of God—because we need to. Sometimes, people find it comforting to personify God in a way that makes that energy more approachable, but this can get us overly mired in the "personality" of God such that we miss the energetic essence altogether. Also, there is actually nothing more tangible than experiencing Source Consciousness within ourselves, and recognizing it in absolutely everything around us. When we come into this perspective, we see that there is nowhere it is absent. And the core reality of all existence isn't based on our wounds, or what we need to do in order to compensate for them; the core reality is one of ineffable beauty, wisdom, love, and peace—and it's waiting to welcome us home.

DO YOU FEEL SAFE RIGHT NOW?

As you already know, healing our trauma directly correlates to healing our relationship with Source—for as we come into greater wholeness, we claim the wholeness that we already are. We open up to embrace the love and peace that have always been there, but that have felt continually out of reach. It is during these moments of stillness that we begin to feel the nature and essence of Source that has always been with us, as us.

So, what is it that keeps us from being able to access this deeper truth of existence? Here's the answer, but it comes in the form of asking yourself a very important question, which I posed in a slightly different way at the beginning of this chapter: "In this moment, how safe am I?"

You might be feeling a lot of different things as you read this, but in most cases, there probably isn't a lot going on that is actively making you feel unsafe. Certainly, such situations exist (and if that's the case, I urge you to stop thinking and start acting on getting yourself into a safe place so you can walk through these suggestions in a healthy way), but most of the time, we are in no immediate danger, even if we've convinced ourselves otherwise. There is a lot of value to creating "safe spaces," as so many people are emphasizing these days, but this can also quickly turn into an overwhelming desire to control one's environment and the people in your midst. Remember, we can reasonably request conditions that help us to feel safer, but we can't force other people to comply with these needs. As an adult, finding safety is your responsibility—but comfort is not the same thing as safety. Just because you are uncomfortable doesn't mean that you are in an unsafe or dangerous place; discomfort is just information, and it's up to you to find a healthy way to navigate your life situations.

I will often ask clients this question about feeling safe when they find it difficult to process their trauma. If their answer to the question is "no," I ask, "Are your thoughts unsafe, or is it the actual environment that is unsafe for you?" Inevitably, their thoughts are the major challenge they run into; they don't trust themselves enough to determine what's safe and what isn't, which leads to a constant state of anxiety.

This might sound discouraging, but it's a good beginning—because it means that some part of them can acknowledge that somewhere within their environment, they are actually safe. I also remind them, "If you say you're not safe with your thoughts, you're actually trusting yourself to say you're not safe; you're developing an inner awareness of what safety feels like, which will make it easier to negotiate and navigate the environment around you and within you." This can be very validating.

Learning to rest into a feeling of safety requires trusting yourself. If you can't trust yourself, you're never going to truly feel safe, even if your immediate environment is safe and you feel the essence of Source as being present within and around you. But if you can honestly respect how you are feeling and perceiving yourself in the moment, you will start to develop a sense of safety.

Sometimes, it helps for people to drop into a sense of safety that comes from relying on the most powerful refuge of all: Source Consciousness. Even if someone doesn't believe in Source or God, every single one of us is connected to something that is much larger than us and much more potent than even the most "powerful" person we can think of. For some of us, that might look like a concrete and tangible source, like the scientific method. But again, while this can be a good way to start to regulate our emotional safety, at a certain point we need to stop externalizing our safety. We have to look within ourselves and gain clarity on whether we are safe right now, inside of us.

Over time, when we practice checking in internally, we might end up saying, "I'm actually okay; I'm a little edgy but I feel safe, for the most part."

One of the things I help clients and participants in my programs do is to engage in a unique process of breathing that helps them cultivate this sense of inner safety. The way it works: After exhaling, they simply sit and pause and wait to feel themselves receiving the in-breath. As they inhale, they consciously breathe in whatever they need to feel; often, this might be safety, empowerment, inner peace and stability, or something else that helps them to feel more connected to Source. As people start to settle into that, they begin to realize that they are not the ones breathing—they are actually being breathed by Source Consciousness, of which they are a part. This experience helps them recognize that they harbor something internally that is much greater than mere matter. People might speak of the breath as being a physical response, but if you look at any spiritual practice or tradition, the breath of God, the voice of God, is an exhalation of a dynamic vital life force that comes into motion and creates the physical universe. Breath is the essence of Source connecting to itself as us; we continue to propagate that pattern of flow when we can genuinely step into the experience of being breathed by the very thing that brought us into form, which has never been separate from us. It *is* who we *are*.

Over time, people can start to breathe out whatever it is they wish to offer the world, so they aren't merely taking in the quality of their true self that they need to feel; they are also giving back what has been so generously given to them. They start to feel like they are kissing the cheek of God and saying, "thank you," which is life-changing for a lot of people I've worked with. That's because the makeup and essence of breath is *the spark of life itself.* Acknowledge you are being breathed, and you can receive what you require. This creates a sense of wholeness and unification, which is healing. It feels like inner peace and centeredness being breathed into form. We can certainly call this healing, but ultimately, it's the creation of your own life symphony. With this experience, you begin not only to heal, but to bring the vastness of your spiritual essence into this physical world. You'll experience ultimate safety, which is an unbreakable communion with Divine Source Consciousness.

WORKING THROUGH SURVIVING AND STEPPING INTO THRIVING

To get to a sense of safety, we must also contend with the part of us that thinks being in survival mode is a noble thing.

The way it works is that a past trauma (it doesn't matter what) is triggered, and people's defenses immediately come up. People move straight into survival mode because they're just trying to figure out how to make it through the pain and shame they haven't processed. This can become a badge of honor that can keep them stuck in a cycle of helplessness and hopelessness. How many times have you heard people say, "I'm a survivor," as if it's something to be proud of? Ultimately, they are saying, "I'm a victim of trauma and I've never gotten through it all the way."

Some people have suggested to me that I myself am a survivor. My response is usually, "I lived with and through that experience, and I put to rest anything that was locked inside me." Of course, I had to create a survivor persona initially, which is what walked me into the healing process. As I got further into it, I began feeling better. With the "better" came safety; with safety came an unconscious part of me that wanted to unload what was locked in me. As that happened, I released a locked-up memory that brought up whatever feelings had been frozen by trauma—sometimes, that looked like rage, or fear, or shame, or sadness. I didn't get too hung up on whatever it was; I just let myself go deep into it. And that's how I came out on the other side.

I often tell people that we don't hit true adulthood until the age of fifty or beyond. Maturity is just the experiential wisdom to do things differently and to bring closure to an unresolved past. I can often see that people are stuck in trauma when I discern their emotional age. I worked with a client in his sixties who continued to boast about how special he was because of all the compliments he'd gotten from people. I realized he was stuck at the age of six, at a developmental point during which his sense of identity was based on what was going on outside himself and how other people reacted to him. What seemed like high self-confidence at first glance was actually indicative of the way he'd lost a sense of trust in himself at a very early age.

As we move through trauma, we'll be asked to face some hard truths about all the ways we came to compensate for the pain and various feelings we didn't have the ability to allow ourselves to feel all the way through. When this happens, we are being called to access our inner warrior, as well as our inner wisdom keeper. The warrior is adept at handling an intense experience without losing their center; they know how to defend themselves, but this is a last resort. The first resort is negotiation and communication. So, when that wound resurfaces, we can begin to see that we are losing our center.

It's never about whether we experience stress or trauma; it's about how quickly we are able to recover. This is true in all circumstances, whether we feel that we are being met by an external aggressor or we are the aggressor in the situation. The inner warrior doesn't mindlessly go into fight mode; they acknowledge whatever is happening in the moment. This might mean feeling something like shame when we are called out for abusive behavior toward someone else. Shame is one of the most difficult feelings to face because the reptilian brain registers it as being equivalent to annihilation or banishment from the group. But if we look at shame carefully, we can start to see that it isn't the enemy;

it is an inner mechanism of checks and balances that allows us to feel where we are being inauthentic. It gives us a chance to course-correct.

Sadly, people who avoid their shame often end up weaponizing it. When we don't let ourselves feel the shame, when we bottle it up instead, it can often manifest as abuse toward ourselves or others (because we are so adamant about protecting ourselves from feeling it that we often end up projecting it onto others—for when we protect, we also project!). It can become a controlling mechanism that causes us to offload the shame we feel onto someone else.

We move from surviving to thriving when we learn to work with shame in a new way. Asking ourselves, "Was I the person I know I am and can be, in that moment?" isn't meant to turn us against ourselves. Shame is often used against us by well-meaning people, but when this happens, our energy is taken away from our mission and purpose. Shame is a way of manipulating us out of our stable point. We lock away the feeling of shame, but we also end up locking away our gifts—our open, precious heart; our curiosity; our enthusiasm; our creativity and passion. We stabilize when we start to recollect ourselves, literally and figuratively, and feel the moment when we separated from the Source that resides within us.

One way to get back into alignment is to create an early-morning practice of focusing on our authenticity and aligned self. We can breathe this into our awareness and commit to carrying that into both simple and complex scenarios. As we do this, we will not falter when we come into contact with someone who does not accept who we are being. We can simply send them compassion and go on our way, recognizing that we are bringing ourselves out to the highest and best of our ability. We can't change the fact that someone else is unhappy about it.

Never feel embarrassed or ashamed when you know you are being your authentic self. If others disagree with or reject you, it's their conflict to resolve. Often, they will attack you because of what you have, what they fear, and who you are, which they cannot control. Sit in stillness and radiate what you want to be inside any given environment—and just *be* that. The universe was created so that we will all eventually come back to our authenticity. This authenticity is much more important than the worthiness or validation that comes from conforming to other people's expectations of us. In knowing this, we can exceed our own potential.

Our authenticity is the natural experience of flowing as the breath of Source. As we are breathed by Source, we become part of a new symphony on Earth. We become part of what it means to create a new environment in which we can engage fluidly; this progressively becomes a part of our journey of being a spirit in finite form. We disrupt traumatic patterns on a cellular structure, and we also move into clarifying our connection with our spirit so we can be the beauty, health, grace, and love we wish to express and experience on this planet. The universe becomes an easier and more joyful place to live in, as it was always meant to be.

COMPLETE WHAT IS INCOMPLETE: A HEALING TRANSMISSION

Allow yourself to breathe in your authentic nature,
your true self, your Divine Source Self.

You are, by design, meant to thrive.
You are meant to live and breathe the highest truth
of your eternal nature and infinite potential.
As you breathe, welcome in from Source
the memory of your authentic nature.

Breathe and embrace that you have always been
and always will be whole.
Let this truth be transformed into physical action.
Let this truth bring to closure all that has remained incomplete,
all that has been impressed upon you,
all that has made you see yourself as a fragment
rather than wholeness incarnate.

All of life's experiences have been opportunities to remember
the truth
of who you are and live it as only you can.
But in a world of survival, you have been shown and told to
be something
that is not authentic to you.

Now is your time to realize that what you have known previously
can be put to rest. Now is your time to bring
love, compassion, and kindness to your life experiences.
You can embrace forgiveness and gratitude,
setting yourself and all of life
free from every incomplete moment.

You are now being breathed by Source
to become part of a new symphony on Earth—
a direct and beautiful expression of the divine song.

Breathe in, and remember
you are the eternal and infinite light, love, and truth
that the world will now experience.

Come into coherence as you breathe in
and embrace all you have ever lived,
knowing it was not meant to break you apart
but to break you open to the truth,

which is uncontainable and eternal,
which lives in, through, and as you.

Feel the flow of Source.
With every breath, live your version of that love.

CHAPTER 5

TRANSCENDING SOCIAL NORMS AND IDEAS ABOUT POWER

THE WAYS WE COME TO KNOW GOD are distinctly related to the ways we absorb social norms and ideas about power. Our earliest human societies were set up around concepts of the sacred, and religion is one of the strongest belief systems around, having been in existence for thousands of years. Religion and our ideas about God are the general bedrock for our moral code of conduct; they provide "rules" for how the world is supposed to work, and what it means to live in a society that allows us to bond with one another in the context of our personal and collective responsibilities.

The ways we've internalized "God"—as an all-powerful being who rains down judgment on evildoers and rewards the "pure of heart," as well as the one who imbues our world with a sense of meaning and order—have played a huge role in the formation of society, culture, community, and every institution on our planet. Granted, many of us recognize that this is an outdated paradigm, but it continues to be the foundation of so many systems still running in the background, energetically—which means that all of us continue to be shaped and influenced by it in ways that aren't immediately obvious to us. This God (who has been in the very pulse of civilization since time immemorial) has touched pretty much everything in your midst—whether it was created as a positive or negative response to that invisible celestial being.

Many of us have learned to go along to get along, so we've taken a lot of the religious beliefs that we were dosed with as children and internalized them rather than actively questioned them. This kind of unquestioning "faith" in God can lead to similar behaviors, such as failing to question authority or accepting at face value the explanations other people give us for "why" things are the way they are.

Humanity's earliest connections to morality hinged on our belief in God's existence. Our ideas about God as a benevolent and compassionate friend (or, alternatively, a wrathful and punitive judge of our moral crimes) have impacted everything from the criminal justice system to how our governments have been built. By attributing our concepts of justice to a "higher power," we traffic in the fiction that the construction of our human world has a basis in "divine law."

While religion can be extremely beneficial in its exaltation of qualities like compassion and kindness toward everyone, our concepts of God start to become problematic when we begin looking at the rash of violence, hatred, and bigotry that have characterized most of our societies. How can we make sense of the idea that we live in a world that is steeped in thousands of years of indoctrination of "us against them," steeped in religious doctrine and dogma that justifies actions like genocide and war while simultaneously putting forward mandates like "love thy neighbor as thyself"? The contradictions are enough to cause anyone's head to spin!

Unfortunately, as many scholars, theologians, and philosophers have noted, religion really is the opiate of the masses. While it can be used positively to expand social cohesion, it has often been used as a tool to institute top-down control of the masses—to invoke fear and paranoia, as well as manipulate our emotions and behaviors.

In a 2011 study, researchers discovered that people are more likely to behave ethically and honestly when they are guided by the belief in a punitive and all-powerful supernatural entity that metes out rewards and punishments in accordance with individuals' behavior.* While some might say that religious doctrine exists to support our moral conscience, it is troublesome that so many of the things we view as natural responses to the world around us are dictated by this sense of fear—which, as we can see in the world around us, is easy to exploit.

So, when we think of how social norms impact who and how we are in the world, we have to consider the ways they can be used or misused. They can help us to build solid institutions (government, education, media, entertainment, commerce, etc.) that bring out the best in all of us—or they can be used to support controlling and destructive beliefs that divide us even further.

This whole process of coming to know Source, or God 5.0, isn't just a "personal" one. It requires that we take a long, hard look at the world we have built, and that we figure out whether it's an accurate reflection of who we are and who we know we are capable of becoming. It requires that we honestly evaluate the social norms we've created, and how they've impacted our ideas of power: who has it, who doesn't, and whether that power will be used as a weapon or as something that has the potential to level the playing field and enable us to live in and as our essence.

Why is this so important? We tend to take our social norms at face value, but the truth is, they change as we come into a greater awareness of our potential. Think about it—the Founding Fathers

---

* Shariff, Azim, and Ara Norenzayan. "Mean Gods Make Good People: Different Views of God Predict Cheating Behavior." *International Journal for the Psychology of Religion* 21, no. 2 (March 2011): 85–96. http://doi.org/10.1080/10508619.2011.556990.

of the United States talked about "government of the people, by the people, and for the people," but it wasn't until many decades later that the concept of "people" extended to women and people of color. If we don't question our social norms, they tend to give rise to imbalance, injustice, and disharmony—as well as morality as a method of social control instead of a tool for communion and connection.

Our social norms give rise to the way we look at power.

Here, it's important to stop and explain what power is. True power is an energy dynamic that is accessed and attained through spiritual growth and awakening. It is expressed through the creation of spirit, and spirit's intention to make itself manifest in the physical world. Currently, power in our world is expressed through taking from another and not working in concert with others, for the sake of everyone's growth.

When we come into Source Consciousness, we start to look at power in very different ways from how we were taught (e.g., power is a zero-sum game that's all about force, wealth, capital, and having "more" of it than other people). As we learn and become more of who we truly are—integral expressions of Source itself—we recognize that we can use our power to change our systems from the inside out; that we can use it to learn to address conflict constructively instead of fueling the same engine of suffering that has been churning since people made God in our image.

SURVIVAL OF THE FITTEST

In thinking about power, one of our most important frameworks comes from 19th-century British naturalist Charles Darwin and the infamous term he coined: the *survival of the fittest*. What this refers to is the continued existence of organisms that have best adapted to their environment, and the extinction of ones that haven't. Taken at face value, this seems to be fairly innocuous, in that species that have a hard time habituating and adjusting to their surroundings are absolutely going to have a difficult time surviving. Change is everything, and our ability to respond to it marks our ability to evolve.

The problem is, the popular interpretation of Darwin's idea is that the "fittest" are made up of the most ruthless, cutthroat individuals of a species—the ones who are willing to annihilate anything and anyone around them if it means coming out on top. I don't think this is exactly what Darwin had in mind—after all, a species doesn't live in a vacuum. It's part of a very intricate web of life, an ecosystem in which a fine balance needs to be maintained among all its parts in order for life to continue.

It would be amazing if our social norms were built on the idea of interdependence, but at least in the West, they are usually informed by "rugged individualism," a doctrine centered around self-reliance, independence, and putting oneself or one's tribe first.

If this is what we're basing the idea of power on, what are the consequences? Well, we can see it in the people whom we choose to idolize or put on a pedestal: billionaires, "influencers" with boatloads of followers, bombastic politicians, and people who seem to lead big and colorful lives. We also tend to collectively gravitate toward people who've demonstrated physical might or who have conquered or out-witted others (or, given the human tendency toward schadenfreude, the pleasure we derive from someone else's misfortune, people who have put others in their place). Often, we also admire those who've shown that they are somehow "special" compared to others. What do these people all have in common? In many ways, they are individuals who seem to have found the answers, who've figured out something or been gifted with knowledge the rest of us don't have.

Humans are patterned and programmed imitators (even when we think all our thoughts are original). We look to the powerful to guide us into survival, to show us how and who to be in the world. We mistake the path they've taken as the path we need to take if we hope to be as successful as them. This is unfortunate, because we could be gaining inspiration from them for totally different reasons. We could be looking to them to see how they've gained strength, courage, power, and charisma—and then, to determine how we can resource similar qualities within ourselves. We could recognize that these qualities come from a noncompetitive, noncontrolling Source of which we are all a part.

I liken it to what Jesus said: "I am the way, and the truth, and the life." This was a metaphor for Christ consciousness itself—something that wasn't particular to Jesus, but that we all have access to when we wake up to the truth of who we are. Jesus was power-filled, but he was not overpowering, nor did he have any interest in exerting his will over others; his entire purpose was to enable people to find genuine power within themselves. Ironically, people ended up building a religion around a teacher whose life was all about dismantling the harmful constructs of religion and governing systems. These people also often blindly followed leaders addicted to their own power.

These days, political frameworks have risen to overshadow and overpower religious ones; sometimes, the two work together in a shadow grab for domination. We have leaders who scorn any sign of weakness and who focus on displays of brute strength. They seem to be saying to us, "Look at me—I've figured out how to be strong and to diminish the other side. I can keep you safe if you follow me." So, in many ways, just as we have social norms and moral codes rooted in fear, we've allowed people in power to prey on and amplify that fear instead of accessing their gifts to help us know and honor our full potential—and to observe natural law, which is all about working together in balance and harmony to create something sustainable.

THE WEB OF THE MATRIX VS. THE WEB OF CONNECTIVITY

Unfortunately, while many of us intuitively understand natural law, we tend to perpetuate imbalance so as not to face the many lies we've created—so as not to feel the enormity of the mess we've collectively gotten ourselves into. I see this when I talk to so many people who express hopelessness and the belief that we're all set up to fail. We can see that the emperor has no clothes, but we don't have faith that our observations will lead to meaningful shifts. Hopelessness is similar to apathy, in that it's an energetic leak that creates holes in our sense of being. We start to feel empty, like there's something missing. We don't realize that the "something missing" is our connection to Source, so we are content to fill the void with distractions that keep anxiety, panic, and guilt over what we've created at bay.

Every single system we have created, from politics to religion to finance to corporate structure, has constructed the stopgaps that help us fill the existential void. It may seem like there's nothing we can do about any of this, but we have a huge share of responsibility in the power we've given these systems. We've essentially bought into the "survival of the fittest" model by saying, "We're empty and we're weak, so please take care of us; show us what to do in order to be happy, successful, [fill in the gap with your desired metric for fulfillment]."

This distorted way of interacting with power has an authentic need at its root: the need to connect with every single soul on this planet. It's little wonder that we've created a literal World Wide Web of connectivity. Connection is a natural law of the universe! However, the current energetic matrix on our planet has created an Internet that is the Wild West of technology; while it's full of opportunities for connection, it's also full of misinformation, hate speech, harassment, and manufactured drama that distracts us from what we really need in order to be who we really are. The Internet reflects the emptiness we feel by creating disruptive programs that perpetuate our dependence on the "powerful." While nature creates interdependence and a beautiful dance of connectivity, our existing structures in the matrix are here to fill a void that emphasizes our disconnection.

All of this goes back to feeling. If we are not willing to feel, we rob ourselves of the chance to connect with ourselves. This creates a sense of emptiness that we try to fulfill by re-sourcing our power in the external world. It's a losing battle, because where Source is infinite, the external games that people play—and that we get so attached to—are finite. It's similar to how drug addiction fuels dependency on the substance, except that substance loses its efficacy over time and people begin to seek out new highs. The things we get addicted to have diminishing returns, and we find ourselves constantly spinning in a hamster wheel that includes both our peak experiences and our crushing disappointments. Once we align with and embrace the essence of Divine Source Consciousness, we begin to experience a satiation that never ends, which becomes the fuel that ignites our inner eternal passion for life.

As this chapter shows, we can use the outside world to help us gain clarity about ourselves instead of just moving through it unconsciously to fill our internal voids. The sense of "I'm not enough" can cease so that we start to see the truth: We've always been connected to Source—and when we realize how we always have been and always will be a part of the magnificent whole, we become who we truly are, which is exactly the same as who we've always wanted to be.

HOW SHAME DISTORTS OUR IDEAS OF POWER AND CREATES A WORLD OF CONFLICT

If we already have access to Source Consciousness, why do we persist in perpetuating mistruths—like the idea that we can fill the void by turning to external "things" and indicators of "success"?

It all comes back to shame. Currently, in our society, shame is used to control, manipulate, and limit others for one's own personal gain. The authentic mechanism or true purpose of shame is that it's meant to be a system of checks and balances that keeps us in harmony within ourselves and the world around us. By design, it surfaces when we are behaving in a manner that is not aligned with our true spirit nature.

The story that shame tells us is that we're not good enough, that we are somehow deficient. But in a lot of ways, shame is an avoidance mechanism that keeps us from feeling those big emotions associated with our story of brokenness, such as fear, powerlessness, embarrassment, or loneliness. When shame comes up, we could certainly choose to investigate the emotions underneath the surface—but more often than not, we tend to overcompensate by "proving" that the voice of shame is wrong. We can see this frequently in people who are in positions of power and who wield it with an iron fist. Think of any of the demagogues who demand absolute loyalty from their followers and who construct clear narratives of "us vs. them." Many of these people in positions of power are ashamed, afraid, and in pain—so they have to use force and aggression to prove that their niggling doubts about themselves are not true.

How do despots come to power? Usually, through a combination of terror, persuasion (they are right and everyone else is wrong), intimidation, and the quashing of civil liberties. They might also use propaganda to gain public support, or to create fault lines in the social fabric—which they then take advantage of. But why are these tactics so successful? How do such people maintain their grip on power? How do they garner public support in the first place?

Maybe you've already guessed the answer, which is also connected to shame. These kinds of leaders mirror back to the populace the pain they feel. When we are mired in shame and other deeply buried issues, we come to identify with our pain; it becomes our adversary, the thing we want to push away at all costs, as well as our weapon, which we wield against those who disagree with us or whom we believe threaten our very existence.

We are no strangers to leaders who come from a very specific essence of attempting to convince the world that the way they see it is correct, while antagonizing anyone who disagrees with them. This essence has vomited itself onto the world stage. Some of our own leaders, in the recent past, have given voice to the pain that a large portion of the populace has been feeling. Such leaders have amplified people's belief that they have been disrespected and sidelined. And they have done it in such a way that has pointed fingers and found easily identifiable culprits—progressives, immigrants, career politicians, you name it.

Such leaders (and we need not name them, as it's less about the specific individual and more about the energetic blueprint that is making itself known across our planet) give people's pain and anger a platform, but they don't actually resolve the situations that led to the pain and anger to begin with. This is another characteristic of people who abuse their power—they rile up the worst of our human instincts without any real desire to fix the problems at hand, because it is this widespread discontent and confusion that keeps them where they are. They come to identify with their position at the top of the hierarchy because it keeps them from confronting the wound they carry around: the possibility they are not as powerful or successful as they believe themselves to be or, more detrimentally, they think they should be because they are entitled to it, or it is somehow "owed" to them.

Just as politicians and others who prey on human emotions can come to identify with that false sense of power, regular people can come to identify with their own stories of being powerless, marginalized, and diminished by the "elite." Ironically, when we identify with such stories, we become susceptible to demagogues who perpetuate that powerlessness, who exploit our suffering with empty promises but are not actually invested in helping us out of it. We use our righteous indignation as a defensive wall against the shame that hides in plain sight.

Toxic shame can be such a destructive emotion because it distorts our capacity to feel our interdependence, and to seek mutual solutions that benefit all of us. We all carry qualities that we disown out of shame—qualities that make us feel unloved, broken, or defective. So, we place our faith in people who profess to be able to deliver us out of this dilemma. We look outside ourselves for validation instead of turning inward and treating our shamed parts with kindness, compassion, curiosity, and forgiveness.

The beauty within this is, we don't have to keep burying our shame by resonating with people who say, "I feel your pain," without actually doing anything meaningful to alleviate it or empower us to move beyond it. When we feel shame (which can be experienced through embarrassment, being withdrawn and quiet, or even taking responsibility for something that is not of your doing, all to halt the sense of failure and rejection in its tracks), we can take it as a sign that we are not being authentic to ourselves, but rather, we are letting someone else's viewpoints supersede what we know is right. This happened to me frequently in my life whenever someone, including my parents, would not understand or accept my viewpoint. Sometimes, they would undermine, diminish, and overpower my viewpoint or knock me down by saying, "How could you?" or "What's wrong with you?" or "That is what you do for family." I came to understand that this was just their way of controlling the narrative of their life and mine, so they could avoid looking at their own past.

Remember, everyone is searching for Source (even if that's not the name we use). We want to know that Source hears and knows us. Those of us who are stuck in the paradigm of God are looking for an external savior as a reminder that this loving Source exists. We don't realize that the only way we can experience an undiluted connection to Source is to fully feel everything in our human experience, including our pain. When we are willing to walk through the briar patch of pain—without identifying with that pain or allowing people with impure attachments to exploit that pain—we discover that Source is within us and all around us; we are all different expressions of the same origin. This experience—of being held, accompanied, and loved through our pain—is the very thing that will lead to the reclamation of our sovereignty. When we have this experience, we no longer feel the need to seek out false prophets who claim to "protect" us from our shame, all while magnifying and exploiting our pain.

We don't need to be protected from our shame; we need to be supported to walk into and through it. The beauty of this is that shame, when we are willing to feel it, can help us to dissolve patterns of protection that keep us locked in fear, pain, blame, and "us vs. them" thinking. When we let ourselves move all the way into and through the shame, until there is nothing left to protect, we experience the relief of release from an endless cycle of avoidance that robbed us of experiencing our full potential.

The moment we hear someone's rhetoric, and we begin to feel righteous, powerful, and justified in our anger and pain at someone or something, this is an indication that we are being manipulated and used. If there is no true caring or compassion for you and what you have experienced, if there is no true sense of empathy, you are likely being exploited. If the focus is not on your personal release and relief from your pain and suffering without personal gain, the person who is stoking the flames of your indignation does not have your best interests at heart.

WHAT IS EVIL?

Another social norm that determines the way we conduct ourselves in the world is the concept of *evil*. Defining evil, determining what is or is not acceptable, is part of the foundation of any society, perhaps even more than defining good. It is how we view evil that determines our laws and the many intricate ways in which we build social cohesion. Granted, it's becoming more difficult to come to a consensus on what exactly evil is, especially as the world is becoming more fragmented and "reality" is no longer a shared perspective.

So, what exactly is evil? I would argue that evil is not a fundamental "truth" of the universe. Evil is a behavioral pattern, just as good is a behavioral pattern. On top of that, our definitions of evil will consistently change in accordance with the society in which we live. Our attitudes will be seen in wildly different lights in accordance with the set of social norms we're operating within. This is why we can't base our concepts of "good" and "evil" on social norms, which are constantly in flux.

Let's go beyond social norms and look at the energetics of evil. Evil itself can take on many forms, but for our purposes, we can define it as a misalignment in our systems that has taken over and thrown us and the world around us out of balance.

If we consider the "old" definition of evil, then based on the way our societies have traditionally operated, evil is the antithesis of God. God lives on one side of the coin of duality, while the Devil lives on the other. Let's take it a step further and think about traditional representations of "hell," a place where the Devil lives and evil abounds. If we think of the Devil and hell as a metaphor, they are merely an outcropping of the perception that we are all alone in this universe, and there is no benevolent entity watching over us with a sense of care for our well-being. Written backward, "evil" is "live." Thus, we can see evil as the absence of life, of love itself; it is the sense that we are bereft of support. This existential loneliness can lead to all kinds of destructive behavior. It is the source of the deepest pain we can experience—and the essence of evil occurs when we allow the worst of our pain to determine who we are and how we engage in this world. If we are no longer congruent with ourselves, we no longer source our sense of value and worth from within; rather, we compulsively feed off whatever is in our presence. This is why acts of evil often evoke images of horrific torture. Evil will go after and feed on the weakest to satisfy its needs. It is a force that seeks to dominate and degrade.

People who behave in an evil fashion are vampiric. They are a fire looking for fuel and they take from others to gain something. They've lost their sense of personal power, which is all about connection to Source and their true nature, so they must derive power from somewhere else. Our most commonly held model of "evil" is individuals who have abused their power egregiously, who have become corrupted. (This can look like a parent with a martyr complex just as often as it can look like a tyrannical leader.) Such people tend to be seen as inhabiting the top of the food chain, but ironically, they don't feel that way. They are steeped in a survival mentality such that they will do whatever they can to keep existing, even if that means annihilating others. This is a model that goes beyond the human framework, and when we begin to explore other dimensions of reality, we see that it exists there, as well.

How do we deal with evil? Well, "fighting" evil doesn't quite work—because, in most cases, we're fighting the evil outside of us from a state of rejection, judgment, righteousness, or avoidance of our own personal pain and suffering. More often than not, we fight evil to get to the root of our personal pain. We fight it so our pain is no longer being resurrected as a reminder of what we felt helpless about in our past, which served to create the pain.

Holding our own sovereignty in the presence of evil is the most effective way to handle it without getting caught in the conflict. We must learn to recognize evil when we experience it, and to hold hard boundaries around it. And if evil continues to "follow" us, this is when we must take congruent action, which might sometimes look like defending ourselves against it with violence.

When is an act of violence congruent? When it can no longer rightfully be called violence, because it is not seeking the annihilation of an enemy, but rather, seeks to bring harmony back into form—like cutting out a cancer using the sword of love.

It's congruent when we act from a place of love—when we have spoken truth to power, when we've tried to walk away, and when none of our solutions to the problem have worked. The evil doesn't cease; it continues to invade our sovereignty. This is a moment in which the divine feminine face of Source, which is all about gentleness and compassion, supports the divine masculine face of Source in cutting the head off evil—and to reactivate and breathe into form the balance that has been forgotten. Sometimes, intense and deconstructive actions are the only way we can bring this imbalance to an end, so that the truth can find a way to rise to the surface. This is not the same as waging a battle from a place of aggression, rage, hostility, or judgment. It is a "last resort" kind of action—reminiscent of the *Bhagavad Gita*, an epic poem in which the god Krishna's advice to the warrior Arjuna is to do his duty by going to war, even though he feels ambivalent and morally conflicted. Krishna understands Arjuna's hesitation, but he also notes that the enemy's aggression will only increase if they are not confronted and brought to justice.

It can be difficult to determine whether our visions of "justice" are coming from Source, or from our own egos. After all, many acts of violence have been waged in the name of "God" or "the common good." However, an act of violence that comes from a place of fear, rage, rejection, and revenge is very different from one that comes from *necessity*—to correct a highly disruptive action, or to respond to unprovoked aggression. This is very important. Violence must never be a first response. It is only something that is resorted to because other options to bring forth balance and harmony have been tested out and none of them have worked.

An act of violence is an act of evil when the person committing it throws others out of their natural state of balance. This can look like exploitation, genocide, or any other act of degradation that undermines another's sovereignty and wholeness. It becomes a game of domination and "kill or be killed" because there is something the person committing the evil is trying to avoid, since facing that thing would be equivalent to facing their own annihilation. We know that the true root of evil is disconnection from Source. In this case, instead of facing the pain that they are all alone in the universe (which isn't really true—and if they sat with the fear long enough, they would understand this), the person committing evil projects that fear onto others. They dehumanize others—perhaps by suggesting that they are, quite literally, "other": aliens, reptiles, illegal immigrants, and any number of other things (meaning separate from self and life)—and are fixated on their absolute destruction. In contrast, an act of violence that emerges from a place of sovereignty doesn't want to annihilate the "other"; it wants to bring closure to the growing imbalance and separation, and to create a world that is genuinely hospitable to and for all beings.

If we are united beings who are part of a massive family, the greatest fear we can possibly carry is a sense of isolation that brings us to mistrust and hate everything in our surroundings. There is no such thing as an intrinsically evil person—but we are all capable of doing evil, depending on how disconnected from Source we are. Coming back into balance requires tearing down the monument of lies and disillusion that has kept us "safe" from our fear (which is simply whatever we choose to avoid feeling and experiencing life in all its textures), while throwing us out of balance and alignment with our true selves, and with one another.

CLEARING OUT THE FEAR OF DIFFERENCES AND WHO YOU WERE TAUGHT TO BE

As this book has been investigating for the last several chapters, stepping into our authentic, whole selves is the very thing that will bring us into right relationship with Source, and by extension, with one another and the world around us. But how do we even know who we truly are, when social norms act as a kind of enforced conformity? How do we begin to separate ourselves from the machinery of the institutions that set the rules for what it means to be "good," "successful," "acceptable," "worthy"?

One of the greatest clues for reaching into our authentic wholeness is looking at how we react to perceived differences. Our reactions to difference might range from appreciation to outright bigotry. When we encounter individuals and groups of people who have been scape-goated and targeted as being "bad" for their perceived differences, it's important to see how we interact with such judgments. Do we go along with them, out of fear of the consequences if we don't? Or do we say no to ostracizing others, and create greater room and more freedom for the expression of our differences?

Unfortunately, even if we ourselves have been cast out or deni-grated for our differences, the effect isn't necessarily that we will be more understanding toward others. Remember, power in our world takes a top-down approach. Those who perceive themselves as being at the bottom of the hierarchy are conditioned to look below them to be assured that someone else occupies the lowest rung—and often, they will not hesitate in "punching down." This is another ugly mani-festation of what it looks like to disown parts of ourselves; we begin to see them in others, and to act in the same violent and debasing ways toward them.

We live in societies that place value judgments on every single quality under the sun. When we take things at face value derived from our head-based referential system, we calculate everything through our minds, whether what we've been told is right or wrong, good or bad, etc. This becomes the lens through which we see other individuals. The way we categorize them brings with it acceptance, judgment, or indifference. Judgment has various gradations—it can look like removal, avoidance, condemnation, or destruction.

I remember being conscious of this from a very young age. When I was in grade school, I wasn't scared of or put off by people who seemed to be outside the norm; rather, they intrigued me, and I was drawn to them for various reasons. In many ways, I was such a person myself, and as a result, I was picked on and bullied relentlessly for being highly sensitive and not fitting the stereotypical mold of masculinity. But I recall that one child I knew had it much worse. He was clearly autistic (which I didn't realize until meeting my wife, Angela, and her son, Nate). He displayed "strange" quirks, but I could see that he was ultimately harmless; he was a child navigating the world in ways that didn't make sense to the people around him. I recall several occasions on which I stepped to his defense, even though I knew I was putting myself at risk. At the age of ten years old, I may not have understood him, but I understood that the way people were treating him was wrong, Of course, I didn't have the skill set at the time to actively engage in helping him, but I instinctively recognized that other kids' violent rejection of this boy was unjust.

I felt this once more when I met my stepson, Nate, who has high-functioning autism. I understood that other people had similarly rejected him, but by this time, I also understood that we push away those qualities that we have not learned to tolerate in ourselves. Belonging to one's tribe is part of our evolutionary nature, and so we learn to suppress or reject anything that might exist outside what our societies and communities have deemed acceptable. When I looked at Nate, I saw a beautiful child with massive potential. I innately knew that all I had to do was look at the best of who he was and help him shift and evolve into those qualities. Certainly, like all of us, he is not without his limitations, and there are certain things he may not be able to shift. However, he is not a broken being, but an individual who came into this world with specific life experiences and his own genetic inheritance, of which he is a product. I understood that if I could show him how to respect and love himself through experiences of pain and rejection, this could help him bring forth his true essence, which was waiting to be expressed. He could then experience his wholeness without wishing he could be someone else, or some other way.

I am also reminded of what Angela was going through when we first met. At this time, she had a continual mantra playing in her head about what might happen when she died, as Nate was an only child and had no close relatives with an interest in helping him. She was beset by an underlying low level of anxiety that never ceased; she continually worried about his well-being at school and other places, and she feared the worst. As she watched me see only his potential, she too began to understand that Nate had come into this life for experience—even if, in our society, we deemed what he was going through to be "unjust" or "difficult." I helped her to recognize that his life is his experience to have, and to see exactly what he needed to activate his potential on a higher spiritual level.

Of course, this can be very difficult to accept, especially when a child like this doesn't grow up in a good family situation. Part of Angela's struggle with Nate was that she, too, had experienced a difficult childhood; she'd been bullied, ignored, and perceived as hyper and odd by others, since she had ADHD during a time when it wasn't really recognized. So, every time Nate was left out, ignored, or treated poorly, Angela was reliving what she herself had not processed in her childhood and young adulthood, which came to be a torturous cycle.

It can be very difficult to witness the suffering and injustice endured by many people who don't fit the mold of what is considered acceptable in our society. It can be even more difficult when we come to acknowledge the ways we, too, might be perpetuating such behavior. When we scapegoat other people, it is because there is some part of our own self that we are marginalizing and that we have deemed unbearable. When we become comfortable with our own quirks (in my case, a wide-eyed, innocent, joyful curiosity about life that can sometimes make others feel ill at ease and even trigger anger, because their own innocence had never been permitted to flourish), we can face others with curiosity rather than rejection. We no longer need them to conform to our standards, because we understand that "perfection" is an individual expression of wholeness, not something that is there to make us comfortable.

In learning to look at and be with the differences that make us uncomfortable, we start to see where we are fractured. Likewise, the ones we've scapegoated become powerful mirrors for our wholeness. If we choose, we can use their particular behavioral expressions to see and know our own imbalances. We can all do our part in walking one another home to wholeness.

FACING THE LIES AND TRANSFORMING OUR SYSTEMS

Throughout this book, I have focused a great deal on the power of knowing life as an experiential process in which we are encouraged to feel every messy or uncomfortable emotion as it arises in our awareness. I don't mean to be Pollyannaish and suggest that stepping into our feelings is an easy process that will turn our world into a paradise overnight. It goes without saying that we live in a world that is steeped in violence. I'm not talking about the violence of a predatory animal going in for the kill. I'm talking about violence that comes from the kind of aggression that is rooted in fear, pain, and ultimately, weakness. True strength and power don't rest in force, but in a deep respect for all life, whereas weakness is always attached to the fear of being "less than," which can sometimes cause people to act out in ugly ways to prove that they are worthy.

We live in a world that has largely become desensitized to violence. On a daily basis, our tolerance for abuse and neglect grow. We have become increasingly numb to stories in the media about war, rape, suicide, addiction. Every system in our world contains some seed of this violence. Violence is a legacy that seeks to perpetuate itself, to keep us stuck in a never-ending conflict between "us and them." Usually, this violence is rooted in so-called wisdom that has trickled down from one very powerful person to everyone else within the system. You can see this not just in our world at large, but in the family unit itself. Rather than respecting that every "part" of the whole has a function and its own wisdom to share, we cut a society off at its limbs and depend on the head (figuratively and literally) to tell us what to do and how to do it.

In Chapter 4, we discussed how we can subvert the idea that wisdom is something that trickles down from an authority figure in the family to everyone else. In this way, instead of just living out the model of "family" that has been handed down for generations, we start to become the embodiment of what family truly is: a system that enables the loving transference of wisdom and truth from one generation to the next. In this way, the next generation can remember who they are—and not be identified as something that "makes sense" to the ones who preceded them.

Just like this model of family, a functional and healthy society embraces both the wisdom of the evolutionary experience (which might hold tradition that's been handed down for generations) and the innocence and openness of the new life that is yearning to be expressed through us. And every single one of us holds both these polarities. We don't need to look to other people to tell us what to do; we simply need to be open to what we are feeling and who we are being.

We must recognize that everything we are, the very state of being we are bringing into the world, influences our external reality more than we can imagine. However, when you pull something out of its environment—similar to a plant that is harmonious within the US but becomes an invasive and dominating species when it's taken to Japan—this throws the entire ecosystem out of balance. This is what we have done to ourselves. We've taken ourselves out of our essence and have created a false egoic environment in which we operate separately from our Divinity.

Because we don't have many social models to help us reconnect (even though many will tell us they have the answers), it's difficult to find frameworks that help us to share our full, authentic selves with the world. We are absolutely meant to take everything we are and share it—both the joy and pain—in uniquely creative ways that allow us to move through our experience rather than get stuck in it. Many of us believe that pain is destructive, and that it needs to be suppressed at all costs. The problem with this approach is that it doesn't take our pain away. We become like pressure cookers, seething with what we've hidden away, until it bursts to the surface in an explosive event. Pain isn't our enemy and keeping it pent up until it eats away at us, until it becomes our very identity, does us no favors. Our pain is not who we are, but it is an integral part of the experiential growth process—which points us in the direction of healing and wholeness. When we learn to process it, we contribute to facilitating change on this planet.

And make no mistake—change is exactly what we need. We are an evolutionary species, after all. If we have the courage to face the lies thrust upon us, as well as the ones we've created, we can shift and transform this planet faster than we even know is possible. However, because truth is the face of consciousness, it can be a scary prospect to people who are operating within the shadows of our own creation, out of fear, shame, and the need to "save face." If powerful yet volatile world leaders could admit to having made an egregious mistake, so many possibilities would open up by virtue of such an admission. Even if these leaders couldn't articulate what they were feeling (and many people living in the shadow of shame can't), they would still recognize that their paradigm is destructive and maybe even antithetical to the very thing they wanted to create: genuine security and a sense of being taken care of in the world (which tends to get supplanted by the desire for absolute power). Recognition of their failure, which would be part of processing their pain, could bring illuminated awareness and understanding to our world. This would be akin to assuming a much greater responsibility than the one these leaders think they have; it would give them a redemptive arc we've seen in none of our dictatorial world leaders.

Government, like religion, is meant to be a guidance system that expresses what we know ourselves to be, or that helps us discover more intimately who we are and all we wish to become. As we discover this through the lens of God 5.0, we come to realize that the systems we have in place are *meant to evolve and support who we are becoming.* Change is often a scary prospect for many of us, but the practice of welcoming the fear and pain, of being curious about it, is what enables us to heal wounds that get resurrected as change occurs. Instead of clamping down on the pain, denying it, doing whatever we can to avoid it, and letting it eat away at us, we can walk through it until we feel whole again. This brings forward an opportunity to elevate not just ourselves, but the society in which we live.

When I talk about change, I am always wary of the tendency to go on a crusade to change the world, which can indicate that we are fighting the very thing we need to learn to compassionately be with, or that we are in victim consciousness and looking to hurt the ones in power who did us wrong. This can be very destructive and take us away from the transformation we long to see and experience. People with a desire to "take down the system" have a tendency to lop off heads. But if they're going in with that kind of intensity, and that kind of intent to destroy or dismantle something, then there is probably something within themselves they are afraid of seeing and feeling—so they want it to disappear in the external world.

We have a different option: to heal the wound that brought about the need to wage a crusade to begin with. When we do this, we don't just destroy what we dislike; we heal what brought it into form and replace it with a better alternative. We can't see that alternative when we are in fight-or-flight mode with our own feelings.

I've had clients ask me, "What you are saying makes sense, but what if you're in an oppressive environment where someone has taken away your rights? Isn't it right to want to destroy your oppressor?" As I've mentioned before, there are going to be times when powerful opposition is the correct (and hopefully last) response, but the impetus behind it does not come from the desire to destroy. It comes from the desire to bring ourselves and life around us into a state of balance.

So, what happens if you don't have the strength to stand within your power in the presence of your oppressor? They may have gotten you to physically acquiesce, but you always have a choice when it comes to whether or not you will give up your integrity. I think of someone like Viktor Frankl, the Austrian psychiatrist and Holocaust survivor who wrote *Man's Search for Meaning*, a remarkable book that demonstrates we can be free in our hearts and minds even when we are subject to abject suffering.* Through this, we become a living, breathing example of what is possible, just as Frankl did for millions of people who read his book and absorbed his legacy.

Jesus is a similar example. Even through the suffering at the end of his life, he became the very thing we all had the ability to be. People both loved and hated him. Many dismissed him, but they simultaneously understood that who he was had the capacity to threaten existing power structures. This fear of the destruction of their false identities kept them from seeing what they were in the presence of—a representation of the healed and whole self. He never stopped being this, even when he was condemned to death.

The only real crusade that we need to go on is the one that will enable us to heal our own pain and bring ourselves into a state of wholeness—which will naturally trickle into every mundane task and every casual conversation. This isn't about slaying the external demon;

---

* Frankl, Viktor E. (1959) 2000. *Man's Search for Meaning*. With an introduction by Gordon W. Allport. Reprint, Boston: Beacon Press.

it is about learning how the demon came into form and healing the pain within us that created that pain of separation in the first place. It is about going into our sacredness and aligning with everything we are. It is about centering ourselves and relinquishing our ideas about who we are, so that we can ask our highest potential to show us the truth of what love, kindness, and compassion are, as well as how we were designed to *be* these very energies and truths. It is about asking to be shown a better way to bring our own unique expression into the world.

We don't know which or how many individuals, once awakened to their potential, will shift the fabric of society so it can become a better place to live. The good news is, there is a more efficient, expansive way to live that can invoke the full capacity of who we are as spirits in this physical world. When we face the falsities we've created, as well as the pain this has generated, we create a magnificent opportunity for everything to be revealed and regarded as sacred. Even if we don't know where we are going, the next best steps for us to take, as a collective rather than a few people appointed to "power," will become clear as day.

DEVELOPING INNER STABILITY AND BEING THE WHOLENESS YOU ARE IN THE WORLD

Maybe by now you are saying to yourself, "All of this sounds great in theory, but the world is a scary, conflict-ridden place. How do I actually sit with the conflict instead of running away from it, if all it does is make me feel worse?"

Indeed, we live in a world with significant violence and a great deal of conflict. The way we begin to shift this is not by running away from it because it makes us feel uncomfortable; instead, we learn to build our capacity for bringing a nonconflicted presence into this conflicted world.

Whenever we are triggered by something in the external world (the words of a certain politician, family member, the person who cut us off on the freeway, or the latest controversy brewing on social media), it is pointing us to something we have yet to heal within us. When we add up all these unhealed internal conflicts within every individual on this planet, that leads to a whole lot of strife and struggle in our interpersonal relationships and societies.

Something I've recognized often among the people I meet is that so many of them are overwhelmed and inundated by the news and all the information that is thrown at us from all sides these days. As a result, I see people take news and social-media fasts or grab on to something that might ease the discomfort they are feeling—like a cookie or a glass of wine. Admittedly, I went through the same thing. In watching the news and recognizing what was happening in the collective, there were times when I felt like I was losing my self and my groundedness. I'd want to scream, cry, and dig a hole in which to bury myself so I could get out of the way of what I was feeling—because it scared the hell out of me. But being who I am, I couldn't let this stand. I had to face what I was afraid of head-on. So, what did I do? I put myself in a position of watching a particular news feed and reading everything in that arena, over and over again. I let myself feel whatever I needed to feel, and I didn't judge anything that came up—rage, fear, contempt, despair, you name it. I simply let myself fully embody the feelings and allow them to lead me to the areas within myself that felt unresolved or incomplete. Sometimes these were just strong feelings, and I didn't necessarily know their origin, but I didn't have to. All I needed to do was be with them, observe them, and surrender to what I felt, without judgment, and let them move through without getting lost or stuck in them.

Sometimes, we fear going into these places because we fear what they might mean about us. When I was a child, there were times when I felt so angry, hurt, and ashamed because of the way my dad treated me that I'd go to my room, slam the door, and scream ragefully about how I wished my parents would die. And I didn't feel bad about those declarations! For years, I couldn't understand why it didn't bother me. But now I recognize that once I got those violent and pain-riddled thoughts and feelings out of my system, I was "clear." I could look at my parents differently. I didn't hold on to my feelings—I let them move through me, as "e-motions" (energy and feelings in motion) are meant to. I took the same principle and applied it to the onslaught of troubling news. I let myself sit with the guttural depths of what I was feeling—until I didn't feel it anymore and came to a healthier state of being.

Now, with those feelings finally released from my system, I could read the articles and watch the shows that I'd been so reactive to from a place of genuine compassion and curiosity. This led to greater clarity and the ability to determine how I could best address the issues in front of me, and to even heal and resolve why the article or piece of news existed in the first place.

Now, I'm not suggesting that you drink out of the fire hose of toxic social media or news shows that are designed to trigger your primal emotions. Try doing it in bite-size chunks. Go through the media you consume and focus on one thing that really triggers or upsets you. Don't turn away from it. Stay with your feelings until they dissolve. Don't judge what you are thinking or how you want to respond. Don't let the tide of emotions carry you away, either. Just . . . stay . . . with . . . it. Observe what is happening, and you will notice that it will start to neutralize. Maybe this will happen when you begin to feel bored, or if your previous emotion has run its course.

Don't fixate on the stories behind the feeling. I've worked with clients who've done this exercise, and they begin to remember childhood memories and past-life issues. They start to cry them out, and I help them to stay focused on what they need to express (in this case, tears), not on what happened to make them feel this way. When they began to process their feelings this way, they realized they could look at the news differently. It got to the point where they'd be able to take in the news without getting triggered. They'd be able to feel whatever they were feeling, enough to get clear and ask themselves, "What do I need to be within myself to stop contributing to the world that this piece of news reflects? What do I need to do to bring about a change for the better—not from my own ideas about what is needed, but from a place that allows me to act in harmony with all of life? How do I create an environment with beauty, grace, and ease?" These are great questions, and they aren't being posed for the purpose of fabricating some kind of alternative fantasy world in which we're free from pain and conflict. Remember that pain and conflict have a powerful evolutionary function. We can use them as tools to guide us into greater curiosity and self-acceptance, and less judgment.

When we are triggered by something external, it is never about that thing in and of itself. Our anger or upset comes from seeing memories played out before our eyes. The energetic conflict, which is connected to our past experiences, is the trigger—but we've chosen to fixate on this particular celebrity who made a blunder, or that particular politician who did something terrible, or this depressing fact about climate change. When we learn to navigate our feelings and surrender to them, we can process the energy of old wounds that have been festering within us for a long time. We can use the news as an opportunity to heal what may have been ignored or neglected for many years. This is why I sometimes joke that, instead of praying for peace, all we need to do is watch the news, identify our conflict, and then observe the feelings that arise from that. Once we allow those to clear, we can *be* peace in the presence of whatever information we are absorbing, which will then radically transform the collective.

I am very much aware that not many people are given the opportunity to express the anger, fear, and judgment they might feel inside. We learn to bottle up those feelings over time; they don't actually disappear, but we become masters at hiding them and hiding from them (and often, we let them spill out in unskillful ways). About two decades ago,

I made the commitment to never hold in feelings that needed to be released. I would literally let myself cry and be shaking on the ground, even when I was out in public, sobbing as people walked around me like I didn't exist. I did this at supermarkets, big chain stores, and anywhere else the emotions happened to arise. I was always amazed that scarcely anybody seemed to pay attention; it was like I was invisible to them. I am guessing that it made many people uncomfortable, so they felt the need to avoid me. However, I really checked in with myself and I came to the conclusion that even if I made others uncomfortable, I wasn't ultimately harming them. I was simply enacting a deep kindness toward myself. And because I committed to heal, I was invisible to being interrupted, for which I was grateful. I could do what I was meant to do, and what so many people unfortunately feel inhibited from doing.

This process is simple, but it isn't necessarily easy. It comes down to this: We don't have to conquer our feelings; all we need to do is practice being with the small, still voice within us that will help us to recognize and observe whatever we are feeling—and to honor it by bringing it forth. As the Gospel of Thomas wisely notes, "If you do not bring forth what is within you, what you do not bring forth will destroy you."

We cannot experience true stability and centeredness until we accept ourselves exactly as we are. This goes beyond individuals and extends into groups. We live in a world full of clashing identity groups, where so many marginalized people are understandably yearning to be accepted for who they are. Yet, we must ask: Is the individual who is seeking acceptance actually doing the work to accept themselves?

An interesting example of this is the growing LGBTQ community, which has gone through a huge evolution in the last decade or so, as more letters and identities continue to be added to the mix—sometimes with pushback from other groups who don't understand or see this as an act of creativity and self-discovery. The desire for a marginalized group to have the right to exist, especially in a world that has often treated it with violence and indignity, is certainly justifiable. However, this sometimes fails to take into account that many of the people who cannot tolerate or accept others can't even tolerate or accept themselves.

Think about it: When we are in rejection of ourselves, consciously or unconsciously, it is virtually impossible to embrace anyone else's viewpoint. Thus, if we are looking for acceptance from the external world, we often miss the fact that we are asking for something that others (especially people who espouse bigoted ideas) haven't even learned to do on the inside for themselves.

People often gravitate toward the polar end of any duality (in this case, "masculine" or "feminine") because these places often hold the highest energetic intensity. However, our true power point is our point of greatest stability, no matter where we are on the spectrum. We experience the full embodiment of our spirit self when we are filled with power—when we are no longer opposing or fighting or competing with anything or anyone else . . . when we no longer need anything from anyone else.

The LGBTQ community has done the world a great service by teaching us about the fluidity of gender identity, as well as other forms of identity. I suspect that in the next couple of decades, so much of the chagrin and conflict we experience around sexual identity will stop existing altogether because it will no longer matter. We will not be stuck between the dualities of "masculine" and "feminine," because we will have come to a place of equilibrium. We also will have come to a recognition that each of us is seeking to uncover the essence of who we are—but that our essence can no longer be defined by rigid labels that can't possibly contain our full self. Rather, we will learn to experience and express ourselves moment by moment, no longer in a choke hold of identities that demand to be seen and known in a particular way, through our chosen framework.

There's a wonderful side effect to all of this: The more stable you become in your own trust and faith in yourself and your ability to bring forth what is within you, the more connected to Source

Consciousness you will be. You will empty out the vessel of your being so that it is filled with what is truth, what is your innermost essence. From this place, you will also be able to hear anything anyone else says without doubting yourself. You might question them for deeper clarity, but you won't be fixated on how "right" or "wrong" they are. Instead, you will be checking for cues on how their way of showing up might be prompting you to become a better version of yourself.

Over time, this will happen faster and faster as it becomes a natural side effect of experiencing everything you feel. Discovering this kind of internal stability is like becoming lucid in the midst of a very active dream. You'll be able to pause and recognize that you can trust the divine universal process that supports the awakening of your true essence. Even if bad things have happened to you, you can practice the art of the pause in the safe and quiet moments of your life. You can remember that you are Love Itself, and you can repeat this like a mantra until you know it to be the only accurate truth, no matter what your mind might be telling you. Over time, even if the world at large is screaming at you, you'll be able to move from an inner core of stability and compassion—for yourself as well as the person or situation creating conflict. You will have done the very thing that will lead us all to an era of peace the world has never before seen, once a large enough number of people do it: You will have reoriented your spirit as your biology.

CENTER IN TRUE POWER TO BRING PEACE TO THE WORLD: A HEALING IMMERSION

*Breathe, as you align with and center into the seat of your soul—
the very essence of Source itself, your true power.*

*Breathe into your heart and feel
the essence and presence of the eternal truth of power itself.*

Pause, and rest into this feeling,
whether it is familiar or not.
Stay with the choice to know authentic power.

Breathe, as you trust your will to feel and align.
Your heartfelt intent is enough.

Breathe, as you remember
you are and always have been enough.

Breathe, and trust that you have the power within.
True power may have no discernible reference to you—
this is good, as the essence of power
is not known to most.

Breathe—
because you have chosen to know Source as yourself,
you will know and remember your true nature as power itself.

Breathe, and stay with this,
until you sense something calm, peaceful, and unwavering,
even if unfamiliar.

Breathe, surrender, and awaken
to the knowing that this is
and always has been available to you, in you, as you.

Breathe, as you settle into this embrace,
that the power of Source is all that you are, have been, and
ever will be.

Breathe,
as you allow your
mind,
thoughts,
body,
feelings,

emotions,
to transmute into the essence of pure power.

Breathe, and become the very expression of this power,
knowing it as you.

Breathe, as you feel the power of Source move around you,
through you, as you.

Breathe, as you feel the very nature
of your light and truth become you.

Breathe, as you open your heart,
mind, and soul to be as one unified truth.

Breathe, knowing that nothing
can ever take this power away from you.

Breathe, as you step into your true essence and nature.
Now is the time to follow your breath
to the heart and soul of who you are.

Breathe, pause, and center in your heart,
in your sacred knowing of your relationship with Source.

Know that your power, your essence, your nature,
all emerge when you are the most quiet.
So pause, and take it in.

Breathe, as you remember
that all of life's experiences come into being
for you to know and embody one simple truth:
that you are the most power filled, loving,
honorable expression of Source there is.

CHAPTER 6

TAKING "SPIRIT" BACK FROM SPIRITUALITY AND THE NEW AGE

A FINAL ASPECT OF OUR CONDITIONING that often requires a clear examination and reframe rests in our existing concepts of spirituality. While many people may consider themselves "awakened" for relinquishing outdated church dogma or seemingly transcending religion, those who are spiritually minded often unconsciously give their power away to powerful substitutes, such as teachers, gurus, organizations, mediums, angels, miracles, and the more "mystical" aspects of the universe. What I would like to shed light on here is that when you take away all of the labels, we are simply looking to become conscious.

This thing we call the New Age gained popularity in a number of occult and metaphysical communities in the 1970s and 1980s. The term *New Age* came into being because many of these communities talked about a new era of love and light (the Age of Aquarius) that would occur through personal transformation and healing. Although it's a beautiful concept, many of the people who got swept up in these communities and ideals (and many who still do) sought it as an escape. Even the tendency to project a time of beauty and love out into some distant point in the future became, for many of them, a way of stepping out of the reality of the present.

Often, the desire to be on a spiritual path stems from the extent of our suffering in the world. But for many people, spirituality can become trapped in an endless hamster wheel of consumerism—as the need for "more and better" can hijack our most well-meaning intentions to locate Source Consciousness within. Other detours from the path can occur when we compare our progress to others, or believe we need to be further along than we actually are.

On my own spiritual path and in my work supporting others in their personal journeys back to Source, I have encountered the many ways people might believe they've broken free from religion, only to find themselves shackled to a lot of the same dogma that characterized their connection to "God." In this chapter, we explore some of the common pitfalls of spirituality and the New Age movement, both in how they've been organized (ironically, in much the same vein as any religion) and how they've been followed.

As you already know, it's my steadfast belief that any meaningful path to Source Consciousness is one that reconnects us to our true power. If we are to connect to that power, it's important for us to begin to question our reasons for being on a spiritual path, and to look at the way we're doing it—otherwise, the work we are doing to clear the path to self-knowledge might end up working against us.

Of course, doing the "work" can be hard in the absence of trusted guides. Ideally, life itself becomes a spiritual guide for us, but many people are confused because we don't live in a world in which the primary reality is respect for life in general. Few of us are taught that each person, and the unique expression of each individual soul, is a precious and necessary gift within our human experience. In the absence of this understanding of the basic goodness and sacredness of life, we tend to get stuck in doctrines that teach us what to think but that don't connect with how we feel. In this way, we might end up bowing down before yet another rigid brand of spirituality that takes the place of religion.

While the desire to comprehend the universe is absolutely understandable, it can lead to even more "rules" rather than the willingness to live inside the mystery of it all—with a deep sense of trust that we will find our path. It can lead to getting caught up in the most recent or trendy spiritual teachings, which might be convenient for the time in which they were born, but that are usually based on current scenarios instead of the highest truth. This chapter offers a more expansive framework for envisioning our spiritual lives, in ways that allow us to play with the spiritual offerings in our midst without becoming codependent and losing an opportunity for connection with Source and reality as it is.

FREEING OURSELVES FROM SPIRITUAL CONSTRUCTS

Much of what we know about spirituality tends to be knowledge-based; that is, we acquire knowledge from a book, a course, or a teacher, and we put it to practical use. There is nothing wrong with the desire to practice a certain path, such as mindfulness meditation, but this is not the point of being an infinite being in a finite body. We tend to use references when it comes to spirituality, which then causes us to say to ourselves, "Well, this is what the teachings taught me!" However, we are not here to learn (contrary to what so many spiritual teachers might say, which makes little sense—if we are already infinite, what is there to truly learn?). Learning is just how spirit utilizes the physical world. That is, we learn about the parameters of matter-based reality—for example, how much of a load a specific metal can carry before its molecular bonds begin to fail. Learning is a study of what different aspects of matter-based reality can tolerate, so that we can create accordingly. In essence, our intellect is built on knowledge that includes references, which help us understand the world of phenomena around us.

It's important to keep reminding ourselves that spirituality isn't about taking another course, reading another book, or getting another certification. In fact, embodied spirituality isn't about references at all; it's about the awareness of self that we are able to exercise *as* every moment. It is about our willingness to bring forth our true nature so we can be in the highest-potential connection with the world around us. In other words, we create the map as we bring more and more of our spirit into and through the creation and expression of the body, which is a temporary vehicle.

We have such a desire to compress and drive spirituality into all kinds of references—angels, gods, guides, avatars, ascended masters (insert your preference here)—and to have our references correlate to something specific and sometimes even measurable—instead of recognizing that these human-made terms are merely words we have chosen to express our understanding of the infinite in the moment. This desire for knowledge-based, reference-based ways of describing spirituality throws limitations on our potential, because instead of opening up to a novel discovery of what our spirit wishes to express in the moment, we are stuck on the need to "know"—meaning, we want a system that helps us to get to enlightenment.

Very often, I encounter people who've actually had profound spiritual experiences that they do not recognize as such, because what they experienced doesn't fit into the current lingo around what "awakening" or a brush with Source looks like. I've also encountered people who might take a course on spirituality, Indigenous healing modalities, or energy work and believe they are experts now that they've been certified—but although they seem to be speaking about spirituality with the "right" kind of language, they have no direct experience with it. They have only skimmed the surface and touched the edges.

You can't encapsulate the universe into what humans can put into language—not until the words are generated from the heart and soul of the person who has experienced, received, and begun living the transmissions. It is then that the words spoken are the essence of what is Divine Source Consciousness.

Many clients have asked me if I have a specific modality I teach people so that they can access Source Consciousness. My answer is always no. I help people get clear as to their own unique way of accessing all that is, so they can relate to Source Consciousness in a way that is true and congruent with who they are. This is all any modality is: a path, identified by a particular person or group of people, that has proved to be effective in accessing higher truths.

Once, I did an energetic exchange with a Reiki practitioner who asked me to memorize and visualize a specific symbol in order for the attunement to progress. I told her, "That's okay, I'm feeling the energy, so I don't think I need to do that." She was surprised by this statement, because she'd been taught that in Reiki, you had to memorize the symbol in order for the energy to transmit and be effective. However, she had already energetically given me the entry point I needed. I tried to explain that the tendency to get stuck on the symbols, which are just a series of individuated frequencies, can hold us back from feeling the actual transmission (the key word here is *feeling*). She had already given me the opening for the vastness that is Reiki, but it was hard for her to accept this without going through the accepted suite of procedures. Remember, it is about stepping into the essence of it, not the mechanics of it.

There is absolutely nothing wrong with any given modality. A modality is just a gateway to a higher truth. However, we have to ask ourselves: Are we going to remain in the gateway forever? Or are we going to use it as a transitional point to greater spaciousness and more aliveness? A modality can give you a set of guidelines or rituals that helps you focus your energy and attention, but it's up to you to embody what the focus brings you to. As we wean ourselves off spiritual dependency on any given set of rituals, we no longer require all the prescribed steps in order to move into an altered state; instead, we become the embodiment of that altered state in the physical world.

One of the other ways I see people getting pulled into the dogma of New Age spirituality is through the creation and perpetuation of distorted or delusional thinking, which is another artifact of turning their constructs around spirituality into something that helps them to feel falsely empowered or in control. This might sound harsh, but let me tell you what I mean by it. To survive in a world where we don't have the capacity or will to *feel* exactly what the things we are experiencing mean to us, in our incarnate form, we create an illusion that acts as a buffering agent for us. We avoid feeling what we must feel in order to embrace what we can be. We tend to create a mythology about our pain that makes it unapproachable. But we also end up spinning a story about ourselves as a spiritual bypass that is compelling enough to take our attention off whatever it is we're avoiding. A lot of people who are in pain might end up developing a false impression of themselves and life, or a God complex that makes them feel special—chosen ones in a sea of abysmally normal folks. There is something protective in nature about the fantasy of a person who believes they talk to God, angels, ascended masters, and disembodied souls. Now, this isn't to say that people don't legitimately have such experiences; I know people who do, but they are not the majority. A lot of what gets generated in the world of so-called spirituality tends to be a way of compensating for a perceived lack of power. It's not unusual for someone who doesn't feel powerful in their life to fabricate a story that gives them a sense of purpose and meaning (take conspiracy theories, for example). That story might have a grain of truth, but if the primary purpose of the story is self-glorification as a method of avoidance, it's not working in their or anyone's favor.

In many ways, people who are caught up in their stories haven't accessed their ability to be humble around what they might *not* actually know—what might belong to the terrain of mystery. Often, if you talk to a psychic who insists they have contact with Source and can tell you absolutely everything about the truth (which might sound a lot like an opinion), you can get a glimpse of where they might be stuck on their own need for certainty and importance.

Once, Angela got a massage with a person who called herself an intuitive massage therapist. At the end of the experience, the woman shared with Angela, "I am picking up that you were sexually abused as a child." Angela has crystal-clear memories and immediately responded, "That has not happened to me, although I've recently worked with a past life where it did, and I think that is what you're picking up on." This made the massage therapist dig her heels in deeper and insist that she knew Angela's reality. This could have been because she was uncomfortable with the prospect of being wrong, or she'd picked up on something she couldn't put a finger on but that she ended up taking literally. She'd turned a construct that could have meant anything into an absolute reality. Imagine the distress this could have caused to someone not as experienced in this realm as Angela is. They would have been highly confused and started a search that they would never find a helpful answer for.

A lot of people go through the process of attempting to find meaning and purpose within spirituality while shutting out the reality of their external lives altogether. For example, I have a client, Christina, who is very empathetic. However, she uses her gifts of empathy not necessarily to serve others or to see more clearly, but to feel more special. I've come to see that while she is a very gifted intuitive, her wounded psyche is running a filter that enables her to spiritually bypass the pain of not feeling special in her own life (a wound that she carries from her childhood). Christina believes that someday, the universe is going to gift her everything she could ever need, because she has followed a selfless spiritual path, but she isn't aware that she needs to believe this because it's her way of affirming her own value and worth. In the meantime, there's a massive misalignment between her story about her spiritual gifts and her actual, day-to-day life, which is filled with pain, uncertainty, and relationship drama.

The stories we create about spirituality, which serve the function of making us feel special or giving us a sense of control and predictability in a mysterious and infinitely complex universe, don't actually lead us to the purpose of spirituality: to know who we are on a fundamental level. If we knew who we were, we would not have to be validated in specific ways to feel our own worth and power. While intellectual constructs and delusions of grandeur can give us a temporary sort of worth and power, they don't allow us to learn to own the power we already have, in such a way that we cannot blame or be dependent on something outside ourselves in order to live in a state of continuous flow and connection with Source.

What happens when we dispense with the need for stories, or for distracting illusions filled with all kinds of magical thinking? We get to sit with the entirety of our lives as they are. We get to *feel the truth of it all to put it into motion for resolution*. Often, we think we might not be able to handle the reality that our relationship isn't what we believed it was, or that our ideas about God are wrong and entangled in our ideas about our personal worth. However, as we sit with our mundane experience, exactly as it is, Source begins to reveal itself. We discover that we don't need a complex origin story, or a map of the universe, in order to navigate our lives and to locate spirit, right here and now, in this earthly existence. We don't even have to understand any of it through our cognizing, rational brain. If we can honor what *IS*, and experience the magic that already lives inside reality, we come to access our own unique connection to the mystery. Free from our own stories and illusions, we come to see that we can enter the mystery with a sense of curiosity, playfulness, awe, and wonder.

IT'S NOT ABOUT BEING SPECIAL

In many ways, although the impacts of social media remain yet to be determined in the long term, the motivation to be famous has always driven human beings. That's because the old viewpoints of God are survival-based. Fame is often equated with being at the top of the heap in what is more or less a zero-sum game, where some people are deemed special and others are not.

These days, "social-media spirituality" is rife with Instagram-friendly accounts of self-proclaimed spiritual teachers, shamans, gurus, and people offering incomplete boilerplate advice in two to three lines of text, accompanied by some attractive image of peace and beauty. And because social media is designed to be addictive, so too are these images that we consume of people with seemingly perfect lives. Often, their lives look a lot like what we aspire to, mostly because media, advertising, and corporate greed at the expense of our quality of life have determined the arbitrary set point for the pinnacle of success.

When we are bereft of ways to embrace our uniqueness (perhaps because we have not learned to fully accept ourselves or weren't raised with the awareness to do so), we might turn this into the need to feel special. The need to be seen as special—to demonstrate our worthiness through a social media account or other ways of documenting that we're successful and have made it—is not a new one. But when we shift into the realm of spirituality, that need can be detrimental to connecting with Source. Source Consciousness is not about the need to be seen through a particular lens and in a particular light by other people. The paradox, of course, is that everybody is special—and simultaneously, nobody is special. When we live inside Source Consciousness, comparison is meaningless.

The spiritual path is not about proving ourselves to be more loving, more conscious, more "together" than the next person. Some accounts can actually be very inspiring and helpful; however, we tend to make comparisons between ourselves and the people we see who seem to have it all figured out. Many of us have succumbed to a mentality of instant gratification and instant transformation. We look to the people who appear to have the best bodies, who are continually traveling to the most exotic places, who have the most fun and least boring careers, and the prettiest and easiest overall lives. (This begs the question of whose standards we've adopted—and if these are truly our own, or simply something we learned from the dominant culture.)

Many of my first-time clients tend to equate spiritual aptitude with instantaneously healing whatever emotional or physical pain they might be encountering. I know that immediate and miraculous transformations are possible because I've witnessed them, but the challenge that spiritual seekers often run into is that they want transformation to look a certain way: the way they've always seen it portrayed in movies. In truth, awakening experiences (which might touch upon near-death experiences, kundalini awakenings, and other "traumatic" and ego-shattering moments) aren't all they're cracked up to be. Sometimes, they are physical hell or they manifest in the type of psychological disintegration that requires a really strong container if we are to integrate the lessons. However, our Hollywood mindset has given us some specific notions about the matter. We forget (or neglect) that the process of spiritual awakening is often nonlinear and generally filled with stepping stones that aren't always easy to cross. And more often than not, they break apart the ego rather than continuing to feed it.

If we are looking at the superficial fruits of spiritual experience, we can get overly fixated on the way everything looks instead of how we actually feel. In addition, we forget that part of the purpose of spirituality is integrating our experiential lessons so that we can serve life itself. Spirituality isn't about being perceived as special or as having unique knowledge and wisdom. It is about being in a space of such clarity about who we really are that we have the capacity to serve others in getting to the same place.

As Chapter 8 will explore in more depth, there's nothing wrong with having the material wealth and the various markers of abundance that are available to us in this human incarnation. But all these things are secondary to who we truly are. They might be rewards we incur along the way, but connecting with Source is meant to help us tap into the wholeness that we already carry within us. Sure, that wholeness might come in the form of a big house or lots of social-media followers. But the true spiritual mindset is not about flaunting what we have, a behavior that often comes from a place of intrinsic lack. It is about being grateful for the opportunities to experience our life in a way that is uniquely ours.

As all spiritual teachings demonstrate, attachment to what we have is a recipe for disappointment, and various levels of upheaval. Remember, change is an intrinsic part of the human experience, and the ability to graciously give up what we have today for what we might experience tomorrow is an enormous part of finding peace in life itself, let alone on the journey of a spiritual path. Desire for attainment tends to come from the trauma and shame of feeling that at some point in our lives, we had nothing—we were lost and alone, empty and hollow. The spiritual path is all about becoming more intimate with that experience of emptiness and hollowness and recognizing that even inside the so-called void, there is vitality and truth. Instead of running away from our experiences of pain and covering them up with acquisitions, we can become more curious and compassionate as we walk into and through every experience life has in store for us.

Presence and curiosity are part of a way of being that occurs when we experience a sense of completeness exactly as we are. From this place, we can be loving, kind, compassionate, peaceful, at ease, and comfortable with the next moment that appears—because this is our nature. And when we can feel that on the deepest levels, our inter-actions with the world become very different. We don't attempt to attain spiritual enlightenment because it will make us feel special and rid us of the feeling that we are hollow and lacking. Instead, we come to all of life with the fullness of who we are. Whatever we choose to experience, whether it is traveling the world or speaking before a large audience, becomes an expression of the overflow that already exists within us. It doesn't come from lack, but from the joy and excitement that we feel within ourselves.

When we shine this intrinsic light, it is contagious; others cannot help but be inspired by it. The key is not trying to emulate the person who is the source of inspiration, but to let them inspire your own unique light to shine forth in whatever expression is right for your own personal soul experience.

This is often what is meant by the Sanskrit term *leela*, which translates to "play." When we are free of attachment, life becomes a beautiful expression, a dance between formlessness and matter-based form that we can joyfully partake in. So often, spiritual teachings fall flat when they emphasize one of two extremes: either the need for more more more, which is often a facade for the emptiness that people feel inside—or, on the opposite end of the spectrum, the idea of living like an ascetic, with absolute minimalism and self-denial of the "good" things in life. Both of these ways can be unhealthy and imbalanced, because both can end up leaving us empty and dead inside.

Spirituality isn't about living with nothing or having no ambitions. It simply means that you are not attached to any of it, but rather, embracing all possibilities of form. A spiritual experience of life becomes neutral in that we are fully expressed and can appreciate every last piece of experience that is available to us. But we also recognize that none of this determines our worth. At the same time, it's important to explore our reasons for wanting the spiritual path to look a certain way—whether it's filled with epic adventures in the rainforest with remote tribes of people and fantastical deities gracing our journey, or having an enormous social-media following and all the material attainments that tend to accompany Western ideas of success. It might not necessarily be your journey to have a multimillion-dollar home or a steady stream of adventures. Perhaps what your soul yearns for is the experience of being connected to Source Consciousness in a different way. There's often a gap between the human way of seeing life and the spiritual way of viewing your experience. Spirituality is about expanding our perspective and consciousness in such a way that we can love who we are, no matter where we are, even when it's simply sitting with your cat or going on a walk through your neighborhood and watching the clouds as the sun sets.

It's useful to aspire to a path of feeling your own intrinsic wholeness and continuing to allow yourself to move in a direction that will bring to you whatever you require in order to express that wholeness in the world, however you have chosen to. *Your intention means everything in this process.* I see many people who get lost in the external destination, and I always gently urge them to come back to the inner sense of how they want to live and how they wish to feel. Plenty of my clients who are extremely descriptive about the places they would like to go and the things they want to experience often come to me feeling totally disconnected from their emotions and true sense of self. This is when I gently inquire, "Do you have a sense of how you will *feel* when you get to that point?" The responses are usually locked inside their mental trappings: "I'll feel accomplished because I have XYZ," or "I'll feel like I can finally relax because I have the life partner I've always wanted."

I encounter them spinning out into lots of thoughts and ideas that are still stuck on the surface appearance of what they *think* the experience will look like. This is very different from remaining in an inner state of attainment—which happens when we start to feel *ourselves* as the abundance, the prosperity, and the joy that we have projected onto the external world. But the paradox is that when we start to embody our wholeness, the expression of it in the external world becomes easier and easier. The thing is, we must clean up what remains to be resolved within ourselves (for example, a fear-based way of looking at the world, or resentments that keep us stuck in the past) before we can generate greater possibilities in the outside world—which is just a mirror of our consciousness, anyway.

This is where the work of connecting with spirituality looks different for everybody. Some people get to this realization of higher consciousness very quickly, and others move at the pace of an inchworm across eternity. Of course, when it comes to Source Consciousness, time is an illusion. In the grand scheme of things, it doesn't matter how long it takes us to experience and know our wholeness and to give up the idea that the spiritual path is about being special. We recognize that it's never about getting somewhere in particular. It is always about the journey of experiencing and getting to know ourselves from within. And at the end of it all, our intrinsic wholeness—which takes us well beyond being merely "special"—*is* both the journey *and* the destination.

SPIRITUAL BYPASSING

One of the major issues people will run into on the spiritual path is the tendency toward spiritual bypassing. I define spiritual bypassing as any kind of so-called "spiritual" behavior we engage in that gives us breathing room from something we're avoiding. In truth, what we really need to do in such a situation, especially for the purpose of connecting with Source Consciousness, is to work a little harder to breathe *through* the uncomfortable experience so we can get to the other side of it.

Spiritual bypassing can often take the form of rote and insincere positivity, which has a lot of people disengaging from reality and using love and light to avoid feeling anything they deem negative or uncomfortable. However, when we engage in spiritual bypassing, we disconnect from the entirety of who we are, which includes the feedback we're receiving from our physical body. Spiritual bypassing becomes yet another way to get caught up in concepts of what spirituality is, as opposed to using our felt, embodied experience to become more intimate with our experience with curiosity, openness, and the willingness to see things in a different way.

Spiritual bypassing is an understandable aspect of the spiritual path because the mind loves to create constructs—so that the next time the storm comes, we can pull out our reference cards and rely on what we've already experienced or been taught, which will give us a sense of safety and shelter. We do this instead of truly trusting that we have what it takes, moment to moment, to face whatever comes up. It can be a lot simpler to bypass with affirmations (which won't work if you don't deeply believe them as truth) than it might seem to move toward the parts of ourselves that are fraught with fear, anger, doubt, or any other uncomfortable emotion, and to offer those parts our camaraderie and care. Often, we end up demonizing those parts of the self rather than breathing with and through them to get to the other side of our experience. We accept the superficial peace of distraction and denial over the profound peace of knowing and touching all parts of who we are.

Once, I worked with a client, Mikhaila, by taking her through an energetic journey that was related to a diagnosis of ovarian cancer. She was very ill but had chosen not to undergo any kind of medical treatment. She was hoping to get some guidance along her path. During her journey, everything associated with her healing process was going smoothly until Mikhaila's vision went black. She felt this was a confirmation that she should absolutely not move in the direction of conventional medical treatment.

I asked, "Why do you think that is? What was it about the blackness that you felt was a no?"

She responded, "The way I see it, the blackness means that if I move in that direction, that's what I'm going to experience."

I inquired further. "It sounds to me that you are equating the blackness with something bad. But what is it about the blackness that you might benefit from? And what's in it that you're afraid of? Also, what if the blackness doesn't represent something like death or the end of your life? What if it just represents the end of your life as you know it, so that you can birth yourself anew in a way that you want? What if blackness is the essence of creation itself?"

As we continued to talk, I also pointed out to Mikhaila that within all the scenarios she had mentioned to me prior to the journey, she had never spoken about being healthy and healed as one of her desired outcomes—which was astounding, given the fact that she was ill. She seemed to have walked in with the unconscious foregone conclusion that her cancer was a death sentence—perhaps because she was a nurse and from her experience the idea of recovery did not seem plausible as a result of the diagnosis. I sensed that she believed she would ultimately die from the illness, and her desire was to simply stretch out her life as much as possible before the "inevitable" happened. I gently said, "You're looking at this from a perspective of limping through your illness, instead of experiencing health and wholeness as a rebirth coming from the illness."

As we continued to work together, I helped her to look more directly into what had created her belief that she could not experience health and wholeness—because, while toxic positivity isn't great, neither is walking around with the haunting expectation that things are just going to get worse. I also helped her to expand her ideas about what the darkness in her vision might have meant, and to not be afraid of moving closer to it.

Moreover, I wanted her to look at her bias against Western medicine. So often, spiritual bypassing can entail looking for a spiritual solution to all of our problems. Of course, the idea of separating spirituality from any aspect of our lives is a fallacy in and of itself. Throughout my work with people, especially those who are very ill, I emphasize that it's possible to integrate both energetic/holistic and Western medical perspectives. For some people, pursuing chemotherapy might be the right choice, and for others it might not be—it's all about finding balance and stability within ourselves, which I assist clients with, and walking ourselves away from fear as our go-to expression and experience.

The story of Mikhaila's discomfort with the darkness tends to be a recurring theme in the work I do. It really exemplifies the importance of being emotionally honest with ourselves—of facing darkness and uncertainty with reverence, compassion, and curiosity, rather than shutting it out. Remember, darkness is just the womb of creation. It is absent of any form we might be familiar with. It is the all-encompassing essence of everything. Because we don't know how to organize this as a concept, it can be difficult to make sense of. Of course, not everybody will take the invitation to walk through the darkness—to acquaint ourselves with it in a friendly, familiar way. It's not always easy because it requires facing the fear that has been generated by our ego, which is scared to death of its own annihilation.

There are worse things than the destruction of our ego as we know it. (Remember, a healthy ego is great, and more often than not, deep experiences of awakening to ourselves don't destroy the ego but help us understand its function and how to use it as a supportive tool of creative expression.) What I often find with people who have preconceived ideas, such as denouncing or declining Western medical treatment, or that darkness is bad or evil, is that such ideas can perpetuate a righteousness that serves to separate us further from each other and life, even as we attempt to find connection and meaning. We must trust ourselves so much and be so emotionally stable that we can actually open up to the vastness and mystery of the universe (as this is where the magic happens) instead of cramming it into a narrow box that keeps us small, safe, and comfortable.

THE GIFT OF SPIRITUALITY:
YOU ARE THE CEREMONY

Recently, at one of the teaching and healing events that I hold, a woman asked me afterward, "Do you teach your method of healing?"

"No, I don't," I said.

She was visibly disappointed. Then she asked, "Do you have any teachers?"

I replied, "I don't."

She seemed confused. "Then, where did you learn your techniques?"

I said, "What I share is something I innately have access to. I wouldn't really call it a technique. When I do my healing work, I realize everybody has an access point to higher states of consciousness and potential. When I work with individuals, I notice what their access point is, and I use it to help them relate to what I'm doing, so they can find their own path. In other words, I don't teach a method, but I do help people get to know who they are and how they operate as clearly and cleanly as they possibly can. People find their own way into the energetics, philosophy, psychology, and perceptions that are connected to Source Consciousness."

She wasn't happy with my explanation. Often, when I reveal that I don't have a program or a series of techniques for people to hone their spiritual awareness, they find somebody else who will give them a step-by-step guide to what (they think) they're looking for. I always wish them well, because I understand that my way isn't for everyone. However, I do believe that one of the great gifts of spirituality is getting to know who you are. I'm not attached to how somebody gets to that place—there are infinite paths that can take people where they need to go. But at some point, we have to drop the path and be willing to step off the edge of what we already know. Again, all of this comes back to accessing your true inner will to relinquish reference points and not reducing the spiritual journey to a series of lessons that can be chunked down into bite-size, bullet-pointed procedures. You might learn how to be a car mechanic by working on a car, but the spiritual path isn't mechanical.

In the work I do, I'm not interested in people replicating my way of being in the world. What I do is bring people back to themselves, which is also what leads them to their unique service in the world. An aspect of this is helping people to let go of their ideas about who they should be, or what their path needs to look like. An ethical spiritual teacher models a sense of openness and curiosity with the person in front of them. When I work with clients, I don't tell them they're making the right or wrong choice. What I do, instead, is direct them to find balance within themselves in such a way that they don't have to be so dependent on someone else's methods.

Much of the work I do is about teaching people to value and use their own discernment. As I alluded to earlier in this chapter, it's a giant red flag if you're approached by anyone who says they are special, who proclaims they've been told they're special by a higher source, or who insists they're the only one who can help you. In truth, on a planet with eight billion human beings, you're going to meet a plethora of people with gifts. Source Consciousness would not create just one person to change the planet. There are many powerful teachers, healers, and practitioners out there. The best thing you can do is simply go to the person or people you feel drawn to. If something feels "off," trust your gut the first time and follow it. You will know the right teacher for you when you feel joy and aliveness through spending time with their teachings.

It's also important to be wary of working with anyone who keeps you in a perpetual loop with their next program, book, or product— insisting that the next thing they have to offer will be the one that gets you over the finish line and into the new life you have always dreamt of. This tactic is one of the reasons chronic gamblers remain stuck on the treadmill of false hope, even though the odds are not stacked in their favor. It's another version of the "sunk cost fallacy"—when you feel you've invested so much time and money that the next "solution" just has to be the one that provides gold at the end of the rainbow. If a so-called healer's marketing style inspires FOMO (fear of missing out) and you feel you have to do almost everything they offer, that's a sure sign that manipulation is at the core of their brand.

As long as we are waiting for a "spiritually advanced" teacher to help us make sense of our lives and give us some kind of foolproof spiritual methodology, we will not be truly free to know ourselves as manifestations of Source Consciousness. The Dalai Lama acknowledged that the religion of Buddhism needs to evolve in order to help people recognize that the answer is not in a monk or spiritual teacher, but within ourselves. It's good to continue to let go of the dogma that holds us back or that gives us the false idea that we must conduct our lives in a particular way, in accordance with a specific set of tenets. All forms of spirituality must evolve to keep up with how humans are evolving, until we get to the point where we don't need spirituality at all because we ourselves are a living, breathing embodiment of Source Consciousness.

Some people I've talked with about this seem to resist the idea. Someone once said, "Our spiritual ancestors would want us to look to ancient wisdom in order to guide our path forward."

This is a point of confusion that's important to untangle. It's not about going back to the wisdom of ancient sages, doctrines, and scriptures. It's about allowing ourselves to integrate all the wonderful knowledge, experience, and wisdom that our forebears embodied, so we can evolve experientially. From an Indigenous standpoint, shamans walked the line between two worlds: the world of ordinary reality and the world beyond ordinary reality. However, as humans evolve, we're moving toward creating a unified sense of being, wherein there is no separation between spirit and form. The paradigms of God 1.0 through God 3.0 still hold to the idea that we are separate from Source. But the current challenge is to learn to come together internally so we can take the essence of spirit and wed it to our physical reality.

It's absolutely beautiful to have reverence, gratitude, and honor for the contributions of our spiritual ancestors. We can see them as embodied examples of what and who we are and be inspired by them as we walk into a new way of manifesting our personal and collective unity. This is not the same as going back to some imagined utopia that our ancestors lived in.

We can accept the processes of change and evolution that are a part of this material reality and live a sense of unity right now, in the present, with all the gifts and challenges that may abound.

As the Dalai Lama implied, we're not meant to go backward. We are meant to recognize that Source is always with us, and we have the capacity and natural ability to draw it to us, through us, as us, here and now, because we are all Source Consciousness.

More than thirty years ago, when I began a path of shamanic journey work, Spirit sent me a message: "We Are Thee and Thee Are We; All That You Are We Are; All That We Are You Are; There Is No Separation." I continued to receive this message that what we perceive as being so separate from us is already part of who we are, and everything in our lives is an opportunity to remember this state of unity.

As the Buddha said, "I am but a finger pointing the way." But instead of looking to the way, we tend to get stuck on the finger. So many people get stuck on the personalities of spiritual teachers and their particular way of doing things. However, I maintain that the biggest task at hand isn't to learn their way of being—it's unlearning all the things that block us from feeling vibrant in our daily lives. I often refer to this as learning to "be the ceremony."

I remember talking to a man who went to an Indigenous medicine person in the American Southwest after deciding he needed some kind of healing ceremony. The man was astonished when the meeting was over in thirty seconds. Dumbfounded, he said, "When are we going to do the actual ceremony?"

The medicine person responded, "I set the intention, and I put it into play. I don't have to engage in a ceremony to do that."

This medicine person understood that every so-called ceremony a person engages in is merely a way to focus our attention on our intention to be and embody Source Consciousness and become all that we are. Because he lived *as* that reality, he didn't need to engage in a long ritual. He got that he was *already* the living, breathing ceremony.

In that vein, there's no need to get stuck on physical rituals (unless you find your deeper connection with Source and experience your internal joy through them, which is a different story). Ritual is just a tool guiding you to remember who you really are. We tend to get attached to the accoutrements of spirituality—the crystals, wands, feathers, and esoteric techniques—because we've been taught that everything of value is outside of us. The key that I usually point out to my clients is that there's a difference between connecting with "who I am" and "what I am"; the *what* still tends to be caught up in external representations, whereas the *who* is what we breathe into and express ourselves *as*. Rituals are a spontaneous and joyful experience that helps us embody our wholeness. It isn't about the words we speak, or the visible signs of spirituality. It is about how we carry ourselves. We can absolutely continue to engage in the rituals and connect with the spiritual teachers, but we don't have to turn it into an intellectual process. In fact, we can feel something powerful ignite within us without choosing to label it at all. We can honor that many different kinds of experiences have the ability to open up our access to something powerful within. It doesn't matter what we're engaged in, but if we feel a sense of gratitude or joy, the "practice" did what it was supposed to.

Every time I have read or experienced something that made a difference to me—that ignited something within me, even if I didn't necessarily know what it was—I simply allowed myself to be with it. So, if you are working with spiritual practices that do not create an ignition within you or open up something deep inside you, and if you're simply gathering information for the sake of gathering information but aren't experiencing a demonstrable shift, consider that perhaps you are still attached to an intellectual construct of spirituality and are not having an experience of what spirituality truly is.

When we experience Divine Source Consciousness, we typically move to the point of our origin, the place through which we are capable of communing with the great mystery, the ineffable, that thing that some of us call God. This can happen in so many different ways: through gardening, art, baking, dancing, writing, singing, being in nature, taking care of our loved ones, and so on. If we can feel the essence of Source within us in these moments, it doesn't matter what we are doing. When we are embodying wholeness, we are living in and *as* Source. In fact, when we open to some of the more mundane ways of connecting with Source Consciousness, we eventually recognize that we can cease seeking altogether. At this point, we get to a place where we can feel and know Source everywhere. We understand in every cell of our body that spirituality is not separate from the elements on this planet, or the experiences of our mundane lives; it's simply a reminder of who we are. Everything carries a vibrational pattern that is an expression of a truth that's meant to call us back to our fundamental nature.

Right now, religion and spirituality exist mostly through the lens of having forgotten who we are. They exist because we feel disconnected, because we believe we need an external set of rules to serve the greater truth that brought us into form. But if we can take the essence of our eternal nature and draw it into our body in order to expand our capacity to be a grander version of what we have known ourselves to be, *everything* is possible.

For many people, this might seem overwhelming or out of reach. How in the world do we feel, live, and breathe alive our divine self every single day? First of all, we must acknowledge the places where we didn't trust ourselves enough to surrender to our Source essence in the past. Perhaps we were paralyzed by our pain, or our fear. It's important that we have compassion for where we've been on our spiritual path—whether we have been fervent seekers, lost our faith somewhere along the way, or momentarily got caught up in shiny appearances. We can acknowledge that in those moments, we just weren't ready. Maybe we were trusting the outer voice of the world more than the inner voice that knows the truth. But we can create an opportunity to simply sit with these restrictive patterns. Or we can move, stretch, scream, and do whatever it is we need to do in order to simply stay with the feeling. No matter what the feeling is in the moment, it is the loving acceptance of ourselves and others that will help us move through every moment of life.

In my role as an intuitive healer and spiritual guide, I am honored to be a witness to people's deep experiences of awakening and integration, which begins with them giving themselves compassion for where they've been. By offering support in that process, I can mirror back to them who they truly are. I can help them to tap into their own heart, and their own intrinsic kindness, understanding, and care. In this way, I hope to remind them that each of us is just as valuable as anyone else. Someone with an emotional or mental disability is just as divine as someone who might not have the same challenges. All of us are born into these magnificent bodies so that we can work with whatever it is we've been given. Everyone has their place and purpose, for the universe exists because of our unique presence, which is the beauty of the great mystery—but sadly, we've created a society that values some people and diminishes others as unworthy.

Unfortunately, spirituality can entrench these referential, comparison-based ways of existing. We tend to use references like success as tools of protection from whatever it is we have learned to be afraid of. However, the references cannot bring us into greater intimacy with Source. In fact, they usually serve to create more separation, as opposed to greater compassion, connection, and awareness. It is only when we continuously learn to surrender our ideas about spirituality that we can come into contact with our naked experience.

Everything you need is already within you, right here and right now. You are and always have been the ceremony. The life you live *is* your ceremony in action. This is your divine gift to life itself.

BECOME THE CEREMONY: A HEALING IMMERSION

Breathe,
and bring into form
your authentic nature and power—
that which has been with you
since before the birth of time,
that which will never leave you, because it is you.

Breathe in,
and know that with every breath,
you are becoming clearer
in your intent to live all aspects of your true self.

Every breath is a recommitment.
Every breath is an acknowledgment.
Every breath is an embrace
of the full spectrum of who you are.
Every breath is your will
to receive from Source
all that you can possibly be.

Breathe,
for this is your ceremony.
This is your heartfelt, soul-felt will to live
from all dimensions of YOU.

As you breathe,
let yourself be love and truth embodied.

When you breathe, remember.
When you breathe, become.
When you breathe, share this with all of life.

Realize
that you are love itself.
You are truth itself.
And with every breath,
you commit to this ever-evolving knowing.

There is no need for validation,
for certainty,
for reference points,
for specialness,
for you have broken free from the cage
of the small "I" who cries out to be seen,
who yearns to feel the sweet waters of Source
because it has forgotten that it is already the ocean.

As you breathe, you are everything.
You are the ceremony of life,
an eternally fluid expression
of Source creation
traversing all forms.

You already contain
what you so desperately yearn for.
Breathe in the reassurance that
you are exactly where you need to be,
lacking in nothing.

PART III

THE RECLAMATION: INTEGRATION

SO FAR, YOU'VE COVERED A LOT OF GROUND. You experienced the Revelation of Part I, which enabled you to prepare for the experience of integrating Source Consciousness into your life by learning to shift into a mindset (and soulset) that will lead to greater balance. After that, you moved through the Revolution of Part II, which was all about clearing your path of the many obstacles that most of us have inherited, especially with the paradigm of survival that dominates in the worldviews of God 1.0 through God 3.0.

Now, you are ready for something wholly new: the Reclamation. This final section of the book shares that which will allow us to reorient our compass to ways of being and doing that are deeply aligned with the new fifth-dimensional paradigm of God 5.0. Thus, we move from a worldview focused on achievement and self-centric notions of enlightenment, and into one that allows us to take responsibility for everything we are creating from moment to moment. This is how we begin to create "heaven on Earth"—through a re-cognition of who we actually are, and what we are capable of when we are allied with Source and connected on the deepest levels.

Reclamation is about authentically becoming who you have always been deep down, beneath all the layers of conditioning. In these final chapters, you will ask yourself the following questions: What is our responsibility with respect to the evolution of human consciousness? How, in this incarnation, can we work to bring in more of the true self? How do we ensure that the actions we are taking account for not merely our personal desires, but for a larger way of being that serves all of humanity, and beyond?

When the path has been cleared and you have opened up and surrendered in such a way that you have gotten to truly know yourself, free of the debris that may have previously marred your reflection in the mirror and served to create pain and chaos, you are ready to live your life in a new way.

For most people who experience a life-changing breakthrough, it's impossible to look at things the same way they used to. Indeed, one has to orient to a new way of living that requires a steady compass. In this section of the book, you will tap into some of the most powerful resources available to us, which will give you the ultimate experience of allowing any final defenses you've built around yourself to fall. This is what will give way to the experience of honoring the precious cargo you've been protecting or guarding your entire life. That cargo is nothing less than your authentic spirit. When you begin to feel the opening that allows you to connect with this part of yourself, which has always been connected to Source Consciousness, you will easily and wholeheartedly say yes: yes to the commitment of living as your true self, yes to the transformations you are sure to experience, and yes to the deliberate creation of a world that allows us to evolve beyond our current systems and into a state of being that truly weds the gloriousness of this human existence with the limitless creativity and abundant nature of Source Consciousness.

CHAPTER 7

RADICAL ACCOUNTABILITY IN OUR RELATIONSHIP TO SELF AND OTHERS

ONE OF THE MOST IMPORTANT ASPECTS of connecting with the Source energy that resides within you is the capacity to take radical accountability when it comes to our relationship to self and others. The first and most important aspect of radical accountability is simply honoring *what is.* This is all about acknowledging our experience for exactly what it is. This may include a one-sided or abusive relationship, whether it's with ourselves or someone else. But it isn't about martyring ourselves or wallowing in self-imposed misery. Radical accountability means that we offer ourselves self-love and self-acceptance, and also that we learn to self-reflect and examine our lives with compassionate, radical honesty. It can be helpful to do this in a community or even with a trusted mentor. But the sincere, heartfelt, surrendered choice—"I am no longer willing to fight what is"—is what brings into action the will to change.

Honoring what is requires being grateful for every instance of our life, because every experience had the power to lead us into a deeper relationship with ourselves. This is very difficult for many people. We tend to either praise or condemn our lives, to focus on the things we like and the things we don't; on the things that went our way and on the things that shouldn't have gone the way they did. But radical accountability starts with honoring every step we have ever taken, every experience we have ever lived through, not because we love the fact that we may have suffered but because *we are willing to embrace all of who we are*. In this process, we come to recognize that, no matter how we may have felt, there was never any point when we were not whole. When we experience this depth of gratitude, the entirety of our life can change in an instant. We recognize that we are not the victims we may have believed ourselves to be; we start to place things on the altar of truth—which is when we place a situation in our lives before Source itself and ask that the truth be revealed to us, not what we want it to be, and to see who we are.

How do we begin to see the truth of who we are, which is the basis of radical accountability?

I think of Cameron, a woman who participated in my 21 Day Catalyst program recently. She had already done a lot of energy work and complained that when she took my class, she felt like she was out of her body. As I listened to her, I had a sense of what she'd experienced. I asked her, "What if you didn't leave your body? What if you simply realized the aspect of who you are that needed to come back into your body?"

This immediately shifted Cameron's viewpoint. She realized that she had had an impression of what was happening to her, instead of taking the time to place her experience on the altar of truth. She realized that she had actually spent a lot of time outside of her body, even though she'd always thought of herself as being embodied.

Many of us might go through an experience like this, where we realize that what we took to be true was not, in fact, truth; that we had been hiding some integral part of our experience from ourselves, perhaps because we wanted so badly for things to be different. The difficult thing with radical accountability is that we have a tendency to be blind to the truth. We don't do this on purpose. It's just that we have grown accustomed to living in a world where we cannot honor and accept what is, and we can't even bring ourselves to see it.

There's a simple way to shift out of our blind spot. I always encourage my clients, anytime they feel confused or like they can't see the forest for the trees, to bring their whole self into the presence of Source and say, "Show me the truth of who I am. What am I experiencing? I wish to see my life and the situation at hand for what it is, and to see myself for who I am."

This is the number one thing we can do to hold ourselves accountable, so we can begin to see ourselves through a well-focused lens, with compassionate clarity; so we can truly recognize the cause of misalignment in our lives. This is what it means to stand before the altar.

Throughout human history, this experience of standing before the altar usually occurred in the spirit of sacredness, a word that has the same root as *sacrifice*. What we are actually sacrificing in this case is our own impression of ourselves, which is limited by ego and trauma, so that we can face the full truth of who we are. If there's only one thing for you to take away from this chapter, it is that radical accountability is knowing and seeing the truth of *you through a lens of compassion and forgiveness.*

So, why can't people accept the truth of who they are, and fully honor the story of their life? When I ask myself this question, I can't help but think of my parents, who simply could not let go of the impression of who they wanted me to be vs. accepting who I actually was. They held on to their desires for me with every fiber of their being because they didn't want to feel the pain of acknowledging how they couldn't see me and might have failed me as parents.

So often, we hold on to a lie because we fear the *feelings* we will experience if we were to acknowledge that our lying caused us to hurt something that was precious to us, others, or life itself. We don't want to live with the possibility that we may have violated a sacred contract. If we were to accept that we had succumbed to a lie, our orientation to ourselves and others would disintegrate in a nanosecond, and we simply wouldn't be able to see ourselves or life the same way. In other words, we would have to change not only our view of life, but of ourselves.

Unfortunately, we build our existence on a fixed way of identifying ourselves in relationships, and in proximity to everything around us. Our persona is terrified of change. It wants the safety of things to identify with, such as predictable thoughts, feelings, and emotions. However, this mentality cripples us and makes us complacent. It holds us accountable not to our true selves or the true selves of others, but to an illusion that robs us and others of our potential. Radical accountability welcomes change, because it will not tolerate the falseness of the identifications we have created. When we create a falsehood, we not only drain our vital life force, but that of the life around us, rather than allowing it to flourish. True accountability requires doing what we can to thrive, and thriving isn't possible if we cannot clearly see ourselves and our lives as they really are.

FROM OBLIGATION TO TRUTH

One aspect of accountability that few people truly discuss is that it requires the integrity to proclaim that we will never abandon ourselves, not even at the expense of a relationship we've been taught to value. For example, there is an enormous taboo around stepping away from relationships with family members, even if these relationships are not healthy. However, relationships that are built on obligation are bereft of truth. It makes no sense to undergo a lifetime of abuse and neglect and then maintain an active connection or contact with the people who treated you this way. This is based on a misunderstanding that love is something that is owed rather than something that should be allowed to flow freely and in a healthy and life-giving way.

Many well-meaning parents love the idea of being close to their kids, and they struggle with the fact that their children might want autonomy, or as they get older, may not wish to have a relationship with their parents at all. Often, parents struggle to see their children as being their own unique souls. This is often true in relationships where we might see the other person as an extension of us, rather than as someone who is wholly independent and on their own spiritual journey. Forcing closeness where there is very little in the way of shared values can be damaging. Love does not require forging the kind of closeness that so many people think is necessary in relationships. Love is about honoring, especially the honoring that allows others their autonomy and their own thoughts and feelings.

Many of us carry regret, shame, and pain around broken relationships, especially if some part of us believes that we were the cause. So, we believe we need to force or fake connection even when it might not actually exist. However, if we are committed to exercising radical accountability, we must keep recognizing that change is a constant. Continuity in relationships is wonderful, but it is possible to outgrow our relationships, whether we are on the receiving end or we have felt the need to move on from connections that do not serve our growth. Radical accountability is not about treating other people as if they are disposable, but it *is* about honoring that every single one of us has a unique path that must be respected, and that people *do* change.

When we are connected with Source Consciousness, we allow ourselves to move in the direction of thriving, but for so many of us, our relationships do not reflect our desire to thrive. They reflect our desire to people-please; to shove ourselves into a tiny little box so that others will approve of us; to belong, even at the cost of our self-respect and true nature. This is a recipe for pain and resentment. Relationships that are built from a space of obligation are not sustainable.

I am not suggesting that if we feel we have outgrown a relationship or we're surrounded by toxic family members, we simply walk away. The first step is radical and truth-based self-expression, which invites an opportunity for things to be different. If we are to live by the idea that we will never abandon ourselves, this must hold true even when we are faced with contrary responses from the people around us.

Radical accountability also means taking responsibility for the decisions that make the most sense to us. For example, Angela has a difficult relationship with her mother that has been contentious at times. Over time, there has been enough transformation that they have created a more tolerable and impartial relationship. However, I learned that there is no compromise possible with my own parents, and I came to the conclusion that the most compassionate action I could take, for them and myself, was to disconnect from them completely. This is a taboo subject that is rarely talked about and is too often tiptoed around in our culture. But in facing our personal relationships, we must be honest with what we are experiencing. What is presenting itself to us? Is there an opportunity for genuine transformation, or will the effort only end up depleting us? In order for there to be a reciprocal energetic exchange between two souls, each person must first know who they are, then state what they want, talk through it, and work on what their personal imbalances are to determine if the relationship can actually shift and evolve. If this does not occur, or if we end up doing the bulk of the work, the relationship will become a source of pain. The relationship is no longer one that is based in love and mutual respect, but one that is imprisoned in projections and expectations that only end up taking us further and further away from our true self.

When we begin to allow ourselves to become intimate with our feelings, even if those feelings include frustration, abandonment, hopelessness, and despair, we come to discover the truth of who we are. I knew this truth at a very young age, but my parents and I differed extensively in our ways of looking at the world and understanding reality. I saw that their rejection of me was connected to their driving need to place me in a box of their understanding to keep their fear and pain at bay. I didn't help matters much. I was so different from them that I may as well have been an alien. In fact, I have often considered that it would have been easier for them if I had been a drug addict, or someone whose life had taken a downward spiral—because at least they would have been able to use judgment, condemnation, and frustration (emotions and states of being they were familiar with) to deal with me. But how could they feel anything toward something that was outside their comprehension? Nobody had provided them with a foundation for how to parent a child like me. Ultimately, my parents never knew how to support me. Their objective in raising me was getting me to fit into society as they understood it to be. They simply weren't willing or able to put in the effort to get to know who I was, or to seek the guidance they'd need in order to support me. They wouldn't even try.

Over the years, I realized I'd remained in the cycle of trying to gain acceptance from my parents, even though I continued to receive nothing but criticism and judgment for my life choices, which they didn't understand. Unfortunately, even as adults, many of us continue to go back to our parents because society insists that we must do this. As I embarked on my own healing process, I began to ask that they welcome me for who I was. I didn't need them to change their own lives; I simply wanted them to change how they saw me and behaved with me.

This simple request was always met with a resounding no. In fact, my parents were often indignant about it. "*You* should respect *us!*" my mother would insist.

Part of why I realized it was necessary to separate from my parents was that over the years, I would need to take weeks, months, and sometimes even up to a year of space from them. After I began a relationship with Angela, I could no longer ignore that whenever I saw my parents, I became emotionally upset as a result of how I was treated and not honored for who I am. I would be imbalanced after I saw them and deeply unsettled even as I was getting ready to see them.

I found myself falling into my old patterns, and it was coming out in our relationship. I also saw that it was impacting my ability to step into my power in all areas of my life—because every time I saw my parents, I stepped out of my power. Then, something happened: I became aware that I was bringing the pain of my past into our relationship, and my heart broke wide open! I could now see clearly that I was allowing my pain to influence who I was in an unhealthy way, causing both Angela and Nate pain. That moment of breaking open freed me to make choices without fear. It was then, out of love, that I decided I would no longer withdraw my power when I was in their presence. This was accompanied by a great deal of pushback, resentment, sarcasm, and hurtful jabs from my parents. At that point, I realized I was no longer willing or able to keep up the charade. It was simply not sustainable anymore. I no longer wanted or needed my parents in my life. And so my parents and I ended up going our separate ways. My distance from them didn't mean I stopped caring, it just meant I chose myself for once.

My brother, Wayne, passed away from cancer seven years ago. During the time he became ill, my parents reached out to me and asked for help. My brother and I had never been close, but we had respected each other enough that we would always reach out and let the other know if there was anything we needed.

When my parents met with me after my brother became ill, I hadn't spoken with them in two and a half years. It was a difficult situation, as they were still extremely hurt and angry. The only thing I was drawn to do in that moment was to thank them for everything that they were, which had helped me to become who I was. I specifically thanked my father for his steadfastness, strength, courage, and power. Of course, in my mind, he had never wielded it in the best of ways, but I knew he had always meant well.

After this conversation with my parents, I connected with Wayne and through our time together it became clear that the cancer had spread too far. It was at this point that we realized the best way I could support his experience of dying was by energetically and spiritually helping him to let go of this physical world with a sense of dignity and peace. I also helped his wife and sons to move through the process in a way that was as comfortable and honoring for them as possible. While I was at the hospital, I also talked with both my parents, and we were cordial. At this point, they began to assume that everything was "good" between us. They didn't realize that I was there for Wayne—not out of guilt or because I wanted to be back in the family.

At the reception after the funeral, my mother asked me, "So, when do we get to see you again?"

I responded, "Mom, you're under the impression that I'm not in the family because of Wayne, but that isn't true. Wayne and I had a very clear understanding of what our relationship was. There was no tug-of-war, and no resentment. We knew where we stood with each other, and we respected that. The reason I'm not around is because of you and Dad. I've given you many opportunities to do things differently with me, and you haven't once taken advantage of that opportunity. So, why would I come back when you don't embrace me for who I am? You keep wanting me to be someone else for you. You wrote an obituary for Wayne. Now, I ask that you write one for me. The person I was is no longer in existence. That Ron is not who I am, or who I've ever been. It was just who I kept being in order to please you. It's what I thought I was supposed to do to get what I hoped deep down I was going to get—which was unconditional love and acceptance. What I came to realize is that if I became that person and was accepted for it, that wouldn't be unconditional love and acceptance anyway. When you are willing to start seeing me for who I am, text me and we'll talk. Until then, please don't reach out."

So far, it's been seven years, and my parents have not reached out with that intent. I honor their choice. But I had come to my breaking point; I could not pretend to be someone I wasn't in order to preserve a relationship that had never been genuine and that had always asked me to sacrifice my truth and to pledge allegiance to a lie. I had come to a place in my own growth journey where I was no longer willing to put myself in scenarios where I could not be respected for who I was, which—to the best of my ability—is a way that leaves only growth in its path. If my own parents could not meet me there, we didn't have a place from which to begin relating.

Because my focus has always been on helping people to unlock and live their potential to be what they can and benefit life as a whole, I recognize that my responsibility is to remain a clear conduit. In relationships, it's so important to honor what is, which means embracing every aspect of our life and not wishing for it to be anything else. This was the gift of authenticity that I discovered and that opened me more fully on my own spiritual path. I learned to surround myself with the people I want to be surrounded by, who also contributed to my growth in the same way I contribute to theirs. I decided I would no longer be a prisoner to obligation, which is why I freed myself and stepped away from my parents.

Do you know what your breaking point is? At what point are you no longer willing to sacrifice your authenticity?

When people have been conditioned to view things a certain way, mistreatment is normalized and they begin to accept that this is just the way it is, without recognizing it was never okay to begin with. A dog that gets beaten only knows how to be beaten. When we become so bound to a power outside of us, we become less capable of acknowledging our true essence, which is unconditional love and a power that exists far beyond the labels that have been slapped on us by our family of origin and society at large.

When you've already gone through the process of the Revelation and embark on the Revolution within, you recognize that the authority was never out there to begin with. But too often, we forget the truth of what is because we have learned to mistrust our own intuition. We have become severed from the authentic, intuitive spirit that lives within us. We simply don't know what authenticity looks like, because the poison has numbed us to the truth. However, as I have already mentioned, every experience that we undergo is an opportunity to come into greater alignment with ourselves.

FROM ME TO WE

Coming into alignment as the true self is the basis of all meaningful and harmonious relationships with the world around us and with all the many manifestations of Source Consciousness that exist in our midst. Unfortunately, to arrive at genuine communion, we must find our way through the manic dance. In almost every culture, the survival mentality is the most primal driving factor. It is perpetuated by the ones who are going to live their lives without any care or attention to each individual's quality of life and potential for thriving. In this way, the legacy of culture and the dynamic of domination perpetuates itself. When we feel caught in this, we tend to sustain relationships that don't allow us to thrive. We become choked off from our own thriving, as we've been conditioned to believe there is something out there in the world that is far more important and stabilizing than us being authentic to who we are.

The dance of the spiritual path is not about simply ripping free from this oppressive dynamic in order to be an independent agent out on our own in the world. The spiritual path is about coming to a center point that allows us to move from "me" to "we"—to engage in a new experience of interdependence and mutual harmony. Thankfully, time is speeding up as we move toward the paradigm of God 5.0 and living in the fifth dimension and beyond. Things are moving so rapidly and changing so quickly, we are no longer construing ourselves subconsciously as mostly finite. We're not attempting to slow down the clock anymore so that we can go back to a time when everything was perfect. The myth of the unchanging society is slowly but surely crumbling apart. Relationships are moving more swiftly. They are no longer anchoring us to a fixed identity. In fact, we are shifting our very relationship with the essence of life. In turn, this is what is occurring in our relationships with each other.

The relationships that do not fit a paradigm of thriving will fall apart more quickly, whereas the ones that support us to step into who we truly are will endure in ways that transcend the present moment. We are coming into a deeper sense of communion with who and what we are, not as labels and identities, but as eternal beings in a dynamic dance with all of life. The point of every relationship that we are in is the emanation of authenticity, which helps us to keep journeying into the essence of our creative self, where compassion exists in a raw and unmediated state, at its purest level. As we work to create mutually harmonious relationships of interdependence, we gain even more clarity on how to bring that compassion and love into the world. We come together to uplift one another, not merely to carry one another's burdens and to perpetuate a legacy of camaraderie through commiseration, which is what many of us know so well.

Part of the challenge is recognizing that there aren't as many models as we would like for this way of being that is mutually uplifting, that serves to mirror the deepest truth of who we are back to the world around us. When I think of the models that exist, I think of the Dalai Lama, whose essence radiates joy, compassion, and peace. At some point in my life, I realized that I needed to be in the presence of people like him: people who help us to find a way of being who we are, simply by being themselves.

As we move into more interdependent and harmonious relationships, we learn to become conduits for authenticity. Unfortunately, most family and social dynamics perpetuate a culture of imbalance that makes it easy for us to become something we are not, so as to find inclusion and a sense of belonging. Authentic intimacy can feel scary because it is unfamiliar to so many of us. However, the more willing we are to step into ourselves, even if that means bringing the relationships in our lives to an end because they do not nurture us into thriving, we become wiser about the relationships and communities we choose to step into in the future.

The more we connect with the true self, the more we discover relationships that lift us up, and that make us aware of where our imbalances are. Of course, that process isn't always fun or harmonious, but we can choose to be mirrors for each other with the utmost kindness and compassion. This is what Angela and I do for each other. I don't need Angela to be anything in particular for me. I simply hold a loving intent for her to be her fullest self, which she generously shares with me, and vice versa. Again, because radical accountability to a new paradigm of life that supports thriving is not possible without the capacity to look at ourselves honestly, the revolution in relating begins inside us when we start to see the patterns we have been stuck in and the places where we have been afraid to fully emerge as our true self.

As I watch the changes that are occurring in our midst, even though they may feel scary and destabilizing, I understand and can honor them. With every generation, there is an opportunity for transformation into a more authentic way of being who we are. Many of us have been conditioned to fear or oppose these changes. But if we remain dedicated to our quest to find an embodied truth, we will become dedicated to every individual's quest to do the same; we will create societies that are inherently stable and balanced because they can joyfully engage in the dynamic dance between "me" and "we." This way, we cannot help but create and nurture societies that honor each unique soul, as well as our intrinsic interconnectedness.

FROM CONDEMNATION TO FORGIVENESS

We live in a world in which the pain, trauma, and wounds we experience, from the moment we are birthed from the womb and into this incarnation, only seem to multiply—especially given our consensus reality that suffering is a way of life. However, one of the most radical things we can do to free ourselves and one another from the weight of resentment, which leads to cycles of violence and suffering, is to let go and embrace forgiveness.

I want to be very clear here: Forgiveness is not the same thing as condoning any of the painful things that happen to us. Rather, it is a completion point that we come to when we have fully honored our pain. By that same token, forgiveness is not something we do; it *is* what we *are*. It is the gift that naturally comes through us when we choose to accept ourselves, our feelings, and our experiences, exactly as they are, rather than telling ourselves the story that they should be different.

Self-forgiveness is perhaps the most important form of forgiveness. As we accept the gift of radical accountability, we come to forgive ourselves for the times we didn't have the courage to say and do what we needed to. When we come to a place of being able to hold our truth as our way of being in the world, we become exemplars of that courage. There is no need to vilify ourselves or anyone else.

For example, in the wake of my experiences of feeling victimized by my family, I was able to gain clarity about where my weaknesses lay. It was a very difficult experience, but I learned that rather than continuing to give in to my weakness, or to believe it was simply a part of my identity, I would no longer choose to be at the receiving end of my or anyone else's condemnation. By the same token, I was not going to turn around and mistreat or harm others in order to keep from feeling the pain that my perceived weakness had caused me, which is something a lot of us can end up doing.

Many of us carry a great deal of unresolved pain about being a victim. Even perpetrators have been victims at some point. Rather than facing this, and transmuting it, they may have learned to weaponize their victimization against other people in whom they saw weakness. The energy of shaming and blaming is what keeps us in a cycle of self-harm and harming others. It may feel like there is no way to rise out of this energy, which continues to blind us to our true power to see and feel and know who we are beyond these temporal experiences. But when we look at any of the higher energies, such as compassion, joy, and forgiveness, we can see that they are simply ways in which the essence of love gets formatted to help us correct an imbalance within ourselves and come into a state of restitution.

Forgiveness is essentially a corrective measure. If we look at the concept of sin that has been put forth in many religions, we can take out the energy of shame and blame and perceive sin as a misalignment with one's true self. In fact, one of the original meanings of sin is "missing the mark." When we miss the mark with respect to ensuring that our actions, behaviors, speech, and thought patterns align with our true self, forgiveness is meant to restore us to that original aligned state of being.

And through forgiveness, especially of the self, we can be grateful for experiences of misalignment because they help us see that our experiences are innately capable of initiating an opening within us—an opening that can help us realize we weren't who we'd chosen to be. Forgiveness allows us to transcend poor or misaligned behavior so that we can step into who we truly are. In fact, forgiveness is our capacity to be who we truly are, and to recognize that others struggle in the same way when they are misaligned.

When I have forgiven others, it has always been in the interest of helping all involved parties to experience an opening that leads all of us to our true selves. However, forgiveness of another does not mean that we welcome them and their behavior back into our lives. I recognized in forgiving my parents that they had to take that journey toward their true self on their own. By that token, I have never viewed an apology as being something that truly matters unless it transcends speech and moves into action. When a person's apology is an act of correction that helps them to honor their true self and move into alignment with that way of being, the words "I'm sorry" no longer matter. The person actually *becomes* the change and has come closer to their authentic self.

In general, forgiveness is an extension of the idea of radical accountability, which allows us to honor what is and to bring it into the light of truth. Even when I think of clients who have overcome extremely difficult childhoods and risen above adversity to find a sense of joy and purpose, I see that much of this is connected to their capacity for forgiveness.

Forgiveness is an act of surrender. When we let go of the idea that things were supposed to be different, we come to truly honor the totality of our experiences and how we feel in response, from our worst pain to our highest bliss. We recognize that all these experiences occurred in order to help us know who we are. And for this, we can actually be *grateful*.

Through forgiveness, we can also bring love to our experience, which draws even more love forth so that we can be all of what we want to be. As I mentioned, one of the greatest difficulties that people have is the forgiveness of self. When we hold forgiveness back from ourselves; when we say, "This is all I am and nothing more"—this attitude creates more of the same poor decisions and stunted behavior. Just as one would find in addictive patterning, a lack of self-forgiveness indicates the presence of shame, which triggers a feeling of unworthiness. When people feel unworthy, this means they don't have to be responsible or accountable for their actions, and they continue to perpetuate harm against themselves and others. However, true forgiveness is not about simply excusing what we have done in the past. It is about bringing the healing balm of love to the places within us that have been wounded. This love instantly transforms us and our way of being in the world.

Many of us go so far down the rabbit hole of self-hatred and heartbreak, especially if we didn't receive the nurturing we needed, that we begin to look at everything through an inverted lens. Sometimes, looking at things in this upside-down way can be a gift, because it means we're being initiated into viewing things differently, and putting the pieces back together in such a way that we can recognize ourselves as the hero in our own narrative. When we actually locate our own power (through sensing and feeling it), even in experiences where we feel broken, there is always an opportunity to reconcile ourselves with Source Consciousness. Sometimes that process is one of extreme dismantling, where we have to hit rock bottom and fall apart in order to discover who we truly are. Whether one is an addict or a criminal, or someone who simply goes through periods of extreme depression—no matter the malady, in order to get out of these cycles, our lives sometimes need to be torn asunder so we can look at it all and realize: "None of this makes any sense!" Within our darkest moments, there are periods of lucidity where nothing feels quite real or right, and these are the perfect opportunities to reorganize ourselves and transcend our survival patterns.

Unfortunately, some people get stuck in the nightmare of the pain, and the journey down the rabbit hole is a difficult downward spiral. However, it is possible to find light in the moments of lucidity. All of us have the potential to experience life in its raw and primal power, beyond the limitations we've placed on it. This is the true power of forgiveness. Even when it feels like we can't forgive ourselves for all we have done, or others for what they have done to us, we can come into the experience of forgiveness, almost as if it were a prayer. This act of true surrender to *what is* creates the opening for transformation, so we can move out of the cycles of acting from our deepest inner pain.

The Hawaiians have a beautiful prayer they call *ho'oponopono*. It is a prayer that can be used for ourselves, our loved ones, and for the world at large. The original prayer goes something like this: "Divine creator father/mother, if I, my family, relatives, and ancestors have offended your family, relatives, and ancestors in thought, deed, or action from the beginning of our creation to the present, we ask for your forgiveness." The contemporary practice of this prayer is four simple lines that we can address to ourselves and others: "I'm sorry. Please forgive me. Thank you. I love you."

The healing frequency of this prayer is extremely powerful, and it can help us to get outside of our mental constructs so that we can continue to expand, even if we might have a tendency to beat ourselves up.

Over time, through my own journey with my family, I have felt shame—and I still have experiences of feeling ashamed of my own behavior—but I don't pummel myself because of it. I am able to respect that I'm human and I make mistakes. The journey of being an infinite being in a finite form is not about having superpowers. It is about focusing on the knowing and inner awareness that I am on an eternal voyage. I have forever—an eternal number of incarnations—to come closer and closer to expressing and experiencing my true essence. Even though I don't want to make mistakes, I must always remind myself that I have lived separate from my true origins for a long time, and I'm doing my best to ensure that the union of form and spirit is as pure and clean as it can possibly be. I am my spirit, and my spirit is me, and even if I don't express this in the way that I wish to in this lifetime, I will ultimately get there.

In the meantime, I will continue to own anything I have done that has compromised my sense of connection to my true self. If I feel cloudy and unclear, I can do what is within my power to clean it up. I will see every moment as an opportunity to take an incomplete experience and bring it into the wholeness that I am. When I do this, I will see my wisdom and my awareness expand exponentially and impact my entire world.

Of course, the word *forgiveness* can be a difficult pill to swallow, even when we understand on a rational level that it isn't about condoning harm. Perhaps you are feeling ambivalent right now, as you read this section. I want you to know you're not alone. Often, I tell clients who are resisting forgiveness that a simple initial step they can take to bypass this resistance is to fully respect the magnitude and amplitude of how *they feel* about whatever occurred. This is especially true if the events entail intensely destructive feelings, like hatred, rage, or wanting someone to suffer for what happened. On a conscious level, we know we shouldn't feel that way, but it can also be a relief.

I always say, without judgment, "Fine, let's walk through this feeling. Let's surrender to the fact that this is how you feel." Sometimes they'll respond, "But if I do that, what if I get lost in it and become a hateful, raging person who wants others to suffer?" I always explain, "If you *don't* walk into and through those feelings, you will become what you fear. If you don't respect that this is how you feel right now, you'll carry it with you like a splinter that will eventually infect you."

Surrender is such a huge factor when it comes to forgiveness, which is not an intellectual process that we can simply talk ourselves into. (For example, I have spoken with many people who insist they have forgiven their abusive parent or spouse, but I can tell from the way they present themselves energetically, emotionally, mentally, and physically that the forgiveness is not authentic because it has not come from their heart.) If we can accept the grief and pain we have encountered in any of our experiences—and if we can honor and embrace that these feelings are so vast that we fear losing the sense of who we are in them—the paradox here is that this moment *will* ultimately come to an end, and the feelings will eventually ebb. Once this happens, we can pause, breathe, and welcome in the experience that brought about so much unsettledness. This culmination happens because we have allowed ourselves to see the experience as it is, not as we prefer it to be. We often refuse to go into the deeper terrain of feeling grief, rage, sorrow—because when we do, we must surrender our viewpoint of ourselves, life, and others, and this loss can feel like annihilation. Even though in the end it is your key to freedom.

The thing is, we come back to life and regain our energy when we are willing to honor what is, and what actually happened. We don't get stuck in what we believed should have happened. In fact, once we finally process the experience, we no longer even have to think about forgiveness. We honor what is to such a degree that we are finally at peace with ourselves and whoever we perceive has caused us harm.

This is where I need to repeat that forgiveness is not an action (a common misunderstanding); it is a state of being, it is the gift that comes at the end of our process of wholeheartedly being with and accepting how we feel within all experiences. Often, forgiveness is something that comes when a person is at death's door, because this is where we recognize that forgiveness has the capacity to free us. Energetically, if we cannot move the pain through our system, we congest ourselves in such a way that we can't let love flow as us and through us. And, as emissaries of Source Consciousness on this earthly plane, we want nothing more than to *be* love itself.

If the word *forgiveness* is tripping you up at all, don't even bother with it. Start with accepting and respecting your feelings about what happened. In fact, you could remove the word *forgiveness* altogether and focus on *acceptance*, *honoring*, and *letting go*. If you do this, you'll come to the same endpoint, the same gift, which is accepting yourself in how you feel and what the experience was for you.

Again, I want to emphasize that if you encountered true harm at the hands of another or even at your own hands, what happened wasn't okay. However, you can always choose your own freedom; you can choose your own precious, beautiful life, which has gifted you so many opportunities to come home to your true self. From this place, worrying about what will or will not happen to the other person (if you were harmed by someone else) is no longer consequential. In freeing yourself, you have set a new pattern of love, compassion, and gratitude for life into motion. That can create the foundation for a new transformation that may not have been previously available.

THE MEANING OF SERVICE

A discussion of radical accountability would be incomplete without an exploration of service and contribution. Many of us see service and contribution as a way of making our mark in the world, but even this concept comes from the notion that we are not worthy unless we do something that is considered important by the world at large.

Over the years, I've come to see the meaning of service in a totally different way. When I'm at the grocery store and I smile at someone and that person smiles back before they can put up the armor of self-protection, I recognize that I have contributed an act of service. I saw that person for who they truly are, and I chose to be who I truly am. I didn't view them as less than in any way, but as another human being on their unique journey having their own experience. I've recognized that service is the act of being the joy, love, and gratitude I am, and living and breathing that when I am in anyone's presence. If we did this more often and simply provided an opportunity for people to drop into themselves beyond their perceived limitations, it would be the greatest service we could possibly offer. It would eventually lead to a shift in our motives for all forms of humanitarian aid—from that of compensation for social imbalances to that of loving support for unforeseen disasters. Simply by being our true self and mirroring that back to others, we would create the kind of world where everyone has a place to rest in their own essence.

Radical accountability is not the same as carrying another person's burden for them. Service needs to be viewed beyond the scope of saviorism, which has a tendency to view people on a spectrum of least worthy to most worthy, weakest to most powerful. However, true service simply occurs when we are the essence of life expressing itself, birthing itself anew every instant. It doesn't matter how we choose to access this, whether we are a CEO or a janitor.

One wonderful way to access the spirit of service is to engage in something that helps to open us up and connect us to the aliveness within us, which we will want to bring into our world when we come to embrace the unique beauty that we are. When we do this, we cannot help but live and breathe our authenticity. This means that we begin to access the courage to say "no" to unhealthy relationship dynamics. The systems that hold up our world become weaker, because we do not need them to make us feel powerful or protected or anything else that keeps us stuck in a false construct of who we are. Throughout this experience of bringing our aliveness into the world, we might fumble and fall, but how we hit the ground and how we get up matter beyond words.

In fact, it is healthy for us to see individuals we admire trusting themselves to make mistakes and to feel pain or shame and ultimately transcend the imbalance. This is why the truth tellers of the world who confront not just the pain and suffering of the collective, but also the pain and suffering within themselves, have the power to mirror back to us our own imbalances so that we can offer compassion and grace to ourselves and others. When we have more and more leaders expressing this beautiful transparency, we'll begin to see changes in how people engage aggressors, and in how we communicate with one another. This will destabilize the fearmongers and the spreaders of hate and rage. When we stop feeding them, they will become weaker. However, if we keep looking to them for validation of our anger and pain, they'll remain in positions of power and visibility.

How do we walk toward an expression of our own aliveness so that we can be responsible for stabilizing the essence of truth on this planet? I recently offered a healing event for my community, and I noticed that so many of the people who came were touched by the atmosphere we had all created, and many of them were brought to tears. I could see that these tears came from the deepest parts of themselves. Such tears are a guidance system to follow and step into so we can grow that feeling that wells up within us. When we step into that which moves us wholly, we can choose to expand it until it becomes everything we are and everything we know ourselves to be. Our community was touched by the experience because, as many of them later shared, it enabled them to feel a sense of inner peace, which is their true selves. Other people in the room shared similar feelings, noting that they felt more aligned and whole within themselves. If we continue to open up our inner authentic essence and let it be the thing that orients us before we take our next step, we will be guided to all of the experiences, the people, the teachings, the lessons, that will open us up to the full truth of who we are—which we need to know if we want to contribute our truth to the world.

Of course, accessing purpose in the 3D world isn't always easy. We might be plagued by a whole host of feelings when we think about "giving back." For many people who long to give their gifts to the world, it is easy to feel justifiably angry or righteously indignant at the horrors that abound around us, and the experiences of pain and violence that are visited on so many of our human and nonhuman fellow beings. There's nothing wrong with this anger. It can, in fact, be holy—for holiness is simply an act of expression that brings us into alignment with our true, whole self. But we are not meant to stay wrapped up in the anger. Rather, we are meant to go deeper—to settle in and feel the heart breaking and to sit with it. As we do this, we notice that we instantly calm down. And if we continue to follow that feeling, we will have the experience of our spirit moving through our body.

This is the point of reorganization. This is the place from which we can ask ourselves, "What should I do now?" An important aspect of service is learning to trust your spirit again. Unfortunately, many people don't trust their spirits, and sometimes they let other people and situations hijack their power to be of service.

When this is the case, we must always look back on our lives and recognize the places where we experienced powerful openings, even if those moments are few and far between.

This makes me think of the movie *Citizen Kane*,* which is a beautiful illustration of how a person can be extremely successful without being of service at all. The primary mystery of the movie revolves around identifying the meaning of "Rosebud," the final word uttered by the newspaper magnate, Charles Foster Kane, as he lies upon his deathbed. The film takes a profound voyage into the pain of the character's childhood, during which he created a fortress that would protect him from being hurt and during which he lost contact with the very essence of his own life force, which was personified by *Rosebud*. He could have lived a life of being in service to that beautiful life essence, but it was only when he died that he recognized it.

Like *Citizen Kane*, we might build a fortress around what we wish to protect because we are afraid of losing it, which is understandable if we have been traumatized. However, by shutting the vulnerable parts of ourselves off to the world, we also shut out our capacity to breathe our aliveness into the spaces of hurt and suffering. We can use these spaces to actively and constructively address experiences of pain and betrayal, and to stay congruent with who we really are. To truly be of service, we must decide whether we are going to stay in the wound, or if we are ready to step into the vitality and love that we are.

Another aspect of service is recognizing that even if we have tapped into our core aliveness, this can still get distorted by our own emotional pain and our sense of lack. This is why it's important to be careful who we surround ourselves with. Are we around people who help others step into their potential, or people who choose to draw power to themselves at the expense of others? Often, the spiritual path may place obstacles in our way that help us to recognize

---

* Welles, Orson, dir. *Citizen Kane*. 1941. Los Angeles, CA: RKO Radio Pictures.

when we are around people who've become consumed by their own egos. It will also periodically give us opportunities to see if we have been consumed by our own egos. (An example I hear frequently is "Why can't I find my soulmate?") By not receiving what we think we want, to fill a void, we begin to realize we weren't clear on what we truly wanted to experience and what would actually complement our lives.

We've created so many systems in our world to do for us what we have the innate capacity to do for ourselves. More of us are beginning to question the solidity, stability, and function of systems, institutions, and leaders that have been operating in the same way for too long. As we find ways to process our fear, and to balance our sense of worth so we can create a system of equitable and loving exchange between one another, we have the capacity to consciously create a world in which all our needs can be met, and our primary service is both an expression of our unique soul essence and a commitment to the highest good of all beings. This is the kind of world in which both the individual and the collective are fully honored.

In this way, our true service is incumbent on all of us reaching our potential in one another's presence. Again, this is radical accountability, because we no longer need the parental figures to tell us what we should or need to do—because we have come to a sense of innate responsibility within ourselves to do what's right for us and for all others. All of us have been impacted by the experience of separation from our true selves, so one of the greatest ways we can be of service is to learn to crack open the armor so we can attend to the spirit and nourish the body with whatever it requires. We can become more healthy and bring that sense of vitality into the world. From this place, we can generate stronger and clearer intentions. We can trust ourselves in the presence of those who may not be trustworthy.

And as we own our personal sovereignty, we will begin to see and respect it in others.

One of the most beautiful original intentions behind most of the world's religions is getting all of us to realize the interconnectedness of life. That is, when one of us suffers, all suffer, and if one is in pain, all are in pain. We have the potential to shift this altogether to the notion that when one is in joy, all are in joy. Even our language can transform so that we are supporting a society full of thriving, not merely surviving.

COMMIT TO LIFE: A HEALING IMMERSION

Breathe,
as you settle into the commitment
that you have been moving closer and closer to:
the commitment to empower yourself,
to become a realized expression of your true spirit nature.

Breathe,
as you settle in and honor
that you are an eternal being.
Yes, you may have lived separate
from your true self,
separate from life,
separate from others,
separate from Source,
but you have now chosen to remember
and embody once more
this truth:
You are separate from nothing.

Breathe, as you feel your innate will
to become unified within,

to hold all parts of yourself intact,
to feel that you are part of everything.

As you do,
you sense your power and energy amplify
simply by owning who you are.

You are taking responsibility
for healing,
for bringing the past, present, and future
into a higher resonance,
into the most sublime aligned expression
of who you are.

You have eternity to bring forth who you are,
as your soul desires,
to express the fullest potential of the love that you are
in honor of your relationship with yourself, others, and all
of life.

Through this journey,
step fully into
your love for God and God's love for you.

Breathe,
and let yourself transform and be transformed by life.

CHAPTER 8

A HEART-CENTERED PARADIGM FOR MANIFESTATION

ONE OF THE MOST IMPORTANT THINGS we can do to truly reclaim our power as living manifestations of Source Consciousness is to respect our infinite potential, which encompasses being able to create with and through the mechanism of our physical bodies. How cool is that?

Leaning into "manifestation" as a blueprint for connecting with God and becoming cocreators with the universe isn't a new concept. Although it's become a big part of the New Age, with numerous books and courses on the Law of Attraction and how to become a money magnet, the idea of manifestation goes way back—into the "Prosperity Gospel" of the evangelical tradition in early America.

If manifestation is something that has helped people to feel in control of their lives, and to connect with spirituality, that probably makes it a good thing, right? Well, it's not so much that I'm trying to be a contrarian claiming that manifestation is "bad"; it's just that the current paradigm we've been using for the past forty to fifty years to get what we want has generally been in avoidance of what we are actually here to experience. (Cue the Rolling Stones song here.) Many people have been manifesting with the hope that if they ask for what they want (perfect job, soulmate, financial abundance, etc.), they will eventually find their spiritual core and *then* be able to navigate through difficult times with greater strength, ease, and openness. But this line of thinking just hasn't worked out for most people.

Most people use manifestation to drift further and further away from the mundane aspects of their lives; they go for the fairy dust, the love, and the light. Again, there's nothing wrong with love and light—except when it becomes a form of escapism, of avoiding the full spectrum of feelings that are a natural part of our human experience. When we're always in love and light, running away from pain or grittiness to get to pleasure, we become lopsided. We cease to see that sacredness isn't limited to one panel of the cosmic tapestry. We were never meant to play at one end of the pendulum swing. In fact, it's ideal when we're neutral and open, so the pendulum can move freely across the diverse scale of experience. After all, manifesting isn't about making one's life easier; it's about creating greater *fluidity* so we can move more easily through any kind of terrain and *every* life experience.

The way I see it, the old paradigm of manifestation is almost like a fantasy *Chitty Chitty Bang Bang* car that takes you up into the clouds, away from the sorrow and challenges of your "real life." In contrast, the paradigm I'm going to be sharing in this chapter is like all-wheel drive, which enables you to keep your feet on the ground as you freely traverse the many paths available to you in this majestic world; to embrace your innate ability to create an infinite number of experiences; and to make manifest your infinite capacity to bring your eternal spirit into form in any way you desire.

The new 5D paradigm is about flow. And yes, with flow comes ease, and with ease comes flow—but when you're trying to manifest in order to keep from feeling or experiencing something (ending up like your dad, for example), or you're repeating the way of the past by wanting "more" instead of striving to experience and be more of who you innately are, the rewards you reap are short-lived. That's because none of us are meant to stay in one place for all time; we are designed to be mobile and fluid, to navigate the ever-evolving landscape of life.

In addition, the old paradigm significantly misses the point of our human experience. We tend to fixate on the thing we believe will change our lives, instead of the experience it's going to bring us into and through. In truth, it's not about having what we're looking for—it's about recognizing who we are when we have that experience. Think of the contrast in these attitudes: Do you want to be in the world in such a way so that you can attain what you want in order to feel better about yourself? Or are you going to feel better about yourself and bring a healthier version of you into the world that will express your completeness and elevate not only your own life but the lives of everyone around you? Getting "stuff" doesn't necessarily elevate anybody; moreover, stuff is finite. It doesn't last forever. Titles, objects, and people can be taken away in the blink of an eye. What can't be taken away are your experiences and your connection to Source Consciousness, which are the only things that will ever enable you to live out your full potential.

Also, while it may be true that you can get anything you want if you work hard enough, that doesn't mean you'll be complete or fulfilled or any wiser. Part of why we tend to focus on manifesting stuff is that we weren't raised to see that we are born *already whole and complete, with everything we need to live our potential.* In many ways, the things we want to manifest are a demonstration of an immature relationship to our true self. We were born with an innate sense of wonder and a limitless capacity for joy. However, few of us were guided to value these qualities when we were young, and we didn't get to experience them in ways befitting our potential. "Stuff" became a substitute for this glorious engagement with ourselves, with all of life.

But we can find a better way to manifest what we truly desire, which is essentially an experience of Source Consciousness in all its vastness and grandeur.

Although the word *manifestation* can often be overused, we're going to be using it quite a bit in this chapter—not for the purpose of demonizing or diminishing the goodness that things like the Law of Attraction have brought to so many people, but for the purpose of clarifying the process so that even more people, not just the "lucky few," can benefit from it. But make no mistake—this isn't going to be a primer on how to get the thing you've always wanted. I'm going to share with you some tools (which I refer to as "truths of manifestation") that I've found to be especially effective when it comes to manifesting the most powerful thing any of us are capable of: the full, authentic version of who we really are.

TRUTH OF MANIFESTATION #1: REMEMBER, IT ISN'T ABOUT BEING "HAPPY"

One myth to dispel straightaway is the idea that whatever we manifest must make us happier. Because often, what we've been conditioned to think of as "happiness" isn't actually the thing that will lead us to greater fulfillment.

Let me give you an example. I have a lot of clients who are naturally wired for constant growth. These are the kinds of seekers who are always looking to understand themselves and bring more of who they are into the world. However, some of them might come to me with the desire to be in a relationship that feels easy and doesn't demand too much from them. Do you see what a contradiction this is? They want to keep growing, but they want their partner to be perfectly accepting, to not make any waves in their life.

In my experience, true happiness is about fully aligning with our nature. If it's your nature to move in the direction of growth, you will be most fulfilled when you bring someone into your life who will challenge you in a compassionate and loving manner to go deeper within and embody more of who you are, and vice-versa. This can make for a vitalizing and spiritually fulfilling relationship, but it's not necessarily going to look like the paradigm of the perfect relationship that you were taught to long for.

A lot of people comment that my relationship with my wife Angela must be easy because it looks so great on the surface, but this couldn't be further from the truth. Throughout the ten years we've been together, both of us have wholeheartedly committed to our growth. This is incredibly challenging, but in a way that nourishes both of us. We understood from day one that our connection was in service of our evolution as two souls on a journey together. As I often tell people, everything about the awakening process is incredibly simple, but it is by no means always easy. The challenge, always, becomes about facing what you would rather not face—holding the integrity of what you want yourself to be, while dealing with the conflicts and challenges that are sure to reveal the areas where you might be out of balance. A growth-oriented partner will not necessarily be the easiest person in the room to get along with because of what may be triggered in their presence. However, you can certainly bet this partner will be your greatest ally when it comes to helping you express your fullest potential and continue to evolve—a reality that Angela and I have lived for the last ten years.

Happiness, the way the old paradigm sells it to us, isn't true happiness; it's only a temporary reprieve, in contrast to authentic joy, which is eternal and creates an environment that supports your ability to manifest a life that allows you to be a better and more expanded version of who you are. Remember it is this eternal essence of who you are that you're seeking to realize in this life.

When we come to understand that life is an evolutionary journey—one in which we will continue to resurrect our perceived limitations in order to grow through them—we will no longer be content lulling ourselves into the fantasy or false sense of everlasting happiness. "Happily ever after" is temporary, unfulfilling, and quite frankly, hollow. We are too magnificent to settle for a storybook version of our wondrous potential.

TRUTH OF MANIFESTATION #2: KNOW YOUR RESISTANCE PATTERNS

I want to be clear about one thing: Manifestation—the way that most of us have been taught—*does* work for some people, but it doesn't work for most of us. Most manifestation techniques hinge on the basic notion that positive thoughts incur positive results in our lives, while negative or self-doubting thoughts incur negative results. It's a specific brand of victim-blaming that isn't appeased when we deny the negative thoughts and just hop on the bandwagon of positive thoughts.

I've met many people who struggle with bringing about the things they want purely through the power of their minds. Here, the struggle begins, and inner shame, blame, and conflict begin to make themselves apparent. People will often start to view themselves as having failed, which couldn't be further from the truth.

It isn't that people are failing at manifestation; it's that they have underlying patterns of resistance, fear, pain, doubt, etc. (basically, the full gamut of the range of lesser emotions we can get stuck in), which they aren't even aware of, buzzing silently away in the background. They're operating at an unconscious energetic level that isn't automatically changed by the attempt to implement "positive" patterns through words and thoughts. For example, they might be swimming in many invisible energetic matrices that interfere with their ability to be fluid (in the form of familial or social lineage patterns, or past-life influences). They might also be plugged into a particular collective consciousness based on the culture into which they were born.

We can't simply reject our genetic and energetic makeup or trick ourselves into believing these have no influence over us. The only way we can truly manifest our deeper desire to experience ourselves in a way that is lighter, more fluid, more joyful, more intimate, is to fully put to rest these energetic patterns we didn't even know we had. And if we're focused on surface-level thoughts and things, we'll never know what those patterns are.

Putting to rest all that we were born into so we can feel ourselves as complete, so we can create in the external world all that we know we are internally, is the ultimate manifestation.

I learned this over two decades of growing my spiritual/healing practice. As my business kept growing, I continued to hit ceilings I couldn't understand. I often felt I couldn't fully address issues that people were presenting to me. My initial reaction of "There's something wrong with me" or "I'm not good enough, gifted enough, or worthy enough to know how to support this person through their issue" persistently got in the way and kept me from following my intuition and heart-centered awareness.

I came to understand that the ceilings weren't my fault, and blaming myself wasn't helping matters any. The ceilings were just part of the generational and social matrix I'd been born into. I grew up in an environment in which I constantly had to adjust how I was feeling and behaving, just to stay balanced within myself and keep the environment as stable and safe as possible. I learned to acclimate to my surroundings, but not to honor how I was fully drawn to be and live. I felt it was my duty to keep the environment around me stable instead of stabilizing and nurturing myself.

Over time, as I settled into trusting myself and my innate awareness, and stepped away from my birth family, I became more stable, clear, and intuitive. This increased my ability to effectively support others, and it increased word of mouth about who I am and what I do for others in my practice, which created a progressive and steady stream of growth in my business. I started to see how I was playing out patterns I wasn't even aware of. I want to share a scenario of how this might manifest in your own life.

You step into a meeting with your colleagues. All of a sudden, you start to feel your system adjust. Something within you shrinks and withdraws. Your back stiffens. You feel nervous. You have a sinking sensation that any words that come out of your mouth are going to be the wrong ones, and everyone is going to fight what you have to contribute. You might start by blaming the people in the room, including peers who are just out to get you. But this isn't about them. It has never been about them. All of this is showing you that you have something that is unresolved within you. It is interfering in not just this moment, but most likely, in all your interactions and exchanges with people. When you are no longer in this situation, you have the opportunity to tap into your connection with Source and ask to see the truth of why you lost your balance, your integrity, your ability to stay connected to the moment. As you do this, everything will begin to reveal itself to you. You will see where you are out of balance, and you will begin to disentangle yourself from the energetic matrix of your imbalanced and unresolved past.

Best of all, there is no such thing as failure in this paradigm. You will *always* draw into your life whatever you need to see how you're either aligned or misaligned. And if you continue to stumble and fall, you aren't getting the full capacity of what your soul wants to experience in this life—you're getting what you're using to avoid that experience.

As my business grew, I began to work with more clients who had detailed and intricate issues, some paralleling my own imbalances that required attention. Through attending to my own weaknesses, I became aware of how to support others into and through theirs. Also, as I became more aligned with my ability to access higher truths, the ways of supporting my clients became crystal clear. This created an opening for me to go deeper within myself and bring my full self to my business. I grew the business from solely one-on-one sessions to adding group healing work and expanding the depth and breadth of what I offered in both areas.

You don't need to know how or why you got out of balance, and you don't need to judge yourself. It's like having an infection and realizing it's there because of a splinter that didn't get pulled out. You simply pivot so you are attending to wherever the healing needs to happen. When you recognize that there's a wound, your method of healing starts to become more apparent.

The process of stepping into a better way of manifesting is all about getting to know who you're not (in this case, the unbalanced, nervous person in that meeting with a group of people waiting to pounce on your every error—at least, in your eyes). From here, you do some inner inquiry to see what happened; then, you walk into and through it, clean it up, decide who you are and how you want to be, and bring this true version of yourself into the world. When you begin to clean up enough of the past (which can only happen by facing the truth of your feelings, not avoiding them), you will naturally draw in the right people, the right opportunities, to help you be more of who you want to be. When you are in alignment with the frequency of your right path, things can't *not* work out for you; this is an infinite universal truth.

And I promise you, if you truly wish to manifest your authentic nature, you will find many ways to do this. You will literally magnetize them.

This is because when you, as a physical being, are aligned with your soul's directive, and you are honoring that subtle, innate guidance that is your spirit essence leading you in the direction of the next greatest adventure of your life, those opportunities to live in and as your true self will never be lacking. This exceeds and goes beyond what your mind wants, which is inherently based on lack and a scarcity mentality.

In general, if you're saying something like, "I want my next partner, or job, or shiny new object that'll make me feel momentarily worthy and validated," you're living through your ego. You're not necessarily living as your spirit essence, because your spirit would simply walk you in that direction—and the ideas of how to manifest it would come either from you or from people walking into your life to spark that awareness of the next step. That is the true essence of manifestation.

When I think of this notion of magnetizing that which will enable you to step into your true nature, I am brought back to meeting Angela. Sometimes, when people talk to us, they assume that when Angela and I met, it was love at first sight—a recognition between two souls. This always makes us laugh, because that's definitely not the case. When she came to work for me, neither of us was looking for a relationship—it simply wasn't on the agenda! I was building my business, while she was trying to heal and raise her son.

Three months after meeting, both of us looked at each other and acknowledged there was something going on here. And as we both began to look at it further, we realized that from the moment Angela came to work for me, we'd both felt like magnets standing a foot apart from each other. Over time, it felt as if the magnets had moved closer and closer together until the attraction was undeniable and irresistible, until they snapped together! And the more we spent time together, the more we drew together—because that was the right manifestation for the next greatest expression of our life's experiences.

If you agree to simply call in the experiences and people who will steward you toward the next greatest expression of your own life experience, this way of manifestation will become second nature and you will begin to bring your full spiritual potential into the physical world—hopefully, with minimal resistance, as you will have surrendered to your soul's deepest knowing.

Of course, the same is true when it comes to who we *already* know ourselves to be. That is to say, if you have surrendered to your ego's knowing, you might view yourself as a "lazy, unmotivated" individual, and you'll draw other individuals into your life who feel the same way about themselves on some level. You'll manifest that which you already know yourself to be. The great thing is, every pattern can be healed. You'll simultaneously be creating an opportunity to choose how you wish to experience yourself differently. If you come to a place of wanting something more, you'll have to recognize that you must love and honor yourself as you explore whatever created a deficiency in your self-appreciation. It's necessary to embrace that it's okay to bring good people and better opportunities into your life. This is the place where so many people falter, because they don't feel worthy, which is exactly *why* they end up turning to manifestation in the first place. The irony is, turning to manifestation keeps them from leaning into the unworthiness they feel, which is the only way they can work through patterns of resistance and discover the very thing they want. However, their avoidance keeps them in a feedback loop of constant unfulfillment.

How do you start to tangibly tackle the mismatch between who you are and what you want?

Let's walk through this together. Let's say you want to bring forth an amazing job that enables you to utilize all your gifts. Even if you've convinced yourself that you are totally aligned with this goal, where are you feeling resistance to it? What's happening in your body when you say, "I am choosing to manifest this wonderful job where I can be more of me"? Perhaps you noticed that something in your system tightened up. You didn't feel joy or excitement. Your mind began to wander. Those are the resistance patterns that need to be brought to a state of closure, of rest.

Resistance patterns are unresolved pieces from our past that cause our energy to leak or congest, and that compromise our efficacy and clarity. When they are resolved, through a process of mindful, heart-filled awareness and inquiry, we become more efficient at every level of existence. Our sensory awareness, biology, and psychology come back to their true nature, because we are no longer disrupted by the fear or worry of an incomplete past and the expression of the pattern it creates. We aren't buoyed by artificial adrenaline rushes, either; instead, we feel the euphoria of being alive, vital, and complete.

Remember, we always draw into our life the very situations that will reveal to us where our incompleteness resides. While this will feel like "failure" or difficulty at first, what it's showing us is exactly what we need to know so that we can begin to resolve old patterns and bring the best of who we are forward. It's not necessary to intellectually identify the things that are standing in our way in order to clear those patterns. What we need to do is become aware of how it *feels* to be congruent or balanced within ourselves, to *know* who we are. We've all had these moments before, when we were living and breathing as a balanced representation of our whole self. When we begin to feel and live those moments in our simple, mundane daily activities, we clear the energetic debris even further and bring our full, harmonious selves into every situation. This is when the magic starts to happen.

TRUTH OF MANIFESTATION #3: BRING MORE OF YOURSELF INTO THE PROCESS

The important thing to remember is that manifestation isn't anything supernatural—it is simply a universal truth. It's a natural part of life's creative process: An impassioned idea gets birthed into action and made manifest and concrete. It's a lot less about acquiring "stuff" and a lot more about creating the situations and circumstances that are favorable when it comes to being who you were always meant to be. The stuff might be fun, but the experiencing of self and others in an infinite number of ways is the heart and soul of life.

In other words, it's not about manifesting what you want *in* your life; it's about manifesting who you are *as* your life.

Here's another example. Maybe you're looking for a kind, soulful partner with whom you can share your life. Wonderful, but let me ask you a question: Do you enjoy being around *you*? If so, great. How can you bring this part of yourself, whom you enjoy so much, as clearly and cleanly as you can, so you can find someone to play with who will elevate you just as you will them? It's not about filling holes with external stuff, including your ideas of the "perfect partner"; it's all about recognizing where the holes exist within you, so that you can work to heal those wounds, nurture the most complete version of yourself, and manifest yourself in such a way that you can share more of you with others—eventually, you will draw to yourself the right person to support you in living your highest potential.

The heart-centered paradigm of manifestation is all about using that compass of feeling we talked about in Chapter 3 to fill up your voids with more of *you*, not with people/titles/accolades/things. This way, even though all of that will eventually come, you won't be attached to it anymore. You'll start to realize that this extraordinary matter-based life is infinitely creative—so why not create something amazing?

I know we are each here to cocreate the world from a place of already knowing ourselves as complete—not from a place of desperately grasping for "more" or "better." So, how do we express and expand this completeness to bring new possibilities into form? Perhaps we are not meant to know in advance. The process of bringing all we are into our lives and embodying it in physical form is a process of creating the path as we go.

In essence, all we need to do is begin with a simple question: "How do I wish to experience myself today?" If you can tap into whatever that might be—as joyful, sensual, curious, wonder-filled—you can work through the process of experiencing yourself this way. You can test what happens in the world around you when you do this. When I began doing this, I started to receive the external support that would help me bring out more of how I wanted to experience myself. I got what I needed to become who I am. And when I did this, I began to recognize that there was nothing I lacked. With this experience of "no lack," my life started to feel more balanced.

All that said, I want to remind you of what the paradigm of manifestation I am proposing is. To put it clearly, where you are is the point of orientation through which you draw to yourself everything you need to experience *yourself* in a more expansive way.

The incredible thing is, when you do this, you start to relinquish rigid control over how things are supposed to look in your world. You can let go of your preferences, which tend to be rooted in ideas of "good" vs. "bad." You can exercise curiosity about your experiences, understanding that they are here to help you recognize the moments when you might be out of balance—and inherently, they are here to help you come back into balance. You can use both "negative" and "positive" experiences to generate who you wish to experience yourself as.

From here, you can actually experience what the world calls "abundance," because you are no longer limited to one stationary position on the pendulum swing of duality. You are now open to infinite possibility. You invite abundance because you are no longer afraid of this or that within the realm of experiential living.

So often, when many of us are introduced to manifestation as a spiritual practice, we choose abundance because we are afraid of not being or having enough. However, when we are no longer afraid, when we open up to the limitless truth of who we are, we discover the meaning of true abundance, which is synonymous with knowing yourself as Divine Source Consciousness.

TRUTH OF MANIFESTATION #4: DISTINGUISH AN EMPTY NEED FROM AN AUTHENTIC PASSION

One of the most important components of manifestation is passion. Passion is often mistaken as desire. However, desire is usually based in lack and want, whereas the passion of the soul is to provide us with the fuel to move in an experiential and evolutionary manner. Desire is centered around physical and psychological needs and the urge to feel better about ourselves, whereas passion activates all that we are into the creative expression of our highest nature to live. Passion is fundamental to the process of change and growth. We change and grow, on some level, because some part of our being wants the experience of moving through the world in an evolutionary way that allows us to bring out more and more of ourselves. Life is governed by passion—the passion for genes to replicate themselves in the next generation; the passion for a bud to move toward the life-giving energy of the sun; the passion for the roots of a tree to find and drink in water.

Passion is a basic inborn quality, but we are so adept at protecting ourselves from whatever we'd prefer not to feel that it's easy to create a false impression of our passion. So often, we are connected to secondhand, or "manufactured," desires that have little to do with who we are and what would actually help us to bring more of ourselves into this life.

Sometimes, when a client tells me there's something they want to manifest, I'll question them about this. "What would happen if you didn't have an opportunity to bring it into your life?" I like to delve in and challenge the idea of the passion to see whether it's a pure passion, which doesn't come from avoidance, or an empty need expressing itself as a passion.

We're amazingly skilled at repressing and avoiding. We'll use all the right terms to make it seem as if we are aligned with a passion, but we might not be aware that this so-called "passion" comes from a place of avoidance and fear. There's a big difference between wanting to pursue your dream of being a doctor because you've always loved helping people to heal and understand their bodies and wanting to do it because you come from a family of doctors and they'd be devastated if you didn't follow in their footsteps. To make matters more difficult, sometimes the distinction isn't always clear. The passion might have initially started out as pure, before it got muddied by the need to compensate for a sense of lack, obligation, or fear.

So, it's important to see where the predominant energy is. I have found that if you start to reflect on the possibility of *not* fulfilling this passion, you'll begin to have a sinking feeling, and you may feel frustrated and upset. If it is a true passion, this energy and intent can become the divine spark to awaken your spirit's drive to express and experience in other ways; it can also act as a guide to help you know when you are accessing authentic awareness rather than an avoidance mechanism to distract yourself from something deeper.

This usually reveals that what you're dealing with is not a true passion but more of a cover-up. You will have a chance to honestly ask yourself if you're pursuing it for the right reasons. Does it come from true passion? Or are you moving in this direction because there's something you're avoiding? Sit and be with it. What is there?

Here's an example. Let's say you want to live in Hawaii. I might ask, "What draws you there?"

"I've always been passionate about it! I think it's the site of the next manifestation of my greatest potential."

I might respond, "With what you have now and where you are, are you complete and at rest? Or are there things you'd rather avoid by going someplace new? Are you trying to get away from something?"

This is where the old adage "Wherever you go, there you are" comes in handy. If there's something you're avoiding, you'll manifest experiences that continue to generate more avoidance. Reminder: Avoidance isn't "bad"! Like any aspect of how we live and behave, we can use it as an indicator to show us when we are out of alignment with our spirit. By bringing a pause to any action, we can redirect our intention and activity. We have the power to shift the direction of our life at every moment.

I bring up the matter of location because it's a very helpful indicator of an authentic passion vs. an empty need. I grew up in New England and was ready for a fresh start, as I had always been drawn out West, but Connecticut and Maine were all I had known as home. Then during a visit to Sedona, Arizona, without any previous desire to move, I knew this would be my next home.

I had been drawn to Sedona (where I currently live) for years. When I sat with why that was, I realized that it just felt like home to me. The energetic dynamic of fluidity, healing, and spiritual renewal seemed to match the dynamic of how I operated. I realized that if I had to stay in New England, I'd be able to manage it, but it wasn't an area where I felt a great deal of fluidity, ease, or passion actively in my life.

When I sat in a spirit of open inquiry to see if there was anything I was avoiding by deciding to leave New England, I realized that the internal impulse to move came from a genuine passion. After all, I'd lived in New England my whole life—and through it all, I'd changed and grown dramatically. My orientation to myself was wildly different, and while it created more spaciousness and helped remove some of the judgments I had about my surroundings, my relationship to the region still felt at odds with who I wished to be.

To gain clarity, I took the time to step into myself and find the true foundation of my peaceful spirit nature. I chose to ask my spirit and Source to help me become aware of, be honoring of, and attentive to the truth around my wish to move. Once I brought that intent into action, I let it go and stopped thinking of it. As I did, the urgency and rejection of where I was currently living began to fade. It was shortly after I let go and I was engaging in something completely unrelated to the surrender when I felt the quiet, still voice within, bringing me to know that the move to Sedona was the next aligned choice.

TRUTH OF MANIFESTATION #5: TASTE THE HEALING ELIXIR OF GRATEFULNESS

Gratefulness (literally, the state of being full of gratitude) is one of the most powerful ingredients in manifestation, because it is a beautiful opportunity to know our own wholeness, to be reminded of who we really are. It enables us to hit the pause button and really *feel* how complete we already are.

This is incredibly important, because sometimes, the need to manifest comes from a draw to fill ourselves from the outside in, to fill the void created by self-doubt and unworthiness that follows us at every turn. Gratitude is the antidote to what ails us.

Sitting in the pause between feeling hunger and satisfying it can take us to being grateful for all that we are and all that we already have. It can also help us identify empty needs. For example, when I went through a divorce twenty-five years ago, I used food as an emotional suppressant that was almost like a pacifier. It kept me from feeling some of the uncomfortable emotions I didn't want to feel. But when I stopped what I was doing long enough to sit with what was actually motivating me, I could tell that I wasn't really hungry. The compulsion was just my way of avoiding uncomfortable feelings, as well as random thoughts and emotions. To step into my truth and power, I got into the habit of going to the refrigerator, putting a piece of food on a plate, and just sitting there and asking myself to feel into *why* I wanted to eat it. Was I truly hungry or was I attempting to avoid feeling something? Sometimes, a distinct feeling would make itself known: sorrow, fear, rage. Fine. I would work to process this emotion, and then I would ask myself if I still wanted to eat the food. Sometimes, the answer was yes, only this time, the action came from a place of nourishment rather than trying to fill a void. Sometimes, the answer was no. The "hunger" I'd used as a distraction and avoidance dissipated altogether.

The thing we have to realize is that people are constantly trying to escape from themselves. We live in a physical world in which we continually feel separate from our physical selves. We constantly search "out there" for what we want, when the real place we need to be looking for answers is within ourselves and our relationship to Source, *as* Source.

Gratefulness is a powerful way to close the gap, in that it helps us to create an environment in which we can truly feel and know ourselves as we are from within. Instead of seeking more, gratefulness enables us to experience and feel into the nature of our own vastness.

Being in a place of gratefulness is the experience of being full of ourselves—full of the beauty, wonder, peace, hope, connection, and infinite joy we naturally *are*. We don't often allow ourselves to experience it. For instance, if you're doing a "gratitude journal," make sure you're not just naming your blessings without really *feeling* them. When we are great-full, we are in touch with the essence of who we are; this sense of in-touchness allows us to draw this essence forth into the world. We can do this at all moments, whether we are acknowledging the goodness in our external lives or simply marveling at the beauty we contain.

There have been moments when I would stop to cry in joy and relief at the realization that I was so deeply in touch with who I am, and to embrace and feel it as fully possible. This can only happen in a moment of pause, when we are not rushing to fill the void or struggling to be something or somewhere we aren't. When I simply focused on this experience of genuine, internally generated joy, it automatically put some of the demons of my old resistance patterns to rest and purged whatever had been previously intervening in my *living* this joy in my daily life.

Gratefulness is so potent when we feel it to our bones, because it's nothing but a reminder of who we are! And the reason it transcends acknowledgment of our physical riches—homes, cars, lovers, friends, accomplishments—is that its true expression is not dependent on any of those things. Gratefulness is the gift that keeps on giving because it enables us to build our resilience, to draw from the wellspring of our deep inner Source.

So, sit in the "uncomfortable" pause, whether you have already manifested something beautiful or you've given over to the urge of distraction. Be with yourself. Feel what is present. It might be very difficult at first, but it is a muscle you must be willing to exercise. Be in awe of what arises. Allow yourself to understand it as part of the magical panorama of who you are. You will come to know yourself beyond this sense of lack, which is just a smoke screen for the abundance you contain. With gratefulness, you will come to know your true wholeness. From this place, you will realize that you were never broken. Even the painful moments were happening *for* you, not *to* you.

This is very different from how we've been conditioned—that is, to only be grateful when we "get" something we want from the world outside of us. However, the essence of Source, of God, is the awareness that guidance and support are always around and within us, even when we've convinced ourselves they aren't. When you are aligned with the essence of Source, you are aligned with yourself and the essence of the fundamental processes that created this universe.

Remember, Source isn't Santa Claus, waiting to hand-deliver the items on your wish list. I recall a great moment in the film *Evan Almighty*,* where God says, "Let me ask you something. If someone prays for patience, you think God gives them patience? Or does he give them the opportunity to be patient? If he prayed for courage, does God give him courage, or does he give him opportunities to be courageous? If someone prayed for the family to be closer, do you think God zaps them with warm fuzzy feelings, or does he give them opportunities to love each other?" And those opportunities aren't always going to be easy.

---

* Shadyac, Tom, dir. *Evan Almighty*. 2007. Universal City, CA: Universal Pictures.

Everything in your life is an opportunity to dig deeper into who you are, to choose to experience yourself as who you are . . . to feel the truth of yourself as the Divine Source energy that surrounds you, *is you*, and runs through every cell of your being . . . to know you are fully connected to the most powerful frequencies of light, love, truth, and power, which are all part of your abundant nature. You *are* that power.

Gratefulness as our natural state becomes the new, infinitely clearer lens through which we see our lives and ourselves. And even if nobody else around us knows what on earth we're gushing about, our gratefulness will be an expression of this clear vision of reality. Because gratefulness is a natural response to knowing ourselves as whole and perfect and unbroken, we'll be in touch with one of the primary operating platforms of creation itself. From here, we will be free to create whatever we truly want and all we are drawn to be.

AN EXAMPLE OF HEART-CENTERED MANIFESTATION

I have been working with Sean for a number of years. He came to me with a desire to create a life that would enable him to feel the childlike joy he knew so well when he was younger—although it took us a while to get to this realization. He was overflowing with curiosity and enthusiasm, and together, we determined that this was the quality he wanted to bring into every interaction in his life.

Sean was a contractor who was great with his hands, as he had a natural knack for making beautiful buildings. However, he was experiencing some difficulty in his business, including pushback from the people he worked with. This was very frustrating to him, because he just wanted *joy*. Unfortunately, it's difficult as an adult, especially as an adult man, to connect to and bring in that infectious childlike joy, which he'd never been fully able to express when he was a child.

I could see that Sean was still carrying pain over having been shut down, repressed, and rejected for his joyful nature. He had figured out how to navigate the world by developing a kind of masculine edginess that was sometimes explosive.

To help him open to this, we went on a journey together to help him experience himself as an expression of that true joy. We had to revisit the places where he had been stifled in his capacity to express his nature, and to resolve everything in him that made it difficult to bring this part of himself into his world so he could be congruent. Over the course of our sessions, we worked to bring that joy and levity into his life, so that he was having joyful conversations with customers, friends, family, and random strangers. Over time, he was bringing joy more consistently into everything he did; the people who wanted no part of it slowly disappeared from Sean's life. Suddenly, he seemed to be presented with opportunity after opportunity to know his true nature. He quickly came to realize that he had healing abilities, which intuitives had been telling him for years. This soon became his primary focus, and he decided he wanted to shift his career to healing.

Sean's story doesn't end there. When he got into healing, he received praise and accolades. He got to bring his light, joyful energy into the work he did, and he genuinely felt good about it—until he didn't. He began to realize that while he'd had fun, this wasn't the work he wanted to do. He didn't really feel passionate about holding space for his clients in the way that he needed to in order to be an effective healer.

Years ago, I'd suggested to him that his talent as a contractor could be used to design homes that were true sacred spaces that would help others be at home with expressing more of themselves. However, he'd been so frustrated with the colleagues and clients he was dealing with that he'd rejected the idea and believed he needed a clean break.

However, now that Sean was truly living in joy, he began to realize that it had never been his work that was the problem. It was who he was being, which resulted in the experiences he was having. When he began to realign himself with his work as a contractor, he began to bring in other colleagues who were softer, gentler, more open. He realized that he could approach his old line of work in a completely different way.

Today, Sean is creating a business that will enable him to design spaces that serve his clients on a much deeper level. Sean went through all five truths of manifestation as I've outlined them in this chapter, albeit in a nonlinear way.

Remember, It Isn't about Being Happy: Although he found praise and accolades in his work as a healer, Sean realized it wasn't bringing him the growth and deeper fulfillment he longed for.

Know Your Resistance Patterns: Sean had to dig beneath his frustration and recognize that the main reason he wasn't getting what he wanted was that he'd learned to suppress his true nature as a being of joy. He wanted to find joy in the external world, but he had to come to terms with the way he'd learned to reject his own joy. He also had to face his resistance patterns later on, when he began to process his resentment toward his work as a contractor, in order to realign with his true purpose.

Bring More of Yourself into the Process: Ultimately, Sean came to realize that he needed to be more of the person he wanted to experience himself as—joyful, enthusiastic, and full of levity. As he continued to do this and to really expand into his nature, he came back to his work as a contractor and had a completely different experience from the one he'd had the first time around. The switch totally flipped from "I want XYZ" to "I want to be an expression of my true potential."

Distinguish an Empty Need from an Authentic Passion: Although Sean turned to healing work, he quickly came to realize that it was an empty need. He confessed to me that, at some point, he'd decided he wanted to be like me and do what I did, which was clearly an avoidance mechanism. In realizing that healing work was fulfilling an empty need, he began to uncover more of his true desire and redirect his attention back to his contracting work.

Taste the Healing Elixir of Gratefulness: Sean had never learned to be appreciative of his skills as a contractor and had actually started resenting them. However, when he came to really value his acumen, he could let it be an extension of who he was and direct it in a new way—as a joyful, loving man whose spirit could bring healing to his clients in a unique way. In recognizing his wholeness, he brought a spirit of gratefulness and awe into his life, which magnetized even more opportunities to feel and know his wholeness in the world.

As Sean discovered, the real key to manifestation is becoming who you innately are. Now, he knows his intrinsic power to manifest a beautiful life, but it is no longer coming from a sense of lack, the desire to get out of debt, or any other avoidance mechanism.

True manifestation is essentially a process of moving from trusting the false self to trusting the spirit self. In this process of manifestation, you begin to feel yourself as complete. You begin to feel and know in your heart and soul that you are intrinsically worthy and whole, and that whatever it is you wish to draw into your life—a job, a relationship, a house—is the next way you wish to experience and express yourself in this world. This is not because the job, relationship, or house will make your life better or more complete; it's simply that you have outgrown your old life, and the thing that you are welcoming into your life is the next opportunity to experience your life anew.

Of course, Sean needed to have all these realizations in his own time. For him, it was a lengthy yet fulfilling journey that enabled him to soak up a great deal of learning, so neither of us would consider it time wasted. In truth, it really doesn't matter how long it takes. As long as we continue to stay in congruence with who we are becoming, life will continue to blossom for us.

INTEGRATE AND EMBODY THE ESSENCE OF MANIFESTATION: A HEALING IMMERSION

Breathe,
as you center into your true spirit nature,
that golden-white sphere that surrounds you,
that is you.

Breathe,
as you allow your whole being,
mind,
thoughts,
body,
feelings,
emotions—
as they expand when welcomed home—
to find balance within themselves
and in relationship to each other.

Breathe,
creating a beautiful and fluid dance
with your true spirit nature.

Breathe,
as you welcome in the essence of Source,
the very nature of creation itself.

Know in every fiber of your being:
You are the eternal essence of Source—
whole and lacking nothing,
in and as your love.

Breathe as you awaken
and become the nature of creation itself,

as you remember you are that which generates
all the celestial bodies in this vast universe;
you are the spark that brings into form
the very heavens in the night sky.

Feel the breadth and depth of your potential
to create your life,
to know that you impact all life.

You are the gift of truth:
that life is eternal and ever-evolving.

You are the infinite potential
breathing itself into form,
to live and love all that is and all that you are.

Breathe in the memory of your ability
to live a full and vibrant life,
bubbling from the inherent wellspring
of abundance.

Breathe as you open to feel and know
that Source has always been
within, around, and as you.
At no time has it been absent.

Breathe as you remember:
You are the greatest creative potential.
You are Source.

CHAPTER 9

DEATH IS NOT THE END BUT A KISS WITH GOD

NOW THAT WE HAVE COME TO the final chapter of this book, it feels apt to visit a topic that is one of the central pillars of most religions and modes of spirituality: death. It's little wonder why. One of our greatest existential fears is death, which marks the end of this finite form that so many of us have been conditioned to cling to, in avoidance of the great unknown that exists beyond this life. For many people who are on the cusp of exiting life, death is a journey into the mystery of the unknown that can surface some of our deepest unhealed wounds. But death is actually an integral aspect of life. Death contributes to the essence of what life is and holds the potential of what it can be. Death is the experience of going into the void, which is simply the potential of all creation.

In many ways, because we don't know how to live, because we do not live in a world that has taught us what it means to be in a mystically aligned relationship with life, we don't know how to die.

In the Introduction of this book, I shared a story about my wife Angela's cousin, Danielle, who died at the age of forty after a cancer diagnosis. For many years, as she dealt with her illness, she was locked in a victim role. Throughout the entirety of her experience, she posted her cancer journey on Instagram, with a desire to heal and get a book deal out of it at the same time. During her process of searching for healing, she traveled, took numerous courses, and worked with a myriad of teachers to gain assistance in opening up to God. Through these various paths, she came to the conclusion that she was hearing the voice of God and could speak with "him" directly. Over time, it became clear that she was desperately searching for a way to stave off her fear of a premature death. She simply didn't know how to surrender to the depths of her pain and fear and to embrace the mystery of life's awe-inspiring journey—and, therefore, trust that every step is meant to support one's highest good to be known. Although she believed she could positively think her way out of her cancer, it came back—and she went from saying she could speak to God directly to being angry at and feeling abandoned by him. The pain and hurt were so great that she threw away all of the healing tools she had acquired, such as her crystals, mala beads, spiritual books, and practitioner manuals.

After her death, someone remarked on social media, "How could God do this to her?" Of course, God isn't a person we can bargain with. God is Divine Source Consciousness: an energy that is neither born nor dies. In accepting this, we too can become fearless about entering death and the realms beyond death, as we begin to recognize ourselves as an intrinsic part of that energy. We also learn the essential ingredients of living a truly meaningful life, no matter how brief it might be. Because Danielle was afraid to feel the spectrum of feelings surrounding her cancer diagnosis, she was in search of a perfect, nonhuman being whom she could wholly trust and who would take away all her problems. These expectations were not realistic, because our pain isn't here to be "taken away"; it is here for us to face and step into and through with gentle compassion. And even if we have lived a life of fear and avoidance, the knowledge of our impending death can be a catalyst for remarkable growth as we find a way to put to rest whatever has been unresolved and to accept what awaits.

I have been blessed to work with a number of dying and terminally ill clients who discovered the "peace that surpasses understanding" when they were on their deathbeds. As I worked with them, I saw that it was possible to free ourselves from the culturally indoctrinated fear of death, and to relax into this inevitability in ways that bring us much-needed healing and prepare us for our own experience of passing from this reality to the next one.

DEATH: A CREATIVE PROCESS

Even if we're afraid of dying, there's nothing more natural than death because it is an intrinsic aspect of life, in the same way that birthing a new life is. Although we may have been conditioned to fear any end of a cycle, whether it's a physical death or the death of a relationship or identity, death is an organic aspect of the creative process. We move from planting a seed or setting an intention, to gestation, to birth, to bearing the fruit of our life experience, to harvesting the fruit, to experiencing the metaphorical plants as they wither, die, and return to the earth so their wisdom can be absorbed into creation for the next season. If we were to view this experience as one that is cyclical and eternal, we would see death quite differently, being grateful for it all, forever trusting the mystery.

Even those of us who were indoctrinated into religion can experience a terror of death, because we essentially view ourselves as finite. However, if we were to embrace the fact that we are infinite, and this specific form is just one of a multiplicity of forms that we may find ourselves being drawn into, we could actually appreciate that death is the process of bringing a specific moment into closure. Closure brings forth integration, then evolution, in preparation for rebirth. As we step off into the next iteration of who we will be, the act of creation requires this full cycle from birth to death, in all its wondrous facets, and all the way back through again.

True experiential creativity is the capacity to die to who we think we know ourselves to be and find new ways to contribute to creation as a whole. When we can trust in ourselves and in our infinite nature, we can move into death with the understanding that it is one of the most intimate exchanges we can experience. In fact, the phrase "the kiss of death" could transform from a morbid idea to an exhilarating one. Instead of being cursed by the kiss of death, we are blessed by a kiss *with* death, a loving exchange with a long-forgotten friend. When we experience death in this way, we realize that although we have come to an endpoint of a particular cycle, it's possible to feel joyous as we appreciate every moment that has led up to this final kiss. We can see that death is a completion of life, which was perfect for the duration of time it existed. And knowing this, we can look forward to the next moment.

Metaphorically, throughout most cultures, death has never marked a conclusive end but a resurrection and a rebirth. Think of the Death card in a traditional tarot deck. Although it can frighten people when it shows up in a reading, it almost never refers to a literal death. It usually means someone is going through a "dark night of the soul" or a "phoenix rising" experience where they are being called upon to relinquish old attachments and welcome a new beginning. In many ways, the Death card is the one that signifies the greatest potential for spiritual growth. Although change can rattle our survival instincts like nothing else, it is an opportunity for dying to the old ways of doing things (which includes many of the patterns that a lot of us were programmed with at an early age and that may no longer serve us) and being rebirthed into new possibilities. In this way, metaphorical death—which we can learn to embrace with gusto and curiosity—can hone our vision for what is occurring on a larger global scale as we move into the fifth-dimensional paradigm.

The way I look at it, this kiss with death (which is nothing more than a kiss with God) can be shared with depth and meaning, enabling us to appreciate the essence of our life as an infinite being in a finite physical form. Regardless of whether we can consciously remember our origins, we have never been separate from the Divine Source within. Each one of us carries a subconscious awareness of this, which we can choose to make conscious. Each of us carries the memory of that eternal embrace with Source Consciousness. This embrace never ceases, but it is in a constant state of divine evolution. With every experience we have as a physical being, we can take the essence of that experience back to the eternal, which also shares its experience, its vast knowing of itself, with us. In many ways, this embrace with death is an opportunity for physical and incorporeal realities to come together into an embrace that brings about a new vibrational pattern and essence. We allow ourselves to be transformed, and we become intimate with all of life and the mystery that is at the heart of Source Consciousness. The Divine wishes to experience itself in physical form, and the physical form wishes to know its divinity. The moment of death allows for this beautiful exchange, a divine interlude. The moment when time and reference cease to exist and all there is is potential as life itself. It is in this moment we are one *as* God.

In this way, we come to the recognition that we ourselves do not have an endpoint because we are in a continual reciprocal exchange between physical and incorporeal reality. It's just that the moment as we have known it has come to its climax, and it's meant to end so that we can become something more reflective and expressive of our divine self—with a yearning to experience something more expansive than what we were before. As we start to sense this, which we can do while we're still alive, we begin to tap into our eternal nature. When we start to feel this eternal nature, the fear of death dissolves. Instead, we celebrate the experience of this lifetime as a glorious series of moments that we can be genuinely grateful for. We come to the realization that life really does continue. As we transition into our next expression, we realize the joy and gratitude of having lived in a physical body, of having shared these precious moments with other individuals in physical form, whether sentient or not, whether human or nonhuman. We get a glimpse of the eternal that exists as the foundation of every transient moment, and we honor the end as it has chosen to manifest.

Although we live in a world that seems to be obsessed with youth and the preservation of the physical form, the processes of aging and maturation are intended to connect us to the eternal. In truth, even in life, every single one of us goes through a series of deaths, both emotional and physiological, so that we can be rebirthed into a new form. We are ever evolving and ever changing. We are the product of every moment that preceded this one. Physical death gives us the ultimate opportunity to create the next great expression of who we wish to be. If we can see and recognize this, we realize that we can move into every moment of life with courage and willingness, with the capacity to heal what may have been previously unresolved. When the human mind recognizes it is going to die, this can bring about either a sense of tragedy or the opportunity to open up and integrate everything that has not been embraced.

I have had the great privilege of supporting individuals who had spent most of their lives angry and lashing out at others and seeing them transform into the most loving and gracious people you could ever meet. In these moments, their family members and loved ones got to see something different from what they had previously known. This has the capacity to change not just the individual who was about to die, but everyone in the family system. Although some people who are facing their death automatically move into anger, disappointment, and heartbreak, it is quite miraculous to witness those who are willing to respond in a completely different way. No matter what they may have done in the past, they are able to transition from this life without any regrets. In the final moments of their life, they have surrendered to the higher truth of their soul: that they are the very thing they have been looking for—the peace and love that *are* the fundamental nature of life itself. It *is* them, not something outside of themselves.

THE FEAR OF LETTING GO

As we've already mentioned, death is a process that is often accompanied by a lot of visceral, fear-based emotions. It can bring up fear in both the person who is on the cusp of dying and their loved ones who are afraid of letting go. Certainly, during the dying process, a great deal of energy can get stuck within a family system, but death also offers a crucial opportunity for transformation. For so many people who are about to lose somebody, there is much that remains unknown. It is the finality of a moment that is connected to a specific identity and way of being that can feel unbearable to live without. Many of us feel lost in the absence of loved ones, and we come to adopt the idea that the other person is such an important part of our own energetic matrix that we cannot live without their physical presence. Many people, even those who don't necessarily believe in an afterlife, connect with mediums and channels to receive assurance that we are all connected beyond just the physical realm. Mediums tend to give humans peace of mind and the ability to grasp what is happening in a way that moves them beyond fear and human preoccupations. Sometimes, a visit to a medium can help a person to begin to accept the jarring change and move forward. Of course, sometimes they resist this and can carry the grief and loss as a badge of honor or an albatross of grief.

Whatever the case, death asks the ones who continue to live on in the human realm to come to some kind of resolution on their own. Whether the person who died is someone they loved dearly, or someone with whom they had difficult, unfinished business, now that the person is no longer physically present, the journey of reconciliation is placed before each individual to honor their experience and find peace within. Will they use this opportunity for transformation of the relationship? It is up to them to choose.

And then, there are those who are going through the physical experience of dying themselves. It is critical that people in such a state allow their mind and body to feel exactly how they're going to feel. Some might say, "I don't fear death," and seem unequivocal about it. But a lot of people have not yet come to embrace the reality of their impending deaths. Most are simply in a state of avoidance and try not to think about it. In many cases, avoiding the reality of impending death isn't necessarily based in fear; there could be shame, regret, or a sense of deep loss over what they were not able to achieve in this lifetime. The incredible thing is that no matter what our belief system, as we get closer and closer to the end of our lives, the spirit becomes much more prominent. The human egoic persona begins to weaken, the walls and barriers we have created begin to dissolve, and the self we thought we were gives way to our one true spirit essence.

I have been among many people in such a transition, and it is heartening to see them begin to rest into the presence of their spirit. When they do this, it creates a sense of effortless ease and release. When I work with someone on the cusp of dying, I help them to truly rest into their spirit, to feel who they are beyond their physical reality. When they do this, they can have a richer and more powerful opportunity of completion, which enables them to feel what they may not have been strong enough to feel in the past because they were so locked within their persona. When the wall between spirit and persona thins, we have the opportunity to put to rest any difficult experiences or beliefs about ourselves and integrate into our lives every aspect of our experience on this Earth. When this happens, we no longer hold on to our regrets. Our trauma can be resolved altogether, or it can become more fluid so that when we transition, we're able to finally put it to rest on the other side—by transcending it. The ease and peace that prevail allow us to experience our own spiritual essence. As our human form comes into proper perspective, we recognize that our humanity and our divinity are part of a single continuum and that life is and was always meant to be an experiential process.

The incredible thing about this experience of letting go is that it is happening on such a significant scale, and it helps us to realize that the healing of our own lineage is possible. That is, it's possible for someone to transition and to heal their traumas so completely that their loved ones—who might include parents, spouse, children, and others—also get the benefit of that healing. The work we do in our life and on our deathbed has the capacity to heal our lineage and transform our DNA both past, present, and future on an evolutionary path.

Without the denser energy matrix of our human persona holding us back, the transition that occurs can have massive ramifications for healing in multiple directions on our lineage timeline throughout all our incarnations. Even if our relatives never did the inner work themselves, we can create the opening to heal our entire ancestral line and the healing can also reverberate into the future, to those yet to be born. The bottom line is, everything that was given to us within the incarnation we've taken is meant for us to embrace and resolve so that everybody in our birth family, as well as the global human family, can receive the benefit of the work we've done. It is only when we are unable to let go of this life and its attendant traumas and challenges that we deal with the issue of our incomplete karma. This is how we continue to carry the pain of the past into new incarnations. However, when we are finally able to put to rest anything that may have served to hold us back in the past, we are free of the weight of suffering. Not only does this free us up for a completely different type of experience the next time we decide to come into form, but it ripples throughout all of eternity. This creates a beautiful cyclical opportunity for all of life to benefit from our experiences, and for all of life to benefit ours.

PUTTING TO REST THE UNRESOLVED

When I work with individuals who are watching a loved one prepare for their transition into the next stage of the life cycle, the one that occurs after death, much of my focus is on helping everyone in the family system—the person who's dying and the people who are witnessing this death—to put to rest whatever conflict they might still be carrying. This includes whatever remains unresolved that isn't necessarily about the individual who is dying, but about what the other family members may have projected onto them.

We have a tendency to endure this type of experience by projecting our pain onto a convenient target, which is why I help family members gain clarity on what they are actually feeling. Is it really about the person who's dying, or are there other things that have occurred that they may be projecting onto the individual or situation? Are there direct traumas attached to the dying individual, or traumas that are connected to the person failing to fulfill a set of (usually unspoken) expectations about who they were supposed to be? Is the person's death bringing up "unfinished business"? Whatever the case, when these emotions, feelings, and energy are amplified during this pivotal time of transition, such moments can truly become catalysts for resolution—even when resolution seems impossible.

In general, these experiences tend to be among family members, because our birth family is, by design, meant to help us remember who we are in these physical bodies. However, as we explored in Chapter 4, few families have the capacity to do that. Still, from childhood and into adulthood, we tend to look to our family members, especially our parents, to fulfill this role, even if we grew up in families that were simply not capable of self-reflection.

However, reflection is often possible in moments of physical death. The conflicts that have been long-standing patterns in the family system can be addressed, so that everyone gets to be who they truly want to be in the presence of one another. The grieving family members are no longer coming to the dying one with the desire for validation, or the wish that things had gone differently. This is very important, because the person who is in transition, even if they are not sentient, will be able to feel the energetic tugs that are coming from family members who still want something from them. Ideally, all family members will work to put to rest whatever resentment, bitterness, or unresolved issues may still exist, so that the dying person can transition into a state of remembering what it is to be held in unconditional love. They can let go of any attachments they might have to this human life so they can transcend.

Even though I've worked with some individuals who haven't always been able to forgive the dying family member, they can usually have compassion for what that person is going through. Forgiveness, on the other hand, can take longer to integrate, but at the very least, the way that the dying person experiences the transitional moment can be eased by a sense of neutrality.

I've watched many people die, and it's mind-blowing how, in these final moments, we have the capacity to resolve issues from this and multiple lifetimes. We can process and transcend hundreds and thousands of years in an instant. I've noticed that even when the body dies, the spirit has the capacity to go through an immediate evolution, so that it is absolutely free to create what it yearns to create in the next phase of its experiential journey. However, this doesn't happen if the energy matrix of the ego is so strong that it becomes welded to the spirit. This is what causes the cycle of karma to continue and to interfere with the cycle of spiritual growth.

Although the spirit creates the mechanism of the body, if there is a fusion between the ego and spirit, that fusion will go with the spirit into the next lifetime. The great news is that the work to dissolve these bonds can still be done even after a person transitions. I've worked with the surviving family members to help the person who transitioned move through whatever is possible for them to move through;

sometimes, they must wait until their next incarnation to resolve what remained unresolved, and other times it's possible for them to heal in the afterlife by fully integrating the experiential lessons from this lifetime so that their next incarnation will be different.

In addition, this can be a time when people (including the individual who is dying, as well as their surviving family members) have the power to unlearn all they've been taught to accept as "right" or "true." We always come to a point in our life when these learned patterns of behavior, which do not ultimately serve us, must be released and cleared; this creates an opening for us to be able to live in the moment of who we are, in each and every experience. It has the power to clear away any old, outdated, dense patterns and energies.

It can be helpful, within the intensity of the dying experience, to remember that we're all eternal beings having an experience that may look like it's couched in the temporal and transient, but that's just because we're not looking at the big picture.

When my brother was in the process of passing away, his body was experiencing a lot of pain and the people around him were upset about this. However, as I looked at my oldest nephew, I told him, "You know, your dad's not here—he's already left. This is just his body going through the physical discomfort based on how the cancer is interfering with his biology and creating certain feedback loops in his nervous system."

Fortunately, my nephew really got this, and it helped him enter the situation with a greater sense of neutrality, which very likely helped my brother, who passed away a couple of hours later, no longer attached to his body. Again, moving into a state of neutrality can be powerful for the family members, as well as the person who's dying. Neutrality can be the space through which truth can be clearly seen and embraced.

One of my clients, James, had been suffering from ALS, also known as Lou Gehrig's disease. He had been in bed for months and was having difficulty breathing and eating. During that time, I worked with him energetically and spiritually and helped him heal various forms of trauma. Through our work together his body stopped degrading, and he began experiencing improvements. There came a point when I looked at him and said, "You've actually turned the corner; it looks like you can recover from this disease." I felt that it would take him up to three years to come back to 80 percent of what his capacities had been. After all, he was seventy-four years old, and the body can be slow to regenerate at that age. After taking in what I stated, James was in a state of disbelief. I left him that day with an opportunity to sit with what he heard.

The next day James was brought to the hospital for respiratory failure and fell into a coma. At his family's request, I spent time with him every day at his bedside. I could sense that internally he had been struggling, full of deep bitterness and in a full-throttle war with God. As most people do throughout their lives, he had created a laundry list of all the injustices he had lived through. And now was his time to bring them directly to the "person" he felt was responsible. With the bond James and I had formed while working together, I was allowed to witness energetically and consciously his experience while he was in the coma. What I could see and sense as a felt knowing was profound.

The essence of day one for James was him reliving what he had been through as a soldier in World War II. I could feel battle cruisers shooting, bombs going off in his psyche, and he was firing all of these weapons at God. He was so rage-filled that every act was to get the deep pain and confusion out of his system and to destroy the very thing that he thought had hurt him—life and God.

The feeling of day two was of de-escalation. Instead of bombs and battleships, it was hand-to-hand combat, where he swung his fists, wielding guns, swords, and knives at God. The rage began to shift—as the fuel for his fire diminished, it was difficult to muster the energy for retaliation without a target. This was the starting point of his letting go, as the initial rage finally released and moved to raw anger and pain.

Day three was akin to an ancient Greek wrestling match. He was going skin to skin, getting dirty, muddy, trying to throw God around, punch him, kick him, beat him—but James himself just ended up on the ground, over and over, alone and sobbing. Again and again, God would gently step aside and imbue him with a feeling of deep and eternal love. God let him do this until he was exhausted, bringing him food and water while he cried and released his last shreds of anger. James finally gave up, as he had nothing to fight against, as nothing was fighting him.

Day four was pivotal, as it started with James attempting to negotiate with God. He remembered what he had seen on the battlegrounds of World War II and was desperately trying to understand the lack of perceived fairness in life. Now he was at a point where he was broken and pleading to understand why. He wanted God to know his greatest fear, that the world wasn't safe or anything he could ever trust. James cried out, life is so painful and hard! How could God allow so much suffering in the world?

A stillness came over James as he felt the true essence of Source beginning to emanate from within his heart. This act of unconditional love for him began to break his guarded heart wide open. As this radiant love expanded, it was like a warm sun enveloping his body, mind, and spirit. He innately understood that suffering happens because *people* allow the suffering of others from their own unresolved fears, pains, and insecurities. Source Consciousness fully honors people's free will to choose their own experiences and then choose again, time after time.

At this moment, he understood that he had only been able to see through the lens of good and evil, and the pain of his conditioning caused him to usually feel the worst. Because we are not meant to live at one end of life's dualistic pendulum, this creates a deep divide within, causing pain, anger, and feelings of injustice to be the only way we see ourselves, life, and others. James could now see with clarity that there were far more options than he had been given in his lifetime. If he had chosen to see the war as a reaction to the pain of man that was unfelt, he could have then slowly started to see a different reality.

Source waited and then gently held James as he came to the realization that he is an embodiment of *all that is*, which is an expression of eternity itself. This higher consciousness let him feel a vast creative expanse that everything is born from and will always be of. He felt unconditional, heart-centered love for the first time—its purity and beauty brought James to his knees with tears of joy. He knew deep within his being that he would never feel alone again. Source Consciousness had filled him with the light and truth of who he *is*. Everything became silent and still as he sat with fresh eyes and saw his very existence in a whole new way.

By day five, James felt deeply at peace; the sensation of a favorite childhood beach filled him, as these were his most cherished memories where he felt safe and loved. James wasn't resisting anymore as Source created an opening for him to feel the truth within him. Source let James know that his life was now his to create. He had finally found the peace he had spent so much of his life looking for. He could feel himself as a Divine Source of Creation, knowing he was with and *as* everything in the universe.

On day six, James came out of the coma. I could feel his deep peace and reverence for his experiential journey into truth. He no longer saw or felt God as God or anything separate from him. He could no longer see God as a mortal figure or a human construct. He knew that the essence of Source was him, and he felt this knowing deep within him, *as* him.

He just sat in awe and peace in my presence.

I continued to help his family process what was happening to him. At one point I looked at James and asked him how his trip with

God had gone. His eyes got big, but he was unable to talk because of the breathing tube in his throat. Instead, he communicated with me through eye blinks: two blinks for yes, and one for no.

I asked, "Do you feel complete?"

He blinked yes.

"And have you thought about whether you want to continue to live or not?"

He blinked yes.

"And do you want to live?"

He blinked no.

I asked him to write on a piece of paper what he was feeling, and he simply wrote, *I am at peace.* As soon as I saw this, I knew he would be gone in the next twenty-four hours. He'd made peace with his life, and therefore, his death.

Amazingly, that growing sense of calm settled over everyone in the family. Everyone was complete and content. The family had the opportunity to put to rest the pain of James's journey, and he was able to put behind him the sense of being disconnected from a God he'd once believed had abandoned him. This was the beauty of everybody being committed to knowing James as a whole being of divine origin, instead of the wounded individual they knew. If all of us could do this, it would change the living and dying process.

If you can recognize what your relationship with God is and process and come to peace with it before you die, as James did, there is no longer a fear of life or death. In fact, one can become grateful and honoring of both. The metaphor of an ocean wave comes to mind. God continuously brings a wave to the shore, and even though we built the castle of our human life on the sand and it gets washed away, we can stop being resentful of God's wave. What God is actually offering us is a chance to rebuild. Source Consciousness is offering us a clean slate of opportunities, so we can realize a greater potential. That clean slate is being offered to us from Source as often as a wave breaks on the shore—which is thousands of times (maybe even more) per day.

The wave is not the enemy. It is just another form of God. God is the wave that comes through and gives us an opportunity to bring that moment to closure by leveling things to the ground so we can integrate that experience, evolve, and start again from a new internal point of origin. It's almost as if Source Consciousness is saying, "This is a wonderful creation, and now, like a Tibetan sand mandala, let's wash it clean. Let's bring closure to what needs to be resolved, integrate it all, and evolve into something new. Then, let's move on to see what else we can create." The powerful thing to remember is that we need not get locked into the sandcastle of our creation. Everything evolves, and we always have an opportunity for a clean slate, so that we can create the next greatest vision of ourselves and how we wish to be.

PRACTICE DYING IN LIFE

One of the most powerful practices we can embark on is to practice dying, even when we are alive and healthy. Here's what I mean by that. I hit a point recently where I felt I was literally dying. So much of my being was simply releasing from my physical, mental, and energetic system that I felt I was dissolving, almost like a caterpillar dissolves into a puddle of goo before it re-forms to become a butterfly. It was extremely intense. My biological and psychological structures were going through some kind of massive recalibration. It was akin to what in shamanic terms might be considered a dismemberment. I felt as if I were being taken apart systematically and then being put back together.

Even though it was physically quite painful and overwhelming, I had hit a place of neutrality as I observed what was happening. I could feel all my emotions, but I was not so stuck on my mind's interpretations. I remained neutral and open to what was occurring.

As I felt the self I had identified as fade away, something else began to come forth—something else that I didn't yet have a word for, but that was clearly starting to work its way through my system.

This is the kind of experience that I have had with others in preparation for the final death of our physical body. It's the recognition that a way of being that we used to identify with and as has ceased to exist. In truth, these moments are constantly happening to us, but many of us are resistant to them, or we misinterpret them as being low points that we need to get some distance from. We might believe that there's something wrong with us or that we're going through some kind of psychosis. However, we go through these transitional moments of closure all the time. We rebirth ourselves constantly. (I sometimes wonder: If we were more open to these moments of transition, would it be possible that we might not even need to go through a physical dying process? What would that be like? How would it feel if we didn't have to endure a hard reset that looks like physical death and birth into a new body or reality? Perhaps our evolutionary process would be one that could allow for smoother and faster transition and transformation.)

For so many people, the death of a loved one or one's own impending physical death is the thing that provides them with the peace that passes understanding—with a sense of surrender they couldn't experience before. Most people who are facing death have learned not to be so attached to what once was; in this sense, death provides a powerful opportunity. However, we can get the same opportunity through the many deaths that we experience in our daily lives. This might include the loss of a relationship, the loss of a job, or the loss of a particular viewpoint or way of life. This helps us practice for the deaths that we will someday experience.

I focus on helping my clients, especially those who are dying or witnessing another person who is dying, tap into a greater awareness of how they view death. Some people simply don't know how to comprehend the fact that they are going to die someday, so I walk them through it as gently as I possibly can. As humans we tend to pride ourselves on being able to prepare for all kinds of different scenarios. We'd like to prepare for what we believe is the unknown. Death is an unknown for almost all of us. But what we can do to prepare for it is to face all of the moments and instances in which we carry a fear of unknown outcomes and possibilities. If the only preparation for death we can take is connecting with all of our deepest feelings and recognizing that it is safe to walk through them, this is enough. Remaining within this alignment is what prepares us for the unknown.

Of course, many people might look to specific practices and knowledge as they consider the big death that will someday come, because we simply want to eliminate as many unknowns as we can. However, we can do this by aligning with ourselves more often, boldly stepping into the everyday moments and transitions, and walking into our final moments on this Earth with a sense of being deeply connected to the part of us that will endure beyond all identities.

When we practice dying to ourselves, which really means dying to our ego and our false notions of who we are, we lose what we believed to be our center only to find our true center, so that we are stable enough to step into the next unknown.

One of the most beautiful experiences I can imagine occurs when the people I work with end up passing away with a smile on their face. I know this is because they have once and for all put to rest their fear of the unknown. They are aligned with their true self, and they're ready to embark on their next journey into the great mystery.

THE OTHER SIDE

One of the most common questions I get from people when we talk about esoteric matters beyond life and death is, "What happens when we die?" Perhaps you've been wondering the same thing since you started reading this chapter. There's no one easy answer to this question, but what I always emphasize is that being in a physical body is *one* experience. However, it isn't the *only* experience. It only makes up a single facet or expression of Source Consciousness, but there are multiple forms and dimensions of life that are not about being in a physical body.

We have come to view life as a three-dimensional dance of flesh and survival. What we think of as life is confined to the body, the mind, and the persona. However, in the simplest terms, there is absolutely more than one life we can possibly experience and encounter, as infinite beings who are unbound by time. We can look at this through the lens of reincarnation in the sense that even if there are certain experiences we don't get to have in this lifetime, we have the opportunity to have those experiences in another.

Our nature is truly infinite, but too many people tend to get stuck on the idea that in the afterlife, the persona they experienced in this lifetime will somehow be preserved. This concept usually accompanies an overly idealized image of heaven, in which we are exactly the same as we were when we were alive, except everything is white fluffy clouds and rainbows.

I recall an experience with a client who died and was reincarnated later as his own grandchild. I was in awe as I felt the energetic imprint of the person I had known. I couldn't understand why this man had chosen to come back to Earth so quickly. But then, I recognized that the work we'd done together had helped him to truly process what he couldn't in his lifetime. In other situations, people need to integrate the experience of their current life as they let go of the body, and it might take time for them to pop back in.

Overall, our ideas about heaven and hell are usually based on our fears and our attachments, as well as everything we have absorbed from religion and society about what death is. However, heaven and hell are things that we experience in moments or sometimes entire lifetimes on Earth.

Hell is a sense of being cut off from our true self as Source Consciousness. Heaven is about wholeheartedly going through the entire life cycle without resistance, from birth to death, knowing you are whole and one with Source. It is only when some pattern within our system interferes with our capacity to fully move through an experience that we end up returning to it in another lifetime so that we can grow and evolve. When we are willing to fully animate our own life—that is, to bring our soul all the way into the creation of our lives and to experience everything fully—we no longer create karmic imprints. This is the power of remaining within the experiential process of living and surrendering to the moment, as it is, in a way that allows us to expand.

In truth, even when we are experiencing a deep sense of pain, even when we are stuck in a personal hell of our making, even when we feel that we cannot go through a cycle for much longer and we don't have the awareness to break out of our patterns, even when the noise of the pain body is filling our senses—there is no way we completely separate from our true self, our soul essence. Divine Source Consciousness is always there holding us in this lifetime and waiting to welcome us back to the beautiful and unprecedented realms that exist beyond it.

THE BOOK OF YOUR LIFE

If there's anything I want you to understand, it's a lesson I find myself sharing with clients over and over again: It's that the end of a physical life is really no different from a scenario in which something comes to a natural closure, such as a conversation, a meeting, or a TV show or movie. In the closure, we get to feel the intent of the experience in action (that is, it was always meant to be a finite experience with a beginning, middle, and end)—and hopefully, instead of attempting to escape the moment or to fill it with empty noise, we get to feel ourselves through that closure. "Wow, that was a really great meeting—we fulfilled what we needed to," or "That experience gave me a new perspective I know has changed me for the better," or even, "This helped me realize that I'm seeking something completely different."

Closure is a necessary aspect of the journey. It's also a huge reason that rites of passage, which are so scarce in our modern world, are so important and valuable; they acknowledge the end of one phase and mark the beginning of a new one. They encourage us to evolve.

Everything comes to its endpoint, but the point of the end isn't to mourn or mark that something is over. It is to take in what we have experienced so we can then begin to share what it *meant* to us. Now that we are winding down that experience, we have the opportunity to truly integrate it. The energy of that moment has come to a climax, and it's time to move in a new, different direction. The experience we just had helps us determine what that direction will be.

We have an incredible opportunity in this journey of a lifetime, as spirit beings having a finite physical experience, to bring the best of what we are into each and every moment. Healing is the opportunity to recognize any incongruities that may reside in our expression, and to birth ourselves anew. We do this by allowing moments, phases, and lifetimes to be put to rest. An experience ends so that we can find new ways to bring even more of ourselves into the moment.

By the time we evolve into an experiential understanding of God 5.0, we have grown in our ability to live and breathe our life as an eternal moment, such that we are no longer held back by our fear of death and we are able to bring all of who we are—our joy, our love, our infinite potential—into our expression. Death gives us a powerful opportunity to do this, because it's the culmination of many moments, brought to a climax. It's the opportunity to surrender any hesitation or pain we carry, and to breathe into existence who we are, based on everything we have ever known.

I am often asked by clients how death factors into karma and reincarnation, and whether how we die impacts how we are reborn. In the realm of spirituality, many people are acquainted with the notion of the "transmigration of souls," or reincarnation. For most of us, the transitioning model of the karmic wheel that we are stuck in entails coming back to the same problems and cycles of pain that we encountered in a previous life. Some part of us is holding on to some level of pain, but each subsequent rebirth gives us an opportunity to put the struggle to rest so that we can regain our power from all the things to which we may have relinquished it. Each lifetime gives us countless opportunities—even in the midst of a seemingly oppressive situation—to breathe our spirit essence into our existence, no matter how the world around us reacts. At the same time, our will is our own, and we may choose to succumb to an overwhelming situation in order to bring the pain to an end, or to pour our energy into a distraction in order to avoid feeling. When we are in a state of rejection or condemnation, we push away every opportunity to evolve. This means that we continue to remain in a cycle of avoidance that will ultimately push us into a corner so we can no longer ignore what is. In this new paradigm, miserable, difficult rebirths are simply no longer sustainable. In fact, what happens is that our human viewpoint shatters as our spirit comes forward. Thus, with each life, we are given an opportunity to take our human will and progressively surrender this energy back to our soul, so that we can live to fully embrace our experience—not avoid it or gravitate toward a specific set of preferences.

In the paradigm of God 5.0, we no longer need to create lifetimes based on avoidance or preference. Rather, our rebirth becomes a powerful willingness to dance with possibility. We are no longer just riding the karmic wheel with no conscious awareness; rather, we choose to bring old forms into closure and new experiences into being. Unfortunately, in the world most of us have been born into, we are not equipped with the wisdom that helps us to recognize when something has come to its end. But if we do not fully bring our experience to closure by integrating and appreciating it, we become stuck in that cycle and carry it into our next life.

Again, conscious choice is always possible, even if we've found ourselves inside a lifetime where we may have severe limitations. Awareness is the salve, and it can always be laid upon the congested, infected part of our life, thus dissolving all the conditions associated with it. If we begin to consistently bring in our awareness and willingness to feel every last experience this life brings to us, we create a life of our own making. We don't simply go through the motions and do what our forebears did; we honor the essence of Source by choosing to bring to life something new that wishes to be born from the infinite palette of the Creator. In fact, we remember that we are not at the mercy of life; we are *both* the Creator and Creation itself.

Once we embody this truth *as* every moment, we free up any congested energy and karma simply ceases to exist. We become the essence of life itself, and we live it so completely that we don't need to come back in our next life to clean up or complete anything that remains messy or incomplete.

I also want to emphasize that when we integrate death in this profound way, we are no longer trapped by some of the dramatics and romanticization that are often associated with past lives. I see this a lot among some clients, who might be justifying their eagerness to hold on to a toxic relationship because they believe they had shared a past life and "we're soulmates." In truth, past lives (if we encounter a resurfaced memory from one of them) and "soulmates" we've traveled through many lifetimes with are simply energetic tools to help us identify where we might be stuck in this life. We are not meant to keep perpetuating the same loops of drama that we may have enacted in previous lifetimes. We are here to recognize where we are stuck, create flow, and reintegrate that energy so we can bring the old story to closure. When we are finally capable of honoring ourselves for who we are now, we can put to rest whatever was incomplete in the past—without unnecessary nostalgia or the mistaken notion that we need to relive or put right the thing that didn't get resolved eons ago. Once we step into the will to honor all that has been and is and allow forgiveness and loving compassion to be the essence of how we live, we close the chapter of karma being a controlling factor in our lives.

I once worked with a client who was adamant that she needed to hold on to a particular partner in her life because she sensed they'd been through many lifetimes together as partners. She was drawn to this man because he was powerful and seemed to know exactly what to do in any given situation, but her perception was skewed. In truth, he wasn't as powerful as she had made him out to be; she had simply never activated her own power. I told her, "Once you've activated that power within, you have to ask yourself: Do you still want to share your life with this man?" Through our work together, she came to find a place of stability and balance, and her attitude toward her lover transformed. After finding the warm blanket of safety, comfort, love, and power that had always existed within her, she ultimately realized it was time to put the relationship to bed, as she was no longer interested in recreating the same toxic dynamic of feeling "less than" or "needing" a partner.

We can come to these realizations in many ways, but the moment of physical death is an extraordinary opportunity for breaking the cycle of karma and of recreating what no longer needs to be created. I like to use the metaphor of a lifetime being a book. By the time our physical life has come to an end, the book of our life has been written and it's time to read it. As we read through this book at the moment of our death, we realize we've written a story that is either complete or incomplete. Death gives us an opportunity to edit the book—to complete that which has remained incomplete, and to make alterations, adjustments, and revisions that open up the necessary energetic pathways that will reorganize the story and extract what doesn't fit, so we can bring forth what we have always longed for.

This process of "editing" your manuscript isn't about changing what happened to you. It is about recognizing and being grateful for all the incredible opportunities that brought you to this moment. It's about appreciating the book, and the entire trajectory of your story, for exactly what it is. Even a life that contains many painful or traumatic moments can be accepted and integrated from a vantage point of wonder and gratitude, rather than regret. It is possible to come to the end of a life with the recognition that nothing you experienced was a mistake, but an opportunity to reconnect with the truth of who you are as an infinite being. Many people who have had near-death experiences report moving through the chronicle of their life as they have lived it and looking upon it with awe and a newfound sense of love for what they may not have previously perceived. We get the opportunity to view our life with the clarity of love, which finally allows us to see ourselves as Source sees us.

This is what it means to complete the journey of a lifetime. It prepares you for a new journey next time around, with a clean slate. It prepares you for a more fluid set of experiences, such that you can consciously create the beginnings of a new journey—by being present and aligned, with all the ingredients you need for living purposefully.

Remember, you are *not* at the mercy of the gods—you yourself *are* an expression of God, so you are only ever at the mercy of yourself, and how you perceive yourself.

As you come to the end of a particular life cycle, you have the opportunity to put everything into complete and total resolution, and to begin the evolutionary process of going into chrysalis form, where everything that was of your old life can finally dissolve. Matter returns to the energy matrix of potential. You have a sense of clarity about what you'd like to experience next, and your spirit naturally gathers the necessary ingredients—not out of rigid preferences or the need for perfection, but from the simple, holy, childlike impulse to create and to play.

Overall, this sacred experience of opening up the book of your life allows you to surrender your impression of what was right and what was wrong, so that you can finally see the truth, which is the lens through which you can see just as Source sees. Namely, you fully understand that there is nothing that happens to you that does not create an opportunity to know who you are and to live that truth. Sensations and emotions such as resentment, anger, and shame are counterproductive because they keep you in a state of rejection that prevents you from seeing that there are no mistakes; that life is an infinite experiential journey in which you are meant to know and embrace your true nature through a multitude of forms.

As we come to the final pages of *The New Freedom of God*, I encourage you to remember that it is you who is writing the book of your life. Like any memorable adventure, that book is not based in some limited human concept of perfection—it is all about capturing the wholeness of who you are. It is about embracing every single thing that has ever been written in your pages from a place of gratitude and grace. When you do this, in each and every moment and at the time of breathing your final breath, you may very well change the world in brilliant and unforeseen ways. And the more of us who are committed to doing this, the more likely it is that we will steward God 5.0 into existence and transform the entire energetic matrix of this world.

EMBRACE AND BE EMBRACED BY DEATH: A HEALING IMMERSION

Breathe, and honor that death
is something to cherish.
Feel that it is something to

love
and appreciate.

Death is a dear friend that holds
the most loving embrace of you and your journey.
Death is Source fully accepting who you are,
have been,
and are becoming.

Death is the highest gift of life:
the chance to fully embrace all you have experienced.

Just as life is filled with potential and possibility,
just as birth is the introduction of that potential and possibility,
death is the welcoming home and the integration
of all that potential and possibility,
so it can be known and realized in a new way.

But the grandest part of this is:
If we allow ourselves to be fully embraced by Source
at the moment of death,
we cease being afraid.

And what we cease being afraid of is not death.
What we cease being afraid of is life—and its end.

Life does not begin after birth,
nor does it end upon death.
Life is the journey itself.

From intent, to gestation, to birth,
through each and every transformation,
you live and breathe and remember.

You are here to recognize
that death is a part of life,
a phase of the experience.
In meeting death's embrace
at every moment,
you may feel life once more.

Breathe and feel the beauty of God
in and as your heart,
knowing you have always been held in love,
sourced in love,
which is the only home
it is ever possible to return to,
beyond this life you know,
over and over again.

A RETURN TO THE WEB OF LIFE

I DIDN'T WANT TO CALL THIS section the "Conclusion," because it isn't. While it is the conclusion of your experience of reading this book, more than that, it's a beginning. It is the invitation I'm extending to you to step into the creation of your next moment with the unadulterated trust that Source is working for you, with you, through you, as you. To that end, as you step into the final transmission of this book, which is meant to help you integrate the essence of this journey, may you have everything you need to be stewarded through the experiential adventure that is life. May you remember that the universal truth of *The New Freedom of God* is and has always been within you to unlock, so that you can feel the exhilaration and wonder that come from the deepest intimacy with your true self. Throughout it all, please remember that I'm here, rooting for you, reminding you that ultimately, there is only one direction home—and you're already on that path, exactly where you need to be.

Your breath is more than just breathing oxygen.
Your breath is a response to Source breathing You.
With every breath, God is breathing into you
the memory of who you are.

Know that every time you inhale,
God is breathing into you
the essence of your true self,
all that you have been, and all that you will ever be.
The knowing that you are Source itself.

Bring your awareness to your breath.
Feel your natural inhale and exhale.

Know with every breath,
you are bringing in the memory of your true self.
Trust with every breath,
you are bringing that memory
to your body,
through your body
and beyond your body
for all life to know and experience.
Throughout the entire Cosmos,
life is sharing itself with existence itself.
It is an innate part of your experience.

This is a journey that does not have a beginning or an end.
Every moment of life is infinite,
every breath is an eternity.
An entire lifetime is experienced as every breath.
For you are an eternal being,
experiencing a lifetime
as every moment

that you are,
that you breathe.

Focus on your eternal heart space.

This is an opening,
a portal to Source Consciousness itself.
An opening to your eternal heart,
through which your spirit and Source
are remembered as one breathes
the One Breath, the Word,
breathing your physical body into existence.

It is this one breath that creates the intent,
manifests that intent,
and births that intent,
as life expressed as this moment.

Calm your mind.
Open your heart.
Become aware of your breathing.
Pause and welcome Source into your spirit,
into your heart.
Inhale into your heart the gift that God is breathing into you,
the memory of your true self.

Pause at the peak of that inhalation.
With gratitude, receive that gift.
Gently and lovingly breathe that memory to your body,
through your body,
beyond your body
to the whole of humanity and all life,
to everything that is part of this awe-inspiring Universe.

Then, bring it all the way back to Source
and offer thanks for this gift of life.

In these moments, pause.
Feel gratitude for the love and gift of wholeness.
Gently and lovingly breathe this into your body,
through your body,
beyond your body,
to the world,
to the Cosmos,
and back to Source with heartfelt gratitude.

As the New Freedom of God.

Breathe.
Pause.
Receive.
And Become.

It is in this moment you know yourself
as the Source of all creation.
Your true self
as God has always known and loved you into being.

"I looked in temples, churches, and mosques.
But I found the Divine within my heart."

—RUMI

ABOUT THE AUTHOR

RON DAMICO is a spiritual guide, innate healer, and conscious channel. For nearly three decades, he has been a wayshower, guiding people from all walks of life through the healing process, and he is at the forefront of advancing the new human consciousness.

A born intuitive, Ron is renowned for his ability to bring profound healing to others simply through the power of his voice, intention, and presence. His energetic abilities are infused with divine healing codes, allowing him to transmit these inherent healing frequencies to others in person, online, and through his written words.

After three significant out-of-body "choice points" in his thirties, Ron's deeper awakenings and healing gifts emerged. Through direct connections with ascended masters, archangels, and soul guides, he continually walks a path of Becoming for himself and for everyone he encounters.

Tens of thousands of people have experienced profound healing and heart-centered conscious awakenings through Ron's love, kindness, and ability to see their true essence at a deep soul level.

WWW.RON-DAMICO.COM